Europe in an Era of
Sino-American Com

C000136615

This book investigates how Europe should position itself in an era of growing Chinese-American rivalry.

The volume explores the contemporary relationship and ongoing dynamics between three of the most powerful players in today's international relations—the United States, China and Europe. It claims that the intensifying antagonism between Washington and Beijing requires a paradigm shift in European strategic thinking and takes a trilateral perspective in analysing key issue areas, such as trade, technology, investment, climate change, the BRI, subnational contacts, maritime security and nuclear non-proliferation. Using this analysis, the work seeks to offer original policy recommendations that respond to a number of dilemmas Europe can no longer avoid, including the trade-off between European interests and values in a harsher global environment, the question of whether Europe should align with one of the two superpowers, Europe's military dependence on a US pivoting to the Asia-Pacific, and possible trade-offs between global and regional governance efforts. The key finding is that Europe must follow a much more pragmatic and independent approach to its foreign and security affairs.

This book will be of much interest to students of European Union (EU) policy, foreign policy, Chinese politics, US politics and international relations in general.

Sebastian Biba is Lecturer and Research Fellow at the Institute of Political Science of Goethe University Frankfurt, Germany, and Visiting Fellow at the School of Advanced International Studies of Johns Hopkins University, United States.

Reinhard Wolf is Professor of International Relations at the Institute of Political Science at Goethe University Frankfurt, Germany.

Routledge Studies in European Security and Strategy
Series Editors:
Sven Biscop
Egmont Royal Institute for International Relations, Belgium
and
Richard Whitman
University of Kent, UK

The aim of this series is to bring together the key experts on European security from the academic and policy worlds and assess the state of play of the EU as an international security actor. The series explores the EU and its Member States security policy and practices in a changing global and regional context. While the focus is on the politico-military dimension, security is put in the context of the holistic approach advocated by the EU.

Europeanisation and the Transformation of EU Security Policy
Post-Cold War Developments in the Common Security and Defence Policy
Petros Violakis

EU-Japan Security Cooperation
Trends and Prospects
Edited by Emil Kirchner and Han Dorussen

European Strategy in the 21st Century
New Future for Old Power
Sven Biscop

Defence Industrial Cooperation in the European Union
The State, the Firm and Europe
Daniel Fiott

European Defence Decision-Making
Dilemmas of Collaborative Arms Procurement
Antonio Calcara

Europe in an Era of Growing Sino-American Competition
Coping with an Unstable Triangle
Edited by Sebastian Biba and Reinhard Wolf

For more information about this series, please visit: www.routledge.com/ Routledge-Studies-in-European-Security-and-Strategy/book-series/SESS

Europe in an Era of Growing Sino-American Competition

Coping with an Unstable Triangle

**Edited by Sebastian Biba
and Reinhard Wolf**

Routledge
Taylor & Francis Group

LONDON AND NEW YORK

First published 2021
by Routledge
2 Park Square, Milton Park, Abingdon, Oxon OX14 4RN

and by Routledge
52 Vanderbilt Avenue, New York, NY 10017

Routledge is an imprint of the Taylor & Francis Group, an informa business

© 2021 selection and editorial matter, Sebastian Biba and Reinhard Wolf; individual chapters, the contributors

The right of Sebastian Biba and Reinhard Wolf to be identified as the authors of the editorial material, and of the authors for their individual chapters, has been asserted in accordance with sections 77 and 78 of the Copyright, Designs and Patents Act 1988.

British Library Cataloguing-in-Publication Data
A catalogue record for this book is available from the British Library

Library of Congress Cataloging-in-Publication Data
Names: Biba, Sebastian, editor, author. | Wolf, Reinhard, 1960– editor, author.
Title: Europe in an era of growing Sino-American competition : coping with an unstable triangle / edited by Sebastian Biba and Reinhard Wolf.
Description: First edition. | New York : Routledge, 2021. | Series: Routledge studies in European security and strategy | Includes bibliographical references and index.
Identifiers: LCCN 2020044899 (print) | LCCN 2020044900 (ebook) | ISBN 9780367441203 (hardback) | ISBN 9781003007746 (ebook)
Subjects: LCSH: Europe—Foreign relations—21st century. | Europe—Foreign relations—United States. | Europe—Foreign relations—China. | United States—Foreign relations—Europe. | United States—Foreign relations—China. | China—Foreign relations—Europe. | China—Foreign relations—United States.
Classification: LCC D2025 .E893 2021 (print) | LCC D2025 (ebook) | DDC 327.4—dc23
LC record available at https://lccn.loc.gov/2020044899
LC ebook record available at https://lccn.loc.gov/2020044900

ISBN: 978-0-367-44120-3 (hbk)
ISBN: 978-1-003-00774-6 (ebk)

Typeset in Times New Roman
by Apex CoVantage, LLC

Contents

Figures

Tables

Contributors/author bios

Sebastian Biba is a visiting fellow at the Foreign Policy Institute, Johns Hopkins School of Advanced International Studies in Washington, DC, and is currently on leave from his position as a lecturer and research fellow at the Institute of Political Science, Goethe University Frankfurt, Germany. His main research interest lies in the area of China's foreign affairs, with special focus on both China's relations *vis-à-vis* Europe (particularly Germany) and the US, and China's behaviour regarding its shared international river basins. He has held visiting fellowships with the School of International Studies, Peking University in Beijing, China, and with the German Institute for Global and Area Studies (GIGA) in Hamburg, Germany. His major publications include a Routledge monograph and articles in *Security Dialogue*, *Third World Quarterly*, *Journal of Contemporary China* and *Journal of Contemporary Asia*. He earned a PhD in political science from Goethe University Frankfurt.

Joanna Ciesielska-Klikowska is assistant professor in the Department of Asian Studies, University of Lodz, Poland. She is a scholarship holder of the Deutscher Akademischer Austauschdienst (DAAD), Technische Universität Chemnitz, visiting lecturer at the Universität des Saarlandes in Saarbrücken and Otto-von-Guericke-Universität in Magdeburg. She is also a member of the Polish Society for International Studies and the Poland-Austria Society.

Mario Esteban is assistant professor at the Centre for East Asian Studies, Autonomous University of Madrid, and senior analyst for the Asia-Pacific region at the Elcano Royal Institute in Madrid. He is the principal investigator of a research project funded by the Spanish Ministry of Economy and Business that analyses the impact of China's Belt and Road Initiative (BRI) on global governance. His research interests are focused on the international relations of East Asia, EU-East Asia relations and the domestic and international politics of China.

Tomasz Kaminski is a political scientist and professor at the Faculty of International and Political Studies, University of Lodz. His research activities are concentrated on the topic of paradiplomacy and city diplomacy, particularly in the context of EU policy towards China. He has worked on numerous research projects funded by the European Commission (Horizon 2020, Jean Monnet Module) and the Polish National Science Centre. His papers have been published in *Energy Policy*, *Asia-Europe Journal* and *European Foreign Affairs Review*. Recently, he co-authored a book *Paradiplomacy in Asia*.

Emil J. Kirchner is Jean Monnet Professor and Coordinator of the Jean Monnet Centre of Excellence, University of Essex. He received his PhD from Case Western Reserve University. He is chair of the Editorial Advisory Board of the *Journal of European Integration*, holder of the Order of Merit of the Federal Republic of Germany, a Fellow of the British Academy of Social Sciences, was awarded a Lifetime Achievement Award by the University Association of Contemporary Studies, and has held fellowships at NATO and the European University Institute, Florence. He has been a visiting professor at universities in various European countries, the United States and China. His recent book publications are (co-author) *The European Union and China* (Macmillan and Red Globe Press, 2019); (co-editor) *EU-Japan Security Cooperation* (Routledge, 2018), and (co-editor) *Security Relations between China and the European Union* (Cambridge University Press, 2016). He has published articles in *International Organization*, *Review of International Studies*, *West European Politics*, *Journal of Common Market Studies*, *European Security*, *European Foreign Affairs Review*, and *Journal of European Public Policy*.

Lara Lázaro Touza is a lecturer in economic theory, Colegio Universitario Cardenal Cisneros (attached to Universidad Complutense de Madrid), an adjunct professor of the political economy of climate change, IE School of Global and Public Affairs, and a senior analyst in the Energy and Climate Change Program, Elcano Royal Institute, Madrid. She is currently working on an EU-funded H2020 research project called MUSTEC, "Market Uptake of Solar Thermal Electricity through Cooperation" and on a research project funded by the Spanish Ministry of Economy and Business that analyses the impact of China's Belt and Road Initiative (BRI) on global governance.

Philippe Le Corre is a research fellow at the Harvard Kennedy School (Mossavar-Rahmani Center for Business and Government), a visiting professor and scholar at ESSEC-IRENE and a fellow-in-residence (Institute of Advanced Studies), CY Paris-Cergy University, specializing in Chinese and Asian affairs. He is also an associate-in-research at the John K. Fairbank Center for Chinese Studies at Harvard University and a non-resident senior fellow at the Carnegie Endowment for International Peace in Washington, DC. He previously worked as a fellow at the Brookings Institution and as a Special Adviser for International Affairs to the French Minister of Defence. His research focuses on China's global rise, with a special interest in Chinese investment and influence in Europe and Eurasia. His last book was *China's Offensive in Europe* (Brookings Institution Press, 2016). His work has also appeared in *Asia-Europe Journal*, *Carnegie Working Papers* series, *China Economic Quarterly*, *Perspectives Chinoises*, *Etudes*, and in an edited volume, *Rethinking the Silk*

Road (Palgrave-MacMillan, 2018). His recent papers include "The Case for Transatlantic Cooperation in the Indo-Pacific" (co-written with Erik Brattberg), "Kazakhs wary of Chinese embrace as BRI gathers steam" (National University of Singapore, 2019), "China's rise as a geoeconomic influencer: Four European Case Studies" (Carnegie, 2018), and "China's global rise: Can the United States and Europe pursue a coordinated strategy?" (Brookings Institution, 2016).

Liselotte Odgaard is a senior fellow at the Hudson Institute, Washington, D.C. She has published numerous monographs, books, peer-reviewed articles and research reports on Chinese and Asia-Pacific security, including *China and Coexistence: Beijing's National Security Strategy for the Twenty-First Century* (2012) and "European Engagement in the Indo-Pacific: The Interplay between Institutional and State-Level Naval Diplomacy", *Asia Policy*, 14:4, October 2019, pp. 129–159. Dr. Odgaard has been a visiting scholar at institutions such as Harvard University, the Woodrow Wilson International Center for Scholars, and the Norwegian Nobel Institute. She regularly participates in policy dialogues such as the Shangri-La Dialogue in Singapore and the Xiangshan Forum in Beijing. She holds a PhD from Aarhus University.

Ramon Pacheco Pardo is reader (associate professor) in International Relations at King's College London and the KF-VUB Korea Chair at the Institute for European Studies of Vrije Universiteit Brussel (IES-VUB). Dr Pacheco Pardo is also Committee Member at CSCAP EU. He has held visiting positions at Korea University, the Lee Kuan Yew School of Public Policy, and Melbourne University. Dr Pacheco Pardo has been editor of *Millennium: Journal of International Studies* and currently sits on the editorial boards of *East Asia: An International Quarterly*, *EU-China Observer* and *Global Studies Journal*. His publications include the book *North Korea-US Relations from Kim Jong Il to Kim Jong Un*, published in 2019.

Michael Paul is a senior fellow of the International Security Division, Stiftung Wissenschaft und Politik (SWP) in Berlin, since 1995 the project director of the Armed Forces Dialogue and a 2018–2019 member of the Expert Team on Maritime Security in the "Seas and Oceans" thematic cycle of the Round Table of the German Federal Government. He has published extensively on international security policy, arms control, nuclear deterrence and maritime security.

Margot Schüller is associate senior research fellow at the German Institute for Global and Area Studies (GIGA). She is a regular lecturer on Chinese and East Asian economics at universities in Germany and abroad and a frequent consultant for governmental and private institutions. Her current research focuses on China's transition to a new economic model and on China's innovation system and policies in international comparison. She was an expert in the Sino-German Innovation Platform until spring 2020, an initiative of the German Federal Ministry of Education and Research (BMBF) and the Chinese Ministry of Science and Technology (MOST).

Øystein Tunsjø is Professor and Head of the Asia Program at the Norwegian Institute for Defence Studies, Norwegian Defence University College. Tunsjø is author of *The Return of Bipolarity in World Politics: China, the United States and Geostructural Realism*, (Columbia University Press, 2018); *Security and Profits in China's Energy Policy: Hedging Against Risk* (Columbia University Press, 2013); and *US Taiwan Policy: Constructing the Triangle* (London: Routledge, 2008). Prof. Tunsjø has published articles in journals such as *The National Interest, Survival, International Relations, Cooperation and Conflict*, and *World Economy and Politics* (in Chinese) and co-edited and contributed chapters to several edited volumes. Prof. Tunsjø holds a PhD in international relations from the University of Wales, Aberystwyth (2006) and an MSc from the London School of Economics (2002). Prof. Tunsjø was a visiting Fulbright scholar at the Fairbank Center for Chinese Studies, Harvard University, during the spring term of 2010.

Reinhard Wolf is a professor of international relations at the Institute of Political Science, Goethe University Frankfurt, Germany. His current research focuses on the role of status and emotions in international relations, as well as on great power interactions in East Asia. His recent publications include "Taking Interaction Seriously: Asymmetrical Roles and the Behavioral Foundations of Status", in the *European Journal of International Relations* (online first); "Debt, Dignity and Defiance: Why Greece Went to the Brink", in *Review of International Political Economy* 25:6 (2018), 829–53; "Donald Trump's Status-Driven Foreign Policy", in *Survival* 59: 5 (October–November 2017), 99–116; and *Eclipsed by Clashing Titans? Europe and the Risks of US-Chinese Confrontation*, special issue 3:1 (Fall 2016) of *European Foreign Affairs Review* (co-edited with Sebastian Biba and Markus Liegl).

Claude Zanardi obtained her PhD from the War Studies Department, King's College, London (KCL) where she researched French, British and German foreign and security policies towards China, and China's military modernisation. Previously, she worked at the European Institute for Security Studies, the West European Union's Assembly and produced research for the OECD-GOV Directorate and the International Secretariat of Amnesty International. She holds a degree with first class honours in economics and another in international relations from the University of Bologna (Italy). She has a MPhil in international relations from both Paris I (Sorbonne), Paris II (Assas), and another in international relations at Bologna University. She studied diplomacy and served briefly at the Italian Embassy in Lisbon. She was part of the European-China Resource Advice Network, a Taiwan Fellow researcher at the Ministry of Foreign Affairs of the Republic of China (2015) and, since 2017, a Global Royster Fellow at the University of North Carolina at Chapel Hill.

1 Introduction

Sebastian Biba and Reinhard Wolf

Over the course of the past decade, the key conditions of Europe's global strategy have been substantially eroded.[1] The rules-based international system had been increasingly under strain even before the outbreak of the coronavirus pandemic and the Trump presidency (Maull 2018). A major cause of Europe's unravelling foreign policy has been the intensifying systemic, economic and military rivalry between the world's foremost powers, China and the United States (US). This antagonism was first highlighted by the Obama administration's "pivot/rebalance to Asia", and has not only stymied the progressive reform of global governance but has also weakened regional and global orders. The world is regressing to a more realist state again, in which zero-sum competition for material advantage and the unilateral pursuit of national security will trump cooperation based on agreed norms, rules and procedures. Europe no longer faces a largely congenial multilateral environment but must adapt to trends that favour self-help at the expense of mutual advantage and reliable cooperation. However, it unfortunately lacks a strategic vision for such a new environment: as a prominent think tank concluded recently, "Europe possesses no robust collective foreign policy position concerning the geopolitical struggle between the United States and China over hegemony in the Asia-Pacific region" (Lippert et al. 2019, 29; also see Otero-Iglesias and Esteban 2020).

Apart from general trends towards suspicion and strife, escalating tensions between the world's two dominant powers present Europe—both the European Union (EU) and individual European states—with profound challenges. What exactly are these challenges and what do they entail? What are the impacts of the intensifying US-China rivalry on Europe, particularly on its security, welfare and values? Worrying scenarios include relative gains considerations that further undermine effective global governance, escalating trade and technology "wars", military escalation in the Asia-Pacific and the US disengaging from Europe to focus its limited resources on containing China. Against such a backdrop, what are Europe's options for action and what then should it do? The list of urgent questions is long. Among other things, Europe must consider whether it can still largely rely on US support for European security, whether it should lean towards one of the two antagonists or steer a pragmatic course, whether it should try to defuse or contain Sino-American antagonism in the Asia-Pacific and beyond, whether it should adapt to a post-liberal world by clearly prioritizing interests over norms and whether it should continue to invest in the maintenance of a fragmenting global order or put more emphasis on promoting regional governance in Europe and its vicinity. Instead of addressing such questions just on a case-by-case basis or avoiding them altogether in the hope that others will solve its problems, Europe needs a thorough strategic debate about how it should position itself in this precarious geopolitical triangle.

This volume's aim is to contribute to this long-overdue debate by investigating the challenges and potential responses to key issues which Europe needs to address. It does not stop at analysing past developments and future scenarios but also takes an explicit policy perspective by asking how Europe should prioritise competing interests, values and options. It brings together well-known experts from various European countries, united in the belief that thinking about European aims *vis-à-vis* the US and China is a matter of great urgency, particularly for the EU if it would remain an active player rather than passively adapt to decisions taken elsewhere; the world will not wait for Europe to "get its act together". Some strategic decisions need to be made now, particularly on instruments (military and other) and institutions that cannot be created overnight. Internal problems such as illiberal trends in several European countries and finding adequate responses to the COVID-19 pandemic—regardless of how grave they may be—must not prevent Europe from looking beyond its borders and failing to prepare for external challenges.

As already indicated, these issues are similarly shared by all Europeans who consider themselves part of what has been the transatlantic community. When we speak of "Europe", we generally refer to the EU as well as individual European countries within and outside of the EU. While we see the EU as the crucial European actor in standing up to the worsening US-China confrontation, we also believe that the European nation state remains relevant (especially after Brexit) and that these share many interests. Hence, the latter have to deal with the question of whether they want to coordinate these interests within the EU or outside of it (e.g., through coalitions of the willing such as the E3). The answer to this question may differ across issues. Consequently, the individual chapters in this volume may focus on different European actors.

All such actors are confronted with the dire reality that global politics has entered a far more antagonistic era, a new phase for which Europe is ill-prepared. This ominous downward trend is most obvious in the trajectory of US-China relations, which provides the rationale and overall context for this volume. As will become clear in the following section, the rivalry between Beijing and Washington has intensified across many issues. It is no longer limited to a number of isolated problems but has now assumed a structural quality and will hardly abate under the new US President Joe Biden. This confrontation is here to stay and may well get even rougher. It will set the stage for global politics for years to come. Unfortunately, Europeans also need to recognise that their own relations with both antagonists have also worsened, if less dramatically. America no longer is the reliable security partner it used to be, while China is now regarded as "a systemic rival" (EC 2019, 1). Both powers have begun to undermine EU cohesion and have applied tougher economic policies which jeopardise European prosperity. To provide the general background for our authors' contributions, we must first map the growing conflicts within this triangle.

Growing US-China rivalry and its impact on Europe

Current US-China relations present themselves to the outside world as the expression of a complex strategic rivalry. Even though the two countries maintain a dense web of bilateral exchanges, the days are gone when pundits would talk about the prospects of Washington and Beijing forming a G-2 mechanism to jointly and cooperatively govern world affairs (Bergsten 2005, 2008; Brezezinski 2009; Zoellick and Lin 2009). Similarly, while the two nations remain economically intertwined, the notion of "Chimerica" (Ferguson 2008)—the long-held impression of a symbiotic economic relationship between the two—has already perished. Over recent years, concepts with such positive connotations have given way to the current widespread and gradually deepening ingrained conviction—by the two antagonists and beyond—that US-China relations are fraught with serious tensions that span a variety of dimensions and a great number of issues, with current trends pointing to a further deterioration of bilateral ties.

At the root of today's growing strategic rivalry is China's unprecedentedly rapid and comprehensive rise to the status of an "emerging potential superpower" (Brooks and Wohlforth 2016) with the potential to challenge US supremacy in the Asia-Pacific region and even globally. Hegemons being challenged by rising powers is a recurring theme in International Relations (IR), with potentially disastrous consequences. More recently, such scenarios have been labeled the "Thucydides's Trap", describing the ". . . severe structural stress caused when a rising power threatens to upend a ruling one" (Allison 2017, 29). Allison (2017) identified 16 of those cases over the last 500 years, 12 of which have resulted in open war between the antagonists.

In IR theory, this phenomenon is best captured by the so-called power transition theory, which sets out to explain and predict the occurrence or absence of war between the hegemonic power and one of its challengers (Organski and Kugler 1981). In doing so, the theory has two drivers: the first is power parity as the necessary condition for a power transition; the second is the degree of (dis)satisfaction of the rising state with its status in the existing regional and global orders. This latter functions as the sufficient condition determining the war-proneness of a power transition. This leads to the underlying issue of present-day US-China relations: a severe and increasingly intensifying status competition between the two countries (Biba 2016; Rudolf 2020).

Generally speaking, status refers to an actor's specific rank within a social hierarchy. It has intrinsic value for a state because the higher its status, the more privileges it can enjoy. As a result, states tend to seek a high status. However, not every state can have this high status, because then none would (Larson et al. 2014). The situation of US-China relations is that US status, both globally and regionally in the Asia-Pacific, remains relatively higher than China's. Additionally, the US is intent on defending and bolstering this status because what is at stake is nothing less than global leadership and regional preeminence, coupled with enormous political and economic gains. Meanwhile, China is not satisfied with its current ranking and privileges, and hence seeks a higher status—allegedly one on par with the US globally and even outstripping the US in the Asia-Pacific region (Biba 2016).

US-China rivalry for status is aggravated by a number of concomitant circumstances. The first is that both nations are highly status conscious. Americans widely share the belief that their country has a distinctive mission to transform the world and that this mission gives their country a superiority over others (Mead 2002; Nau 2002). At the same time, an increasingly bipartisan consensus, comprising a majority in US business and society, has emerged which sees China as a serious threat to this US self-perception (Zhao 2019). For example, the December 2017 US National Security Strategy overtly labelled China a "revisionist" power that would aim at shaping "a world antithetical to U.S. values and interests" and would seek to "displace the U.S. in the Indo-Pacific region". The Chinese, meanwhile, have traditionally considered themselves the centre of the civilised world and currently understand their country's renewed rise to great power status after its "century of humiliation" as natural and regaining something lost (Yan 2001). The US is perceived to stand in China's way and as denying China's rightful place in the international system. A "sentiment of insecurity and sense of being threatened" by the US have increased in China ever since former US President Barack Obama unveiled his "pivot/rebalance to Asia" strategy in November 2011 (Wang and Yin 2014).

Related to this is a second aspect: agency. While the US-China status competition is principally rooted in the anarchical structure of the international system, it has recently been intensified by factors of agency. That is to say, while this rivalry has preceded former US President Donald Trump and will stay under new US President Joe Biden, Trump's "status-driven foreign policy" (Wolf 2017) further accentuated the problem. His "fixation with personal prestige" and his "desire to look like a 'winner'" necessitated him making America the undisputed "number one" again (*ibid.*, 99–100). Chinese President Xi Jinping certainly cultivates a very different approach to leadership than Trump; however, his sensibility to status concerns is arguably little different. It remains to be seen in how far Biden will adopt a different tone.

The third concomitant is that of ideological differences. From the US point of view, it has not been beneficial to its perception of China's rise that the latter is neither a liberal democracy nor a market economy (Friedberg 2011). China's recent "handling" of the Uighurs in Xinjiang, as well as of protest in Hong Kong, has underlined the US' standpoint and nourished widespread American frustration about China's failure to democratise any time soon. There have also been growing US concerns about China establishing, and possibly exporting to the world, a new development model that is capable of merging autocratic rule with sustained economic growth. Conversely, the Chinese Communist Party has long feared US "missionary zeal" to democratise the world and hence has cautioned Washington against both overt and covert endeavors to subvert and transform the Chinese political system.

Consequently, US-China relations have been characterised by increasing mutual distrust about the other's intentions (Lieberthal and Wang 2012). This state of affairs might escalate existing security dilemmas between Washington and Beijing. This is particularly so because both the US and China seem to be relatively insensible to the actual existence of such dilemmas, with each side claiming purely defensive intentions and not realizing that their respective actions could also be perceived otherwise—as offensive tactics (Rudolf 2020). In addition, the current state of affairs has already led a number of distinguished observers to conclude that we are now entering a new cold war era (Leonard 2018; Kaplan 2019).

As previously mentioned, the ongoing and worsening US-China conflict—including status competition, security dilemmas and even cold war mentality—plays out on different levels and comprises a number of crucial issues. Regionally, it is all about supremacy and spheres of influence in the Asia-Pacific (Mearsheimer 2010). While the US retains its post-World War II claim to leadership in the region, a rising China is less and less willing to accept this claim that, historically, was its own. Due to the status concerns illustrated above, as well as significant economic interests, neither side is likely to back down, while the possibility of a peaceful condominium has also been questioned (Friedberg 2011; Mearsheimer 2010; Wolf 2012). Importantly, it is also in this regional context that military confrontation between the two powers is most likely and cannot be ruled out. The two cases that stand out in this regard—the South China Sea and Taiwan's status—have both become more intense over recent years. In the South China Sea, China's rapid and large-scale building of artificial islands and its subsequent stationing of military equipment on these have provoked repeated US "Freedom of Navigation Operations" through these contested waters. Physical military encounters between both sides have become more frequent in recent years and could well produce some inadvertent clash that might then spiral out of control. Regarding Taiwan, former President Trump exemplified the increasing US lack of sensitivity to Beijing's "One China policy" when he caused a major diplomatic stir in December 2016 over a phone call with Taiwanese President Tsai Ying-wen. Additional international security problems in the region, such as the North Korea nuclear issue or the Sino-Japanese conflict over the Diaoyu/Senkaku Islands, could also entail a US-China military face-off.

Globally, the likelihood of military confrontation has receded; however, the number of controversial issues is increasing, as do their interconnectedness and complexity. Even areas where there was still cooperative interaction between Washington and Beijing under the Obama administration—such as over climate change mitigation and nuclear non-proliferation—have faded since Trump assumed office. The most significant complex of problems in 2020 is what could be termed the "economy-finance-technology triangle", which is most evident in escalating diplomatic confrontation between the two countries in recent years and plays out not only bilaterally but also in multilateral organisations such as the World Trade Organization (WTO).

In light of his protectionist "America First" approach, former President Trump has brought a great amount of zero-sum thinking to the field of broader US-China economic relations, which is unlikely to go away under the new Biden administration. Already during his election campaign in 2016, Trump called China a "currency manipulator" (Forbes 2016) and repeatedly lamented America's huge trade deficit *vis-à-vis* China, infamously proclaiming, "[w]e can't continue to allow China to rape our country, and that's what they're doing" (*CNN Politics* 2016). Since the beginning of 2018, the US has drawn China into a protracted trade war which particularly features US special tariffs on a large number of Chinese export products. Superficially, this conflict is about reducing China's bilateral trade surplus and about recreating jobs for American workers. More profoundly, it is the epitome of a growing competition for global geo-economic dominance between the US and China that is further underlined by their different economic models and conceptions of the international order. Consequently, the US has been wary of China's Belt and Road Initiative (BRI), condemning it as a potential "Trojan horse for China-led regional development and military expansion" (Chatzky and McBride 2020) and has also warned third countries, particularly in the Global South, against Beijing's alleged "debt-trap diplomacy" (Chellaney 2017).

Crucially, this competition has also featured an increasingly important technological dimension. This is mainly because both the US and China consider technological superiority key to economic and military strength—even more so in the present digital age (Schulze and Voelsen 2020). Driven by its industrial policy strategy "Made in China 2025", which aims to transform the country into a "high-tech superpower" (Wübbeke et al. 2016), China has already started to seriously challenge America's leading position in a number of pivotal dual-use technology industries, including artificial intelligence and robotics. As a result, the US has been considering a partial economic and technological "decoupling" which is meant to guarantee US national security by establishing strategic supply chains independent of Chinese producers. The most prominent example of this US policy so far has been the blacklisting of China's telecommunications giant Huawei Technologies, which bans US firms from selling high-tech components (such as chips) and software (e.g., Google's Android operating system) to this Chinese company that is perceived as a significant long-term competitive threat to US dominance of future wireless technologies such as 5G.

The deep strains in US-China relations is best illustrated by the COVID-19 pandemic. Despite the grave negative effects of the pandemic across the entire globe, and unlike previous emergencies regarding infectious diseases like the SARS outbreak in China in 2003, the US and China have not been able or even willing to collaborate in providing public goods and joint leadership to steer the world out of the crisis. Instead, we witness a mutual blame game, the nadir of which was reached when Trump, on a number of occasions, used the phrase the "Chinese virus" and when China's foreign ministry speculated about the US military having brought the virus to China in the first place.

For Europe, the growing US-China rivalry—which may well lead to military confrontation, deglobalisation and the bifurcation, or even collapse, of international order—does not bode well. As a weighty potential partner in their contest, both Washington and Beijing have begun stepping up the pressure on Europe— both the EU and individual European states. However, this situation has already prompted increasing political fragmentation across Europe. With the danger of Europe being ground between these two more powerful antagonists, the "old continent" is faced with tough choices. This is not least because Europe's bilateral relationships with both the US and China have more recently encountered a number of serious and growing difficulties.

US-Europe relations

Not so long ago, most European pundits would have argued without hesitation that Europe should position itself much closer to America than to China. Notwithstanding temporary disagreements between the George W. Bush administration and some West European governments, transatlantic cooperation was deemed essential at the time. General alignment with Washington seemed to be necessary for a number of reasons: common values, institutions and various common interests— particularly in maintaining a rules-based global order—in combating climate change and in safeguarding free trade and sea lanes. Last, but not least, there was also a shared interest in stabilizing Europe and its periphery (Garton Ash 2004). Europe's dependence on US military protection, the dollar system and American leadership in international forums reinforced the European preference for the US. Moreover, the Obama administration's renewed commitment to multilateralism (Anderson 2018; Indyk et al. 2012; Mann 2013) seemed to suggest that Europeans and Americans could return to a stable transatlantic relationship, reinforced by their common intertest in containing a more assertive and aggressive Russia.

However, Obama's 2011 pivot to Asia already foreshadowed the negative repercussions for transatlantic ties arising from US-Chinese competition for predominance in the Asia Pacific. This rebalancing raised European concerns that Washington would gradually reassign scarce resources (military and other) to that region at the expense of American contributions to the North Atlantic Treaty Organization (NATO). It also indicated a shift in focus that might reduce American interest in and attention to European and Mediterranean challenges and issues (Gareis and Wolf 2016; Polyakova and Haddad 2019; Witney 2019). While Russia's military interference in Ukraine may have temporarily dampened such concerns, some Europeans came to realise that an escalating Chinese-American rivalry could entail new geopolitical risks for a dependent Europe which lacked a cohesive foreign policy backed by sufficient capability (Joffe 2012; Rifkind 2011).

The arrival of the Trump administration was a tremendous boost to such worries. Trump's personal diatribes against fundamental Western institutions—above all NATO and the EU—his open support for Brexit, his questioning of US membership in the Western alliance and his blanket threat of illegal trade restrictions broke with fundamental principles of US foreign policy, thus calling into question traditional American commitments to a secure, prosperous and democratic Europe. European leaders started to realise that the continent could no longer count on crucial American support. As German chancellor Angela Merkel admitted in a 2017 beer hall address, "The times when we could completely rely on others are a thing of the past" (ARD Hauptstadtstudio 2017). French President Emanuel Macron went even further and called the transatlantic alliance "brain-dead" when Washington refused to consult its European allies on Syria (The Economist 2019).

Beyond the assault on the transatlantic bond, the Trump administration increasingly undermined multilateral institutions and transatlantic efforts that provided collective goods, such as global prosperity, world health and effective arms control (Dworkin and Gowan 2019). Among other things, Washington imposed illegal tariffs on China and Canada, weakened the WTO by blocking the appointment of arbitration judges, obstructed global cooperation on the economic consequences of COVID-19, cancelled American contributions to the World Health Organization (WHO), abstained from an international pledge conference for developing a coronavirus vaccine and withdrew from numerous institutions and agreements, including the United Nations Educational, Scientific and Cultural Organization (UNESCO), the United Nations Human Rights Council, the Transpacific Partnership (TPP), the Paris Climate Accord, the Open Skies Treaty and the multilateral agreement on Iran's nuclear programme (JCPOA)—even though Iran was still in compliance with the latter's obligations.

While this unsettling trajectory may now be reversed to some extent by the new Biden administration that is committed to "rally the free world to meet the challenges facing the world today" (Biden 2020, 76), such repair efforts will take much time and effort, while the loss of trust will be hard to undo. Even with Trump no longer in the White House, the legacy of Trumpism is here to stay. Trump's allies in Congress will not be quick to bury an "America First" rhetoric that appealed so much to their voters. Elite support for open markets will hardly return to its previous levels. And calls for a pragmatic China policy, which seeks common ground wherever possible, will continue to face an uphill battle. The notion of a systemic antagonism between the two giants is likely to persist—with all the sobering consequences that such a cold war perspective entails for America's commitment to a stable Europe. Hence, Europeans must accept the fact that the "good old days" of transatlantic cooperation may be gone for good.

All in all, the growing Chinese-US antagonism and the weakening of transatlantic ties mean that America and, even more so, Europe need to adjust their relationship to the new realities. American leaders must consider whether they want to preserve a weak and dependent Europe, which willy-nilly accepts US leadership or domination, or a more forceful and autonomous Europe, which can largely take care of its own region and might more effectively cooperate with America where their preferences coincide. Correspondingly, and more importantly in the context of this volume, Europe needs to decide to what extent it should reduce its risky dependence on America by pursuing strategic autonomy in defense and foreign policy, bearing in mind that such projects might accentuate transatlantic disagreements on global issues, accelerate the hollowing out of US commitments to Europe and might further marginalise NATO.

China-Europe relations

Relations between China and Europe have been principally characterised by quite different dynamics than those between the US and Europe. This is because the key parameters that have traditionally bound Americans and Europeans together—joint historical experiences, shared values, cultural proximity and military dependence—are virtually non-existent in Sino-European relations. China and Europe have therefore been much more distant partners, not only conceptually but also geographically. On the one hand, this situation has, until recently, resulted in an almost complete lack of geostrategic competition and military entanglement between the two sides. On the other hand, it has enabled China and Europe to focus their relations almost exclusively on economic issues. As long as economic ties were (perceived to be) mutually beneficial, the overall relationship between China and Europe generally prospered, despite a few bumps related to human rights, such as when individual European leaders received the Dalai Lama.

Recently, however, the economic engine driving Sino-European relations has increasingly faltered, especially from a European perspective. In addition, the overall relationship has become more complicated, with the negative trends in the economic realm spilling over into politics and creating a sort of rivalry that is increasingly strategic. While Europe still believes that cooperation with China on a number of global challenges, such as climate change and nuclear nonproliferation, serves European interests, Europe is at the same time "wak[ing] up to China's rise" (Smith and Taussig 2019) and its potentially adverse impacts on the old continent. Consequently, the EU has recently labeled China "an economic competitor in the pursuit of technological leadership and a systemic rival promoting alternative models of governance", in addition to seeing China as a "cooperation partner with whom the EU has closely aligned objectives" (EC 2019, 1). French President Emmanuel Macron, moreover, proclaimed that "the period of European naivety [*vis-à-vis* China] is over" (Reuters 2019).

From Europe's point of view, a crucial term for understanding the recent troubled state of Sino-European economic relations is reciprocity—or, more precisely, its absence. As China's economy has rapidly modernised and started to move up the value chain, the formerly close-to-symbiotic relationship, in which China provided the market for European exports in exchange for European investments and technology, has in many industries ceased to exist and given way to an increasing amount of competition. However, from Europe's perspective—which is not, after all, very different from that of the US—this competition is not fair, with European businesses facing much higher restrictions to market access and related areas in China than vice versa. This "facilitat[es] the economic dominance of Chinese enterprises and . . . disadvantag[es] foreign competitors" (Wübbeke et al. 2016, 7).

Repeated European requests for China to create a more level playing field have been largely unheeded by Beijing.

As a result, Europe has started gradually pushing back. In 2016, the EU did not keep its promise to grant China market economy status under the WTO, 15 years after the country's entry. In addition, after a spike of Chinese foreign direct investment (FDI) into Europe in the same year, several European capitals grew worried about a potential "technological sellout" (Handelsblatt 2019) to China and the lack of intervening tools at their disposal; this eventually led to the adoption of a new EU investment screening mechanism in early 2019. Meanwhile, the conclusion of a bilateral investment treaty between the EU and China that was to address European concerns about opening China's market and eliminating discriminatory laws and practices continues to be out of sight, with China reluctant to accede to European demands.

That said, it must also be recognised that European countries are not, in fact, united in their stance towards China. In recent years, this has become most pronounced with regard to China's BRI and the 17 + 1 mechanism. In April 2018, all 28 (at the time) EU ambassadors to China, except Hungary's, signed a report critical of the BRI for hampering free trade and effectively being a "one-way street" that favoured Chinese companies and left European countries without a say (Handelsblatt 2018); however, this unity has since crumbled, with around half of EU Member States—including Greece, Hungary, Italy and Portugal—breaking ranks and supporting the BRI. Similarly, the 17 + 1 mechanism has been perceived very differently across Europe: whereas its participants, including 12 EU members, have largely welcomed Chinese funds for infrastructure development, others— especially Germany—have made no pretense of their regard for the mechanism as a potential Chinese divide-and-rule tool that further erodes EU unity (Europe Online 2017).

A big problem for Europe is that, with China's growing geo-economic footprint particularly on its eastern and southern flanks, Beijing has increasingly sought to influence European domestic politics in its own favour. However, despite a continued lack of European unity and some resultant Chinese successes in promoting Chinese interests—such as Greece torpedoing an EU statement on China's human rights violations in 2017—many European countries seem to be growing more and more disenchanted with China (Otero-Iglesias and Esteban 2020; Smith and Taussig 2019). The most recent illustration of this possible trend is the shifting attitude of European countries towards Chinese involvement in the development of their 5G infrastructure by acknowledging the national security vulnerabilities this might present. It is notable that even some Central and Eastern European countries which are members of the 17 + 1 mechanism have lately signed agreements with the US on 5G security that would limit the role of Huawei in their markets (Haenle and Tcheyan 2020). Similarly, China did not score points for its "mask diplomacy" during the COVID-19 outbreak in Europe (Brattberg and Le Corre 2020). In fact, Europe has increasingly pushed back against China's propaganda and disinformation surrounding the pandemic. At the same time, however, the EU has also toned-down rhetoric that implicates China in spreading the coronavirus, following pressure from Beijing.

Together with the by and large hesitant response from European leaders to China's treatment of the Uighurs in Xinjiang and protestors in Hong Kong, Europe's mixed behaviour demonstrates that, despite all difficulties, most countries in Europe are still willing to maintain a balanced approach towards China, due mainly to hopes that economic benefits will continue to accrue. A key question for China, therefore, is the extent to which Beijing is willing to seriously accommodate European concerns in light of its increasing rivalry with Washington and growing concerns, at least from some quarters in China, that it should not forfeit relations with both the US and Europe at the same time. Meanwhile, Europe is confronted with the question of how important its economic relationship with China really is for its positive future trajectory—especially if European countries are faced with mounting American pressure to make a decision on which side they will stand in a potential US-China showdown.

Key challenges/dilemmas

Europe is thus faced with a very challenging international environment where (a) the two foremost powers seem to be on a collision course, and (b) where neither of these appears a natural partner which shares the bulk of Europe's interests and concerns. While the historic Cold War also put Europe in a difficult position, this time it lacks a reliable protector and a straightforward supporter for its vision of a stable global order which upholds key values and facilitates the production of vital collective goods. Europe must therefore accept that it faces a number of painful questions and dilemmas:

1   Should Europe opt principally for one side in global governance or should it pursue pragmatic case-by-case cooperation, more closely collaborating with China on some problems while partnering with the US on others?
2   Should Europe concentrate on salvaging or promoting global institutions, or should it resign itself to their stagnation and decay and, rather, hedge its bets by building regional order(s) in order to prevent destabilizing developments in its vicinity which could otherwise hurt it?
3   Should Europe prioritise efforts to strengthen NATO or should it rather focus its initiatives and resources on the quest for strategic autonomy—even though this policy might (further) undermine US commitment to European security?
4   Related to this is whether Europe should try to play a more meaningful diplomatic or military role in the Asia-Pacific or whether it should concentrate its military assets and activities even more on Europe and its neighbourhood?
5   Finally, will Europe still be able to afford the "luxury" of promoting its values in the global arena, particularly in the Asia-Pacific, or should it accept that material interests take precedence whenever interests and values are at odds?

It is these hard questions that Europeans can no longer escape and which we have therefore asked our contributors to consider in their areas of expertise. While we certainly cannot hope to provide definitive answers to them, we hope that the volume's chapters, along with its conclusion, provide some valuable insights into how Europe could and should respond.

Structure of the book

Following this Introduction, the first three chapters of the volume address Europe's agency in the light of ongoing structural shifts in the international system. Øystein Tunsjø's contribution argues that Europe is confronted with a new bipolar system which forces a weaker Europe to adapt to the structural effects of a Chinese-American power contest. After making the case for a bipolar understanding of the current international system, Tunsjø examines the effects of this new power structure, with special emphasis on the geopolitical features of the Sino-American rivalry, which unfold primarily as a contest for maritime supremacy in the Asia-Pacific. In this unfolding antagonism, Tunsjø sees Europe largely as a bystander torn between its traditional military dependence on the US and its growing economic dependence on China. Due to its interest in salvaging transatlantic security ties, Europe might eventually feel compelled to support Washington in its economic contest with Beijing. Nevertheless, such American pressure could also strain transatlantic relations since Europe, unlike the US, could continue to view China less as a military threat and more as an economic opportunity. According to Tunsjø, such transatlantic differences would become even more pronounced if Beijing and Washington were to become involved in yet another regional conflict. In considering this predicament, Tunsjø concludes that Europe should cautiously support Washington in upholding the current economic order while stepping up its capabilities for providing security in its own region rather than preparing for an active military role in the Asia-Pacific.

Liselotte Odgaard concurs with Tunsjø that Europe is not in the same power league as China and America. However, drawing on the English School's concept of a "middle power", she comes to more optimistic conclusions regarding Europe's influence on the Chinese-American confrontation. In Odgaard's understanding, great powers need the support of middle powers for stabilizing regional security orders. The competition of dominant states for ideational and material backing thus opens independent space for middle powers to advance their own visions of international order. Such powers may thus promote international norms which curb the great powers' usage of hard power and help ameliorate military tensions. Applying these insights to Europe's structural position in the Chinese-American context, Odgaard investigates options for the EU and its major members to promote a peaceful resolution in the Asia-Pacific. As she points out, Europe is not too weak to play a meaningful role, especially if it cooperates with other middle powers in the region. Even in the South China Sea conflict, active involvement by European states that threatens neither side's core values and interests can exert a stabilizing influence. By demonstrating the value of maritime codes for unplanned encounters, European navies can help to defuse regional military competition without backing one side into a corner. In Odgaard's view, instead of withdrawing their forces from the Asia-Pacific, Europe should capitalise on its diplomatic potential.

Similarly, Tomasz Kamiński and Joanna Ciesielska-Klikowska paint a somewhat more optimistic picture of Europe's influence in the Asia-Pacific region. In their investigation of sub-state contacts between Europe and China, they alert readers to a largely untapped potential for promoting cooperation and European norms. After reviewing the dynamic evolution of subnational contacts between Europe and China, the authors analyse how cooperation between regions, cities, universities and other sub-state actors can help stabilise overall Sino-European relations. They then substantiate these general points with a more detailed discussion of sub-state contacts between Chinese provinces and German *Länder* (states) as well as between cities in the two countries. Kamiński and Ciesielska-Klikowska argue that such paradiplomatic activities can constrain the effects of tensions that emanate from interactions between states or between Brussels and Beijing. Such forms of cooperation, being less politicised than high-level contacts, are more likely to "weather the storm" of official confrontations and might alleviate setbacks in the field of global governance. This may prove especially useful if the EU and its member states feel forced to support US positions against China. Moreover, such contacts can be an important low-level tool for promoting European values and good practice without provoking a backlash from the centre in Beijing. Kamiński and Ciesielska-Klikowska use these findings to call European authorities to make a more systematic effort to harness the advantages of these instruments.

The following group of chapters analyses key issues related to Europe's role in Asia-Pacific security, with a view to Europe's main interests and options. Emil Kirchner's contribution discusses the EU's Asia security policy in an ever more challenging environment which seems increasingly at odds with the multilateral *modus operandi* that has characterised European diplomacy. Following an overview of the EU's current role in East Asia, Kirchner first analyses the impact of the Chinese BRI project and the Trump administration's move to open confrontation with China and, albeit to a lesser extent, with Europe. He then investigates the strategic implications of closer Chinese-Russian relations before examining the general prospects for a meaningful EU Asia security policy. Notwithstanding the turn towards Sino-American confrontation, Kirchner advocates a more autonomous EU policy that should aspire to amity with both antagonists. Only in the case of a major military confrontation between the two superpowers should Europe opt for the US. To forestall such a conflagration, Kirchner favours systematic efforts to uphold the multilateral global order as well as regional European security initiatives in the Asia-Pacific aimed at conflict resolution and confidence building. In both endeavors, the EU should strengthen its impact by teaming up with like-minded states, especially regional democracies that also stand to lose from escalating superpower confrontation that would further destabilise both regional security and multilateral institutions. Kirchner thus acknowledges the growing challenges to Europe's diplomatic approach in the Asia-Pacific but argues that it is still too early to discard such diplomacy altogether.

Following this general policy outline, Michael Paul's contribution focuses more specifically on the EU's potential role in the South China Sea conflict. After summing up the historic origins and legal features of this complicated dispute, Paul investigates its key implications for European interests in trade and regional order. He then addresses Europe's past military and diplomatic involvement in the region and its limited options for fostering a peaceful resolution. Although well aware of the significant constraints that European actors face in this difficult security environment far from European shores, he does not advocate a passive approach. Instead, he makes the case for more active involvement. He particularly sees a useful role for a European naval presence, coupled with diplomatic efforts to promote respect for international norms that regulate maritime governance, freedom of navigation, confidence building and dispute resolution. In line with the previous authors, Paul suggests closer cooperation with like-minded states, including eventual collaboration with the new Biden administration. Symptomatic of his support for more European involvement in regional security affairs is his call for a more active German role, including regular deployments of *Bundesmarine* frigates to the Asia-Pacific.

Ramon Pacheco Pardo analyses European interests and options with regard to the second multilateral security flashpoint in East Asia: the conflict over North Korea's nuclearisation. He does so by taking a decidedly realist point of view, arguing that Europe should primarily cater to its own interests: to the overall stability of the non-proliferation regime and to the dangers implicit in a nuclear North Korea for nuclear proliferation to jihadists or states in the Middle East, where Europe's security interests are even more strongly affected. Pacheco Pardo first puts these ideas into perspective, showing that the EU's relevant strategy documents indicate a gradual shift from liberal assumptions to a more realist worldview, one which puts more emphasis on Europe's self-interest and "the language of power". He then discusses Europe's stakes in the conflict and its past contributions to international denuclearisation, including its participation in the global sanctions regime and the Proliferation Security Initiative (PSI). The author then goes on to investigate differences and commonalities between Europe's stance and those of the region's key players, such as the US, China and South Korea. Based on this review, he concludes that Europe should not prioritise close cooperation with one of these states. Instead, he makes the case for a pragmatic approach that gives precedence to European interests rather than values, uses all tools available and seeks collaboration with any actor whose priorities and tactics happen to coincide with those of Europe.

Following the analyses related to matters of traditional security, the next four chapters of this volume turn to examine major geo-economic issues affecting Europe's welfare. Margot Schüller's contribution tackles two (geo-)economic issues that are becoming increasingly intertwined in US-China-Europe triangular relations: the rather traditional topic of trade, including the multilateral global trade regime and the rapidly emerging problematic of technological competition.

In the first part, Schüller outlines the details of the ongoing US-China trade conflict, with a particular analytical focus on Europe's perspective. Discussing the WTO, she argues that, while Europe shares some of the US concerns about China's mixed compliance record, unlike the US, European states also continue to see China as an important partner for preserving and modernising the global trade organisation. According to Schüller, this is not least because Europe could be the next target of US trade sanctions. The second part of the chapter delineates China's pursuit of global technological leadership as well as pertinent US countermeasures. With regard to Europe, Schüller finds that the old continent is caught in the crossfire of this "tech cold war", as she calls it. Considering this difficult situation as well as European interests and dependencies, Schüller advises Europe to develop its own nuanced China policy that differs from the current and confrontational US approach. Altogether, Schüller reaches the conclusion that Europe should not take sides in the US-China rivalry, but instead must build the capacities for acting as a global power in its own right.

Philippe Le Corre focuses on China's outbound foreign direct investment (FDI) to the US and Europe, which has recently become a growing concern on both sides of the Atlantic. Le Corre starts by describing the challenges Chinese FDI presents to both the US and Europe. The two sides have in fact been confronted with different scenarios: in the US, Chinese investment has been largely driven by private commercial incentives and the acquisition of advanced technologies firms, whereas in Europe it is primarily Chinese state-linked entities that have been interested in investing in critical physical infrastructure. Le Corre then argues that, mostly due to different perceptions of the challenges, early US and European responses to Chinese FDI also diverged, with the US screening and effectively banning deals that were seen as affecting US national security at a time when Europe's response still was generally lax. Meanwhile, however, Le Corre welcomes the hardening in Europe's more recent approach, which has therefore moved much closer to US positions. Nonetheless, he sees Europe as still disunited on the matter. He writes that while big EU member states (such as Germany, France and Italy) have sought to mend fences and have driven the launch of a EU-wide FDI screening mechanism, smaller members and certain European countries outside the EU continue to embrace Chinese investment and are hence increasingly dependent on Chinese money. Despite the trend of decreasing Chinese FDI, Le Corre concludes that the US and Europe should better align their future approaches towards the subject and also seek to coordinate their policies with like-minded third countries.

The following chapter, authored by Claude Zanardi, deals with China's BRI and its impacts on Europe. Using the Central and Eastern European Countries (CEECs) as a case study, Zanardi maintains that the BRI, particularly through the huge financial resources attached to it, has not only enhanced China's economic footprint in Europe but has also increased its political leverage in the region, up to the point where the (further) undermining of democratic institutions has become a possibility. Zanardi then turns to discussing the connectivity aspect of the BRI, especially its digital dimension through the so-called Digital Silk Road (DSR).

Here she contends that the DSR's strong focus on new technologies, such as 5G, might help spread authoritarianism and curb fundamental human rights. However, by detailing recent developments surrounding China's role in building 5G infrastructure in Poland and Serbia, Zanardi also reveals how different the outcomes on the ground may actually be, with Poland eventually banning Chinese Huawei Telecommunications from its domestic market and Serbia endorsing the company. As Zanardi does not perceive much cooperation potential with China on the DSR, she recommends that the EU strengthen democratic institutions in the CEECs and make greater efforts to provide its own digital infrastructure. More generally, Zanardi reaches the conclusion that the BRI is a much more important challenge for Europe than diverse security problems in the distant Asia-Pacific, which is why the EU should, in light of its own resources, give priority to managing its own neighbourhood.

Finally, Mario Esteban and Lara Lázaro Touza investigate the current cooperation potential between the US, China and Europe with regard to global climate change mitigation. They firstly analyse the likely consequences for climate-related cooperation between the three actors now that US abandonment of the Paris Agreement has actually taken effect. What they find is that, to date, US-EU climate cooperation has continued to some extent, despite Trump's decision to leave the Paris Agreement. According to them, this is, however, unlike US-China climate cooperation, which was marginalised by the Trump administration, thereby opening the door for enhanced China-EU cooperation on the subject, including emissions trading and joint cooperation in developing countries. Consequently, Esteban and Lázaro discuss the potential drivers of and barriers to China-EU co-leadership in the realm of climate change mitigation. They argue that, while there are a number of domestic reasons on each side as well as international pressure that would militate for joint leadership, it remains to be seen if such a trajectory actually materialises. As the two authors explain, this is mainly due to a recent loss of momentum on the part of China, which sees itself confronted with changing domestic conditions: above all, a slowing economy, resulting in the prioritisation of pro-growth policies at the expense of sustainability. All said, Esteban and Lázaro conclude that the EU will and should remain open to collaborating with both the US and China on climate issues because, from Brussels' perspective, and unlike many other areas of concern in this volume, climate cooperation includes neither a values-interests dilemma nor geostrategic competition.

Based on the findings of the individual chapters, the conclusion by Sebastian Biba and Reinhard Wolf makes a comprehensive assessment of Europe's options in the light of intensifying US-China rivalry and then offers long-term policy recommendations for Europe's self-preservation within the US-China-Europe strategic triangle. To map out the range of Europe's possible responses to a deepening US-China face-off, the first part summarises the key agreements and disagreements among the chapters' authors. In doing so, Biba and Wolf identify major trends among the experts and propose a number of follow-up questions that need to be addressed in greater detail to yield substantial answers to the guiding questions of this volume. On this basis, the editors formulate key lessons for Europe. They argue, firstly, that elites need to convince their citizens that an escalating Sino-American confrontation entails serious risks for the very sustainability of the European way of life; secondly, that a less stable global environment forces Europe to bolster its resilience by pooling more sovereignty, by boosting its autonomous military capabilities and by using its economic capabilities more strategically; thirdly, that Europe must take more responsibility for stabilizing its vicinity; fourthly, that Europe must intensify its efforts to win over new partners for salvaging the rules-based multilateral order; and, finally, and perhaps most importantly, that Europeans must soon overcome their strategic complacency and agree on long-term plans for Europe's self-preservation. Reviving Franco-German co-leadership will be essential in this regard.

Note

1 The volume editors would like to thank Markus Liegl for his most valuable contributions at the early stages of this book project, as well as Franziska Kasten, Irene Opaterny, Emil Suhrab and Simon Westphalen for their highly appreciated help with the references.

References

Allison, Graham. 2017. *Destined for War: Can America and China Escape Thucydides's Trap?* Boston and New York: Houghton Mifflin Harcourt.

Anderson, Jeffrey J. 2018. "Rancor and Resilience in the Atlantic Political Order: The Obama Years." *Journal of European Integration* 40 (5): 621–636.

ARD Hauptstadtstudio. 2017. "Merkels Trudering-Rede—eine taktische Glanzleistung." May 29. https://blog.ard-hauptstadtstudio.de/audio-46952/.

Ash, Timothy Garton. 2004. *Free World: America, Europe, and the Surprising Future of the West*. New York: Random House.

Bergsten, Fred. 2005. *The United States and the World Economy: Foreign Economic Policy for the Next Decade*. Washington, DC: Peterson Institute for International Economics.

Bergsten, Fred. 2008. "A Partnership of Equals: How Washington Should Respond to China's Economic Challenge." *Foreign Affairs* 87 (4): 57–69.

Biba, Sebastian. 2016. "It's Status, Stupid: Explaining the Underlying Core Problem in US-China Relations." *Global Affairs* 2 (5): 455–464.

Biden, Joseph R. 2020. "Why America Must Lead Again: Rescuing U.S. Foreign Policy After Trump." *Foreign Affairs* 99 (2): 64–76.

Brattberg, Erik, and Philippe Le Corre. 2020. "No, COVID-19 Isn't Turning Europe Pro-China (Yet)." *The Diplomat*, April 15. https://thediplomat.com/2020/04/no-covid-19-isnt-turning-europe-pro-china-yet/.

Brezezinski, Zbigniew. 2009. "The Group of Two That Could Change the World." *Financial Times*, January 13. www.ft.com/content/d99369b8-e178-11dd-afa0-0000779fd2ac.

Brooks, Stephen, and William Wohlforth. 2016. "The Rise and Fall of the Great Powers in the Twenty-First Century: China's Rise and the Fate of America's Global Position." *International Security* 40 (3): 7–53.

Chatzky, Andrew, and James McBride. 2020. "China's Massive Belt and Road Initiative." Council on Foreign Relations Backgrounder, January 28. www.cfr.org/backgrounder/chinas-massive-belt-and-road-initiative.

Chellaney, Brahma. 2017. "China's Debt-Trap Diplomacy." *Project Syndicate*, January 23. www.project-syndicate.org/commentary/china-one-belt-one-road-loans-debt-by-brahma-chellaney-2017-01.

CNN Politics. 2016. "Trump: We Can't Continue to Allow China to Rape Our Country." *CNN Politics*, May 2. http://edition.cnn.com/2016/05/01/politics/donald-trump-china-rape/index.html.

Dworkin, Anthony, and Richard Gowan. 2019. *Rescuing Multilateralism*. London: European Council on Foreign Relations. www.ecfr.eu/page/-/7_Rescuing_multilateralism.pdf.

The Economist. 2019. "Emmanuel Macron Warns Europe: NATO Is Becoming Brain-Dead." *The Economist*, November 7. www.economist.com/europe/2019/11/07/emmanuel-macron-warns-europe-nato-is-becoming-brain-dead.

Europe Online. 2017. "German Foreign Minister Warns EU against Divisive Chinese Tactics." *Europe Online*, August 30. http://en.europeonline-magazine.eu/german-foreign-minister-warns-euagainst-divisive-chinese- tactics_574948.html.

European Commission (EC). 2019. "EU-China: A Strategic Outlook." March 12. https://ec.europa.eu/commission/sites/beta-political/files/communication-eu-china-a-strategic-outlook.pdf.

Ferguson, Niall. 2008. "Team 'Chimerica'." *Washington Post*, November 17. www.washingtonpost.com/wp-dyn/content/article/2008/11/16/AR2008111601736.html.

Forbes. 2016. "How Far Can Trump Go on Chinese Trade Policy?" *Forbes*, November 14. www.forbes.com/sites/sarahsu/2016/11/14/how-far-can-trump-go-on-chinese-trade-policy/#59b6820c1dd1.

Friedberg, Aaron L. 2011. *A Contest for Supremacy: China, America, and the Struggle for Mastery in Asia*. New York and London: W. W. Norton & Company.

Gareis, Sven Bernhard, and Reinhard Wolf. 2016. "Home Alone? The US Pivot to Asia and Its Implications for the EU's Common Security and Defence Policy." *European Foreign Affairs Review* 21 (3/1): 133–150.

Haenle, Paul, and Lukas Tcheyan. 2020. "How the World Is Responding to a Changing China." *Carnegie Endowment for International Peace*, June 10. https://carnegieendowment.org/2020/06/10/how-world-is-responding-to-changing-china-pub-82039?utm.

Handelsblatt. 2018. "EU Ambassadors Band Together Over Silk Road." *Handelsblatt*, April 17. https://global.handelsblatt.com/politics/eu-ambassadors-beijing-china-silk-road-912258.

Handelsblatt. 2019. "Altmeier will Ausverkauf deutscher Industrie verhindern." *Handelsblatt*, November 29. www.handelsblatt.com/politik/deutschland/industriestrategie-2030-altmaier-will-ausverkauf-deutscher-industrie-verhindern/25282996.html?ticket=ST-6357969-WTVlF5gRdoHagSmuoWxb-ap5.

Indyk, Martin, Kenneth Lieberthal, and Michael E. O'Hanlon. 2012. *Bending History: Barack Obama's Foreign Policy*. Washington, DC: Brookings Institution Press.

Joffe, Josef. 2012. "The Turn Away from Europe: Rebalancing US Forces Is Inevitable—and a Threat to World Stability." *Commentary* 134 (4): 11–15.

Kaplan, Robert. 2019. "A New Cold War Has Begun." *Foreign Policy*, January 7. https://foreignpolicy.com/2019/01/07/a-new-cold-war-has-begun/.

Larson, Deborah, T.V. Paul, and William Wohlforth. 2014. "Status and World Order." In *Status and World Politics*, edited by T.V. Paul, Deborah Larson, and William Wohlforth, 3–29. Cambridge: Cambridge University Press.

Leonard, Mark. 2018. "The US and China Are the Closest of Enemies." *Project Syndicate*, November 27. www.project-syndicate.org/commentary/america-china-closest-of-enemies-by-mark-leonard-2018-11.

Lieberthal, Kenneth, and Jisi Wang. 2012. *Addressing U.S.-China Strategic Distrust*. Washington, DC: Brookings Institution Press, John L. Thornton China Center Monograph Series Number 4, March. www.brookings.edu/wp-content/uploads/2016/06/0330_china_lieberthal.pdf.

Lippert, Barbara, Nicolai von Ondarza, and Volker Perthes, eds. 2019. "European Strategic Autonomy: Actors, Issues, Conflicts of Interests." SWP Research Paper, March. www.swp-berlin.org/fileadmin/contents/products/research_papers/2019RP04_lpt_orz_prt_web.pdf.

Mann, James. 2013. *The Obamians: The Struggle Inside the White House to Redefine American Power*. New York: Penguin Press.

Maull, Hanns W., ed. 2018. *The Rise and Decline of the Post-Cold War International Order*. Oxford: Oxford University Press.

Mead, Walter Russell. 2002. *Special Providence: American Foreign Policy and How It Changed the World*. New York: Routledge.

Mearsheimer, John. 2010. "The Gathering Storm: China's Challenge to US Power in Asia." *Chinese Journal of Political Science* 3 (4): 381–396.

Nau, Henry R. 2002. *At Home Abroad: Identity and Power in American Foreign Policy*. Ithaca: Cornell University Press.

Organski, A. F. K., and Jacek Kugler. 1981. *The War Ledger*. Chicago, IL: Chicago University Press.

Otero-Iglesias, Miguel, and Mario Esteban. 2020. "Introduction." In *Europe in the Face of US-China Rivalry*, edited by Mario Esteban, Miguel Otero-Iglesias, Una Aleksandra Bērziņa-Čerenkova, Alice Ekman, Lucrezia Poggetti, Björn Jerdén, John Seaman, Tim Summers, and Justyna Szczudlik, 19–32. European Think Tank Network on China Report. www.ifri.org/sites/default/files/atoms/files/etnc_report_us-china-europe_january_2020_complete.pdf.

Polyakova, Alina, and Benjamin Haddad. 2019. "Europe Alone: What Comes After the Transatlantic Alliance." *Foreign Affairs* 98 (4): 109–120.

Reuters. 2019. "EU Leaders Call for End to 'Naivety' in Relations with China." *Reuters*, March 22. www.reuters.com/article/us-eu-china/eu-leaders-call-for-end-to-naivety-in-relations-with-china-idUSKCN1R31H3.

Rifkind, Malcolm. 2011. "Europe Grapples with U.S. Pivot." *The Diplomat*, December 1. http://thediplomat.com/2011/12/europe-grapples-with-u-s-pivot/?allpages=yes.

Rudolf, Peter. 2020. "The Sino-American World Conflict." SWP Research Paper, February. www.swp-berlin.org/fileadmin/contents/products/research_papers/2020RP03_rdf_Web.pdf.

Schulze, Matthias, and Daniel Voelsen. 2020. "Strategic Spheres of Influence." In *Strategic Rivalry Between United States and China: Causes, Trajectories, and Implications for Europe*, edited by Barbara Lippert and Volker Perthes, 30–34. SWP Research Paper, April. www.swp-berlin.org/fileadmin/contents/products/research_papers/2020RP04_China_USA.pdf.

Smith, Julianne, and Torrey Taussig. 2019. "The Old World and the Middle Kingdom: Europe Wakes Up to China's Rise." *Foreign Affairs* 98 (5): 112–124.

Wang, Dong, and Chengzhi Yin. 2014. "Mainland China Debates U.S. Pivot/Rebalancing to Asia." *Issues & Studies* 50 (3): 57–101.

Witney, Nick. 2019. "Building Europeans' Capacity to Defend Themselves." *European Foreign Affairs Council*, June. www.ecfr.eu/page/-/5_Building_Europeans%E2%80%99_capacity_to_defend_themselves.pdf.

Wolf, Reinhard. 2012. "Auf Konfrontationskurs: Warum es zur amerikanisch-chinesischen Konfrontation kommen muss." *Zeitschrift für Politik* 59 (4): 393–409.

Wolf, Reinhard. 2017. "Donald Trump's Status-Driven Foreign Policy." *Survival* 59 (5): 99–116.

Wübbeke, Jost, Mirjam Meissner, Max Zenglein, Jacqueline Ives, and Björn Conrad. 2016. "Made in China 2025: The Making of a High-Tech Superpower and Consequences for Industrial Countries." MERICS Papers on China Number 2, December. www.stiftung-mercator.de/media/downloads/3_Publikationen/MERICS_PAPER_ON_CHINA_No.2_MadeinChina_2025_Dezember_2016.pdf.

Yan, Xuetong. 2001. "The Rise of China in Chinese Eyes." *Journal of Contemporary China* 10 (26): 33–39.

Zhao, Suisheng. 2019. "Engagement on the Defensive: From the Mismatched Grand Bargain to the Emerging US-China Rivalry." *Journal of Contemporary China* 28 (118): 1–18.

Zoellick, Robert, and Justin Yifu Lin. 2009. "Recovery: A Job for China and the U.S." *Washington Post*, March 6. www.washingtonpost.com/wp-dyn/content/article/2009/03/05/AR2009030502887.html.

Part I

Europe's agency in the international system

2 New US-China bipolar system

What role for Europe in security and defence?

Øystein Tunsjø

Introduction

Against conventional wisdom and the mainstream view that the international system is either unipolar (Beckley 2011–2012, 2018; Brooks and Wohlforth 2008, 2016; Hansen 2011; Monteiro 2014; Wohlforth 1999), multipolar (Layne 2012; Mearsheimer 2014; Murray and Brown 2012; Posen 2009; Schweller 2014; Waltz 1993) or nonpolar (Haass 2008, 2017; Zakaria 2008), this chapter contends that the structure of the international system has changed from unipolarity to US-China bipolarity (Tunsjø 2018). China's rise has altered the underlying distribution of power in the international system. While China is not the equal of the United Sates (US) in power aggregate, it has narrowed the power gap significantly and vaulted into top ranking. Of equal importance is that no other state is strong enough to serve as a competitor to these two. Since the top two states are now much more powerful than any third state, the structure of the international system has changed from unipolarity to bipolarity. No studies have examined how the return of bipolarity affects the European Union (EU) and European states and how they are likely to respond to such a global power shift.[1]

The emergence of a US-China bipolar system and the contemporary power shift from the West to the East is unprecedented. For the first time in centuries, we are now living in an Asia—and especially an East Asia—centred world. Asia's share of the global economy and the world's defence spending now outpace Europe's. China is the biggest and most important driver behind the global power shift from the West to the East. East Asia has become the key strategic area in contemporary world affairs. Europe was at the centre for centuries but not anymore. When Europe was the core strategic area, Lord Ismay, North Atlantic Treaty Organization's (NATO) first secretary-general, could famously announce that the key objectives for the allies was to keep Germany down, Russia out and the US in. To paraphrase these words: Europe today has only a marginal role to play in keeping China out (that is, from controlling vital sea lanes in East Asia), in keeping Japan down (that is, preventing Japan's remilitarisation, fuelling a regional arms race and war between Japan and China) and in keeping the US in (that is, as a counterweight to China).

The global power shift provides the key starting point for examining Europe's role in a new bipolar system and its implications for European states and transatlantic ties. Divided into three parts, the chapter first shows why the distribution of capabilities in the international system is bipolar. I have elsewhere established the return of bipolarity thesis (Tunsjø 2018). However, the current literature contains so many misunderstandings, different interpretations and misguided views on polarity that it is necessary to highlight why the international system has shifted to bipolarity. I develop the case for contemporary bipolarity not only by examining the current distribution of capabilities, but I contend that the contemporary distribution of capabilities in the international system is roughly similar to the origins of the previous bipolar system in the 1950s.

The second part explains why polarity matters to international politics. Establishing the contemporary polarity of the international system is important because the superpower(s), great powers and other states and institutions behave differently within different structures. In the words of Waltz, structure "shapes and shoves". The distinct role and pattern of behaviour of European great powers prior to World War II (multipolar system), the role of European states and the EU during the Cold War era (bipolar system) and their different room for manoeuvre in the post-Cold War period (unipolar system) suggest that a new international system is likely to push the EU and European states in new directions. Structural realist theory maintains that a polarity perspective cannot explain much, but it can explain and predict the most important aspects of international politics—how the systemic distribution of capabilities shape state-balancing behaviour and the risk of war among the top-ranking states. Waltz argued that balancing differs between bipolar and multipolar systems. He further maintained that a bipolar system of two is more stable than a multipolar system of three or more (Waltz 1959, 1964, 2010).

However, Waltz's neorealist theory only compared bipolar and multipolar systems. He never compared two bipolar systems. Thus, neorealism is insufficient to explain and predict balancing and stability in a new bipolar system in the 21st century. Drawing on a newly developed geostructural realist theory,[2] the final part of this chapter focuses on how a new bipolar system might affect European security and defence policy. It examines whether European states are likely to be a balance against China, and the risk of European states being drawn into a future conflict in East Asia.

Some scholars, including some contributors to this volume (Brattberg and Le Corre 2019; Casarini 2020; Odgaard 2019; Pejsova 2019; Stumbaum 2014), advocate that Europe should take a balanced approach and not choose sides in the growing rivalry between the United States (US) and China. Simultaneously, it is argued that Europe should combine such a posture with a more significant role in Asian security affairs. I think these propositions are untenable. A new bipolar system is likely to polarise, and it will become more difficult for European states to have their cake and eat it too: they will increasingly be compelled to choose sides between the US and China. When confronted with this dilemma, one should not forget that the US has played and, in comparison with China, continues to play a decisive and much more important role in European security, stability and prosperity. However, since the US is likely to retrench from the Middle East and Europe in order to concentrate more of its resources on China, its only peer-competitor, Europe needs to differentiate between its core and peripheral interests.

Core is Europe's ability to sustain security and stability in Europe and its neighbourhood. Currently, European states are not able to fulfil this objective and they remain dependent on the US. Therefore, instead of pursuing a stronger security role in Asia, European states should retrench from Asia, similar to how the US is seeking to pull back from other regions besides Asia. No Asian states will consider European states significant security actors in the region, and Europe does not have the capabilities to play a major role in disputes over North Korea, the East China Sea, Taiwan, the South China Sea, between India and Pakistan or between China and India. A stronger European role in Asian security will overextend Europe's resources in pursuit of peripheral interests and undermine its core interests.

Such a grand strategic approach does not imply that Europe cannot trade with China, the US and the world or that Europe should not compete in developing innovative technology. Europe can also sustain its cooperation with the US in upholding the liberal international order and can play a role in non-traditional security affairs, including managing pandemics, cyber-security, migration and climate change. However, by avoiding traditional security entanglements in Asia and instead strengthening Europe from within and advancing their cohesion, European states might pursue a strategic goal similar to how the US benefited from its isolation from conflict and wars in Europe and developed itself into the world's leading power in the 20th century (Tunsjø 2013). It is unlikely that Europe will manoeuvre into a preeminent role in world affairs in the 21st century, but a stronger focus on taking responsibility in Europe and its vicinity can prevent it from becoming marginalised in the periphery. It remains the best strategy for maintaining an important role for Europe in international affairs and the new bipolar system.

In summary, this chapter contends that Europe has a marginal role to play in an increasingly crisis-prone Asia-Pacific theatre and concludes that, with growing US-China confrontation, Europe should side with the US. However, in order to combine these two objectives of maintaining a marginal role in the Asia-Pacific and siding with the US, Europe needs to prioritise norms and values with the US and take a pragmatic approach whereby it takes more responsibility for security and stability in Europe and in its own neighbourhood.

The contemporary bipolar distribution of capabilities in the international system

Three developments suggest that the international system has shifted from unipolarity to bipolarity. The first is the narrowing power gap between the US and China. The second is the widening power gap between China and the third-ranking powers (Russia, India, Japan, Germany or any other state one might conceivably conceive for such a ranking). If this gap is larger than that between the first and the second ranked power, then the system is probably bipolar. Thirdly, the distribution of capabilities between the contemporary international system and the origins of the previous bipolar system in 1950 is roughly similar. If the current distribution of capabilities resembles those at the start of the previous bipolar system, then the contemporary international system is very likely bipolar.

According to Waltz, we can measure state power and how power is distributed in the international system according to how the top ranking powers "score on *all* of the following items: size of the population and territory, resource endowment, economic capability, military strength, political stability and competence" (Waltz 2010, 131). It is beyond the scope of this chapter to assess each factor in depth, and I focus mainly on measuring the distribution of economic and military power. It should also be noted that the EU as a non-state actor cannot be regarded as a pole in the international system. However, the EU and other institutions and regimes are shaped by polarity. The origins, consolidation and enlargement of European integration were strongly affected by the origins of the previous bipolar system, superpower rivalry during the Cold War period and the post-Cold War unipolar system. For instance, EU enlargement into Eastern Europe was simply impossible when the Soviet Union existed; French and German integration was very much shaped by the threat from the Soviet Union in the 1950s. The development of a new US-China bipolar system and a power shift from the West to the East are likely to shape the EU and European states in new directions in the 21st century.

The gap between number one and number two

China is not overtaking the US, even if the Chinese economy is now the world's largest measured in terms of purchasing power parity (PPP). The US economy is still larger than China's if we measure nominal gross domestic product (GDP), although China is narrowing the gap at a remarkable rate. China's nominal GDP is currently 64 percent that of the US.[3] This contrasts sharply with the early 1990s, when US nominal GDP was about 15 times larger than China's, or in 2000, when it was approximately eight times larger (The World Bank n.d.). Currently, according to the Stockholm International Peace Research Institute (SIPRI), US military spending is about two to three times that of China. This differs from the turn of the century, when the US defence budget was more than ten times that of China, not to mention the early 1990s, when US defence expenditure was more than 20 times higher. China is obviously more powerful than in the past: its share of the distribution of capabilities in the international system has increased considerably, and it can now be ranked in the top tier in terms of its economic and military capability, even though it has not obtained power parity with the US.

The narrowing power gap between the US and China is only one aspect of the shift in the distribution of capabilities in the international system. We cannot know whether the international system has become bipolar or multipolar until we examine the power distribution between China and other great powers contending for a place among the top-ranking nations.

The gap between number two and number three

Over the last several years, China has pulled ahead of all the other powers that might have been considered for a place at the high table. The size of the Chinese economy in 1990 was about 1.5 times that of India and roughly half the Soviet Union's and, in 1993, China and Russia's economy in nominal GDP was roughly the same. Today, China's nominal GDP is about *ten times* larger than Russia's and more than *five times* India's (International Monetary Fund 2015). It seems illogical to argue for a transition to multipolarity and not bipolarity when India has about one-fifth and Russia one-tenth of China's nominal GDP, while China has obtained more than three-fifths of US nominal GDP. The Chinese economy is almost three times as large as Japan's, the same for Germany, and more than four times as large as France's and the United Kingdom's (UK's) (*ibid.*). These other powers are unlikely to see the necessary rate of growth to catch up economically with China, and the gap in economic strength is likely to further widen in China's favour.

SIPRI estimated in 2017 that China's and Russia's defence spending amounted to \$228 billion and \$55 billion respectively. China's defence budget is roughly four times that of India, Great Britain and France and almost six times larger than that of Germany and Japan, as also estimated by SIPRI. China has now achieved superiority over any power next in rank for designation as a superpower. A bipolar system, as Waltz pointed out, is "a system in which no third power is able to challenge the top two" (Waltz 2010, 98).

No great or major power measures up to China's combined score, and these powers are even much further from catching up with the US. Since no other countries are able to match China's aggregate power, two states—the US and China—are now much more powerful than the rest. If we base our analysis on the customary definition of pole and polarity by international relations scholars, the multipolarity—a system in which three or more great powers have roughly equal capabilities—is nowhere to be seen in the current international system.

Comparing two bipolar systems

China is not as powerful as the US, and it is far from dominating or ruling the world. But China does not need to overtake the US before the international system can be considered bipolar. The Soviet Union was never as powerful as the US during the previous bipolar period, but it was still regarded as a superpower and a pole in a new bipolar system. As Barry R. Posen writes, the

> Soviet Union was only barely in the US league for most of the Cold War in terms of economic capacity but we think of the era as a bipolar order, in part because the gap between the Soviet Union and the third ranking power in the immediate aftermath of World War Two and for much of the Cold War was so great.

(Posen 2011, 321)

More importantly, it was the widening power gap between the two top-ranking powers (US and Soviet Union) and the third (UK) that shifted the international system from multipolarity to bipolarity in the 1945–1950 period. Morgenthau recognised Great Britain as a great power at the end of World War II but argued in 1948 that, in the aftermath of the Second World War, "British power has declined to such an extent as to be distinctly inferior to the power of the US and the Soviet Union, the only two great powers left at present" (Morgenthau 1948, 271). In Morgenthau's revised and enlarged second edition of *Politics Among Nations*, published in 1954, he added, concerning the decline of the relative power of Great Britain that the US and the Soviet Union, "in view of their enormous superiority over the power next in rank, deserved to be called superpowers" (Morgenthau 1954, 324).

While the Soviet Union remained inferior to the US in its combined capabilities, they were sufficient to give it top ranking. It was the decline in Great Britain's relative power and the shifts in the distribution of capabilities between the second-ranking superpower and third-ranking great power that transformed the international system from multipolar to bipolar between 1945 and the late 1940s and early 1950s. This is an important but often underemphasised point in the current polarity debate, which correctly focuses on whether China's combined capabilities are sufficient for top ranking status but neglects the equal importance of measuring the power gap between China and the power next in rank for determining the polarity of the contemporary international system.

In sum, it is the narrowing power gap between the US and China and, even more importantly, the widening power gap between the two top-ranking powers (US and China) and any third-ranking power that has shifted the international system from unipolarity to bipolarity. The comparatively roughly similar distribution of capabilities strongly suggests that the international system has returned to bipolarity with the US and China as the two superpowers that are much more powerful than any other state.

Why does polarity matter?

There is broad consensus within the field of international politics that whether the international system is multipolar, bipolar or unipolar shapes states' behaviour and conditions the possibility of peace and stability. Determining polarity is important since it allows for predictions about the prospects for stability and patterns of state behaviour depending on whether the international system is multipolar, bipolar or unipolar. Behaviour follows from the changed position of the top-ranking powers and the new structure of the international system. European states acted differently in multipolar systems prior to World War II, when they were considered top-ranking great powers, than in the bipolar post-World War II era. The US and the Soviet Union acted differently from Britain and France following the emergence of a bipolar system in the post-World War II era because the latter pair were not superpowers.

The end of the bipolar system in the 20th century and the emergence of unipolarity fundamentally changed the EU's role in international affairs and European states' defence and security policies. These states restructured their armed forces in order to contribute towards wars in the Balkans, Afghanistan, Iraq, Libya and Syria. These policies and actions were unthinkable and almost impossible to carry out during the previous bipolar system but became possible in the shadow of US primacy. The unipolar era compelled European states towards new policies and the EU's enlargement policy was initiated. A new bipolar system will not resemble the past, but it will shape the role of the EU and European states' foreign and defence policies.

However, a structural approach has explanatory limits. It may account for why it became possible for the EU to initiate its enlargement policy but not why certain new members were accepted at a particular time. A structural view explains why it became possible for a small European state like Norway to send troops to military operations in the Balkans, but it cannot explain what type of soldiers or capabilities Norway contributes. It explains how it becomes possible for Norway to participate in the war on terrorism in Afghanistan but not why Norway refused to commit troops to the 2003 invasion of Iraq. The emphasis on polarity also explains why Norway could conduct air strikes against Muammar Gaddafi's regime in Libya but not why it refused to participate in air strikes against President Bashar al-Assad's Syrian Armed Forces.

Geostructural realism: refining Waltz's structural realist theory

The structural realist theory of Waltz sought to explain and predict how polarity shapes states' patterns of behaviour (balancing) and stability (risk of war). Waltz's core argument was that balancing differs between bipolar and multipolar systems and that a bipolar system is more stable than a multipolar system. According to Waltz, his theory explained and predicted why superpower balancing behaviour and stability during the bipolar Cold War era differed from great power politics and war during the previous multipolar era. However, Waltz's structural realist theory could not explain the unipolar era (Brooks and Wohlforth 2008; Monteiro 2014; Wohlforth 1999). More importantly for this chapter, Waltz never compared two bipolar systems, nor have any other studies compared two bipolar systems. Thus, Waltz's structural realism cannot explain why contemporary US-China rivalry/balancing differs from US-Soviet rivalry/balancing during the previous bipolar system or predict whether there is a higher risk of war between the two superpowers in the 20th compared to the 21st century.

The return of bipolarity matters if we wish to gauge the possibility of war between the US and China over the course of the 21st century. When we first compare the stability of two bipolar systems, we find variations primarily because of the geopolitical differences between a bipolar system concentrated on East Asia rather than Europe and with superpower rivalry concentrated more on the maritime domain than on land (Tunsjø 2018). During the previous bipolar system which concentrated on Europe, the US was inferior to the Soviet Union's land power. The former had to rely on nuclear weapons in order to deter and prevent a potential Soviet attack on Western Europe. There was a high risk that any crisis or conflict could escalate into a major or nuclear war. An arms race, severe tension and hostility followed, but Europe remained stable and peaceful.

The military rivalry between the US and China is primarily in maritime East Asia, not on land. In contrast to Europe, none of the US' most important allies in East Asia (Japan, South Korea, the Philippines and Australia) border China. Instead, water and the US naval preponderance protect theses allies from China's formidable land power. The US does not need to rely on nuclear weapons as heavily as it did in Europe in order to deter China. One might think that this is good for peace and stability; however, instability and the risk of war increase when deterrence is based more on conventional instead of nuclear weapons.

A future conflict might erupt in the South China Sea, the East China Sea or the Taiwan Strait. The most likely scenario is a limited war at sea that would not result in an invasion of China, the US or its allies, but would likely result in devastating attacks on the military infrastructure of both sides. Decision makers might risk a limited war or battle at sea in maritime East Asia, calculating that the possibility of a major war is less likely. Few believed that a limited war in Europe would not escalate to a major or nuclear war during the previous bipolar era. In a limited war at sea, because there is a limited existential risk, this constraint is absent. The risk of escalation to the use of nuclear weapons is, therefore, less likely.

Geopolitics can take its place as one element that complements structural realism, enhancing its explanatory and predictive power. I have labelled such a reconfigured theory "geostructural realism". Geostructural realism contends that, although it is important whether the international system is bipolar or has some other structure, stability and balancing is heavily affected by geopolitics and the way in which geography affects the two superpowers and their relationship. However, few studies have examined how geopolitics shapes how European states balance the potential for European involvement in conflicts in East Asia in a new bipolar system

Balancing and the risk of war: what role for Europe?

A geostructural realist perspective holds that geopolitics are likely to compel European states towards a limited traditional balancing of a rising China. Conversely, European states are likely to be pushed towards a stronger balance to China in realms other than the military. Since the risk of war between the superpowers is relatively higher today than under the previous bipolar system, European states could face a potential military conflict with China in the Indo-Pacific theatre.

From traditional to non-traditional balancing

While Waltz argued that superpowers in a bipolar system mainly rely on internal balancing, US allies in Europe contributed to balancing the Soviet Union. Most important was their role in providing a forward presence for US troops in

Europe, but their internal balancing, such as nuclear capability and conventional arms build-up, also contributed to deterrence and US war-fighting capabilities. Geographically, China does not border Europe like the Soviet Union bordered US allies in Europe and East Asia during the Cold War. Thus, European states today are unlikely to have as strong a role in containing China as they did in containing the Soviet Union in the past or as Japan did containing the Soviet Union in the Far East during the previous bipolar system.

Geopolitics explain why Europe and the US have different threat perceptions of a rising China and why European states have very limited military capabilities that can balance, deter or contain contemporary China (Tunsjø 2014). In the past, European leaders and NATO considered a potentially stronger role in the Asia-Pacific.[4] Standing shoulder to shoulder with the US and its Asian allies in the aftermath of growing Chinese assertiveness since 2008, the US pivot seemed sensible to some decision makers (Tunsjø 2013). It was argued that Europe should no longer have a free ride on US defence commitments in preserving freedom of the seas and counterbalancing China. Russia's annexation of Crimea and involvement in the civil war in Ukraine in 2014 shifted the debate and undermined any suggestions about a European pivot to Asia.

Being a counterbalance to China, a rising power that dominates the Asian mainland and which is increasingly turning its attention to Asian waters, seems to be a farfetched and ill-considered strategy for Europe. The few military capabilities possessed by Europe are needed in Europe and its neighbourhood, especially as the US becomes preoccupied with China. European countries are likely to manage in the future without the same American commitment to maintain European security. Consequently, Europe and the US need to acknowledge and come to grips with defining the role of Europe and NATO in a bipolar and Asia-centric world. US allies in Europe can compensate for their lack of shared threat perceptions of China by taking more responsibility for their own defence and keeping the NATO and EU "houses in order" by maintaining stability in Europe. They can also more effectively participate and assume leadership in out-of-area operations to provide security in Europe's neighbourhood and at vital choke points and sea lines of communications (SLOCs). Rather than European countries taking part in superpower balancing in Asia, a more realistic ambition is that European states, NATO and the EU seek leadership for security in Europe and stability in its neighbourhood, which will be conducive to Europe's own interests and contribute most to US rebalancing towards the Asia-Pacific. Such a division of labour in transatlantic relations might complement a US strategy that focuses on China's rise and the long-term challenges from its peer-competitor (Tunsjø 2014).

European states seek to sustain strong security ties with the US while simultaneously maintaining strong economic ties with China, in contrast to the largely independent relationship European NATO members maintained with the Soviet Union during the Cold War. While such a policy is possible within the new geo-structural conditions, this response might undermine transatlantic relations. Is it realistic to expect closer cooperation between the US and its European allies if their preferences in trade and security diverge? If Europe resists US pressure to support US economic policies that deal more forcefully with Chinese trade policy, will the US tolerate European resistance? If pushed to choose sides under new structural constraints and intensifying US-China confrontation, European countries should, and are most likely, to stand with the US and in support of the Western liberal order.

Two developments of the balancing role of European states and the EU are likely to be the result of a new bipolar system. Firstly, systemic effects might push the Western alliance to cooperate more strongly in economic affairs and in upholding the international order, in which it has invested so heavily. This would also include stronger coordination across the Atlantic on issues such as cyber security, international law, global governance, space, restrictions on Chinese investments and access to dual-use technology. Stronger cooperation in these non-traditional domains could compensate for Europe's lack of a role and capability in the traditional military balance with China. European states can no longer provide bases for a US forward-enhanced military presence or develop military capabilities that can deter China, similar to its role in the previous bipolar system. Instead, US allies in East Asia are likely to fulfil this balancing role in the contemporary bipolar system. Taking stronger responsibility for its own security and cooperating with the US in balancing China in non-traditional security might therefore sustain the transatlantic alliance.

Secondly, Europe's growing economic dependence on China, and the US request for higher European defence spending, have the potential to compromise transatlantic relations. In 2017, China had become Germany's most important trading partner. As Germany is simultaneously pushed to take more responsibility for its own security and gradually invest in a military build-up, ties between Germany and the US are likely to diminish almost irrespective of the personal chemistry between their leaders. If Germany spends 2 percent or more of its GDP on defence in five to ten years—not an unlikely scenario but still not very much defence spending for a major power—it is likely to have the highest defence spending in Europe by a large margin. This, in combination with strong economic ties with China, would strengthen Germany's independence and prominent role in Europe, which also suggests that transatlantic ties could wither.

Geostructural factors fuel diverging threat perceptions of a rising China across the Atlantic. This is the principle cause of Europe's limited traditional balancing role and the major strains in working out a common China policy in transatlantic relations. Growing economic ties between China and European states are an important indicator of divergence, alerting us to the possibility that Europe and the US could take different paths in their relations with China. New geostructural conditions pose a major challenge to transatlantic ties. The ties across the Atlantic are not only important for supporting the West's liberal order and in traditional and non-traditional counterbalancing of China; the US will remain a vital security guarantor for peace and stability in Europe. Since the US became involved in European security affairs in the post-World War II era, Europe has remained stable, peaceful and prosperous. Future stability in Europe is likely to depend on strong transatlantic ties.

The risk of war

The risk of war between the superpowers, today relatively higher than under the previous bipolar system, will have important implications for the EU and European states. European states can be affected both directly and indirectly. The outbreak of the Korean War in 1950 had important implications for European security and NATO. We cannot rule out NATO involvement should a conflict erupt in East Asia—for example on the Korean Peninsula, in the East China Sea, in the Taiwan Strait or in the South China Sea. Based on the assumption that North Korea can target the continental US with intercontinental ballistic missiles, the Trump administration contends that North Korea poses the greatest immediate threat to the US. While a North Korean missile strike against the US remains unlikely, such an attack would most likely trigger NATO's Article 5. While the diplomatic efforts on the Korean peninsula could provide more stability, there could easily be setbacks during the negotiations and in the aftermath of any agreements. Many difficult issues are likely to be unresolved for the foreseeable future, including North Korea's arsenal of nuclear and biological weapons and the strong US military presence on the peninsula.

While a conflict on the Korean peninsula is unlikely to affect Europe in similar ways as the conflict of the early 1950s, the implications for Europe of another war are significant. If the US does not defend its ally South Korea from an attack by the North, it could indirectly undermine the credibility of US alliances and security in Europe. In addition, any deal that allows the North Korean regime to maintain short and medium range conventional and nuclear missiles, but not inter-continental missiles, will also undermine the credibility of US alliances. Conversely, if the US launches a preventive war against North Korea without the consent of its close ally in the South, it could also indirectly undermine US alliances in Europe. For example, states that border Russia and seek to deter and reassure their neighbour will be alarmed by such an eventuality, fearing in the future that the US might strike Russia against their own interests. Finally, European investments and citizens in South Korea and North-East Asia are likely to be at risk in a wartime contingency.

A potential conflict between China and the US over Taiwan could have both direct and indirect implications for Europe. European states could be dragged into a war to support the US, or Europe could be affected by the havoc a war involving the two largest economies in the world will have on trade and financial stability. Similarly, a conflict in the South China Sea, where about 30 percent of world trade transits—a large proportion being European trade—will have a significant impact on European interests.

Russia might use a military conflict in East Asia as a pretext to intervene in NATO countries in the Baltics or in Eastern and Southern Europe. Conflict between Russia and NATO could then spill over into the High North as Russia is likely to mobilise its Bastion defence in any war with NATO. Such a scenario would force the US to balance and prioritise between conflicts in two theatres and potentially prevent the US from enhancing its military presence in Europe.

It remains to be seen whether US-China rivalry in East Asia or the North Korean crisis will trigger any conflict, and whether Russia will take advantage of any potential conflict in East Asia to advance its interests in Europe. Nevertheless, developments in East Asia are likely to shape US and NATO defence planning and their responses to any future conflicts.

How the US responds to China's anti-access and area denial capabilities in East Asian waters is also important for understanding how it might address a similar challenge from Russia in the North Atlantic. US military concepts, such as the Third Offset, AirSea Battle and the Multi-Domain Battle, inform US thinking about the functions and usage of military force. The US Joint Doctrine, signed and approved in October 2016 and termed Joint Concept for Access and Manoeuvre in the Global Commons (JAM-GC), will not only guide US operations in its rivalry with its peer competitor, China, in East Asia but also describes how US forces will operate in Europe. Such concepts and doctrines seek to support and inform US and allied forces in countering rising threats to US access and manoeuvres, in sustaining conventional deterrence and in maintaining US technological superiority in both of its flanking regions.

The development of war-fighting capabilities, new technologies and military platforms in one region does not take place in isolation. Advances in missile technology, the development of missile defence and radar systems, and enhanced space and cyber capabilities all demonstrate that the effects of military modernisation are global. The new superpower rivalry will drive developments in new technologies, ranging across artificial intelligence, quantum computing, big data, biotech, nanotech, unmanned capabilities, robotics, 3D printing and e-commerce. The future of the US grand strategy, the credibility of its alliances, the role of deterrence, secondary states' adjustments to superpower rivalry, military modernisation and the emergence of a new world order are issues shaping current strategic thinking in Europe and in East Asia. In order to gain a better understanding of these core themes, we need to examine how they overlap in the US' two flanking regions and understand the effects of a new bipolar international system.

Conclusion

If rivalry and conflict continue to increase in US-China relations and in East Asia, it should be no surprise if the US asks its European allies whether they are with or against it. Threat perceptions of communism were largely shared across the Atlantic in the post-World War II period, and the US and European powers more or less agreed on the various strategies of containment during the previous bipolar system. Indeed, one of the important implications of the Korean War in June 1950 was that it cemented transatlantic relations and contributed to the creation of NATO. The geostructural conditions of the new bipolar system suggest that Europe has a marginal role in balancing a rising China. In preventing geostructural effects from undermining the transatlantic alliance, European states need to step up their non-traditional balancing of China and take more responsibility for their own defence and security. However, if Europe actually undertakes such measures, it might equally lead to a more independent European role in the new bipolar system. In addition, if a conflict erupted in Korea, the Taiwan Strait or the East and South China Sea today, it is unlikely to reinforce transatlantic relations as did the Korean War in 1950. Different threat perceptions and strategies for dealing with China's rise suggest that another conflict in East Asia would probably constrain and weaken transatlantic ties rather than strengthen the relationship. Common norms and values, however, might sustain close transatlantic ties; the growing military, economic and technological threat from a rising China could reinvigorate the transatlantic alliance.

Notes

1 Although previous studies have examined the effect of global power shifts on US-China-EU relations and sought to analyse the implications of global power shifts for Europe and transatlantic relations, no studies have examined the effects of a new US-China bipolar system on the EU and European states (see Alcaro et al. 2016; Biba et al. 2016; Falkner and Anheier 2017; Rodrik et al. 2017; Ross et al. 2010).
2 The geostructural realist theory reconfigures Waltz's structural realist theory in order to explain and predict patterns of behaviour and stability in a new bipolar system. It adds geopolitics to Waltz's emphasis on anarchy and the distribution of capabilities as the structure of the international system (see Tunsjø 2018).
3 This is based on a US$11 trillion estimate for the Chinese economy and a US$18 trillion estimate for the US economy.
4 Former High Representative Cathrine Ashton seemed keen on discussing developments in the Asia Pacific region at the July 2012 ASEAN meeting. Former US Secretary of State, Hillary Clinton, and former Assistant Secretary of State for East Asia, Kurt Campbell, pushed for Europeans to stand should-to-shoulder with America on economic, diplomatic and security issues in Asia.

References

Alcaro, Ricardo, John Peterson, and Ettore Greco, eds. 2016. *The West and the Global Power Shift: Transatlantic Relations and Global Governance*. London: Palgrave Macmillan.

Beckley, Michael. 2011–2012. "China's Century? Why America's Edge Will Endure." *International Security* 36 (3): 41–78.

Beckley, Michael. 2018. *Unrivaled: Why America Will Remain the World's Sole Superpower*. Ithaca: Cornell University Press.

Biba, Sebastian, Markus Liegl, and Reinhard Wolf, eds. 2016. "Eclipsed by Clashing Titans? Europe and the Risk of US-China Confrontation." *European Foreign Affairs Review* 21 (3/1).

Brattberg, Erik, and Philippe Le Corre. 2019. *The Case for Transatlantic Cooperation in the Indo-Pacific*. Washington, DC: Carnegie Endowment for International Peace. https://carnegieendowment.org/2019/12/18/case-for-transatlantic-cooperation-in-indo-pacific-pub-80632.

Brooks, Stephen G., and William C. Wohlforth. 2008. *World Out of Balance: International Relations and the Challenge of American Primacy*. Princeton, NJ: Princeton University Press.

Brooks, Stephen G., and William C. Wohlforth. 2016. *America Abroad: The United States' Global Role in the 21st Century*. Oxford: Oxford University Press.

Casarini, Nicola. 2020. "Rising to the Challenge: Europe's Security Policy in East Asia amid US-China Rivalry." *The International Spectator* 55 (1): 78–92.

Falkner, Robert, and Helmut Anheier, eds. 2017. "Europe and the World: Rethinking Europe's External Relations in an Age of Global Turmoil." *International Politics* 54 (4).

Haass, Richard N. 2008. "The Age of Nonpolarity: What Will Follow U.S. Dominance." *Foreign Affairs* 87 (3): 44–56.

Haass, Richard N. 2017. *A World In Disarray: American Foreign Policy and the Crisis of the Old Order*. New York: Penguin Press.

Hansen, Birthe. 2011. *Unipolarity and World Politics: A Theory and Its Implications*. London: Routledge.

International Monetary Fund. 2015. "World Economic Outlook Database." www.imf.org/external/pubs/ft/weo/2015/02/weodata/index.aspx.

Layne, Christopher. 2012. "This Time It's Real: The End of Unipolarity and the *Pax Americana*." *International Studies Quarterly* 56 (1): 203–213.

Mearsheimer, John J. 2014. *The Tragedy of Great Power Politics*, 2nd ed. New York: W. W. Norton & Company.

Monteiro, Nuno P. 2014. *Theory of Unipolar Politics*. Cambridge: Cambridge University Press.

Morgenthau, Hans J. 1948. *Politics Among Nations: The Struggle for Power and Peace*. New York: Alfred A. Knopf, Inc.

Morgenthau, Hans J. 1954. *Politics Among Nations: The Struggle for Power and Peace*, 2nd ed. New York: Alfred A. Knopf, Inc.

Murray, Donette, and David Brown, eds. 2012. *Multipolarity in the 21st Century: A New World Order*. London: Routledge.

Odgaard, Liselotte. 2019. "European Engagement in the Indo-Pacific: The Interplay Between Institutional and State-Level Naval Diplomacy." *Asia Policy* 14 (4).

Pejsova, Eva. 2019. "Europe: A New Player in the Asia-Pacific." *The Diplomat*, January 19. https://thediplomat.com/2019/01/europe-a-new-player-in-the-indo-pacific/.

Posen, Barry R. 2009. "Emerging Multipolarity: Why Should We Care?" *Current History* 108 (721): 347–352.

Posen, Barry R. 2011. "From Unipolarity to Multipolarity: Transition in Sight?" In *International Relations Theory and the Consequences of Unipolarity*, edited by John G. Ikenberry, Michael Mastanduno, and William C. Wohlforth, 317–341. Cambridge: Cambridge University Press.

Rodrik, Dani, Eva-Maria Nag, and Andy Sumner, eds. 2017. "Europe and the World: Global Insecurity and Power Shifts." *Global Policy* 8 (Supplement 4).

Ross, Robert S., Øystein Tunsjø, and Tuosheng Zhang, eds. 2010. *US-China-EU Relations: Managing the New World Order*. London: Routledge.

Schweller, Randall L. 2014. *Maxwell's Demon and the Golden Apple: Global Disorder in the New Millennium*. Baltimore: Johns Hopkins University Press.

Stumbaum, May-Britt U. 2014. "How Europe Matters in Asian Security—Addressing Non-Traditional Security Threats Under Climate Change Conditions: Towards a New Research Agenda on Norm Diffusion in EU-Asia Security Relations." NFG Working Paper 9. www.asianperceptions.fu-berlin.de/system/files/private/wp914-europe-asia-nontraditional-security-threats.pdf.

Tunsjø, Øystein. 2013. "Europe's Favourable Isolation." *Survival* 55 (6): 91–106.

Tunsjø, Øystein. 2014. "China's Rise: Towards a Division of Labor in Transatlantic Relations." In *Responding to China's Rise*, edited by Vinod K. Aggarwal and Sara A. Newland, 151–174. Cham, Heidelberg, New York, Dordrecht and London: Springer.

Tunsjø, Øystein. 2018. *The Return of Bipolarity in World Politics: China, the United States and Geostructural Realism*. New York: Columbia University Press.

Waltz, Kenneth N. 1959. *Man, the State, and War: A Theoretical Analysis*. New York: Columbia University Press.

Waltz, Kenneth N. 1964. "The Stability of a Bipolar World." *Daedalus* 93 (3): 881–909.

Waltz, Kenneth N. 1993. "The Emerging Structure of International Politics." *International Security* 18 (2): 44–79.

Waltz, Kenneth N. 2010. *Theory of International Politics*, reissued. Long Grove, IL: Waveland Press Inc.

Wohlforth, William C. 1999. "The Stability of a Unipolar World." *International Security* 24 (1): 5–41.

The World Bank. n.d. "GDP (Current US$)." http://data.worldbank.org/indicator/NY.GDP.MKTP.CD?page=1.

Zakaria, Fareed. 2008. *The Post-American World*. New York: W. W. Norton & Company.

3 Europe in between US-Chinese strategic competition

The role of a middle power

Liselotte Odgaard

Introduction

This chapter addresses Europe's role as a middle power in the US-Chinese strategic rivalry in Asia. I argue that, in a conflict-ridden region, Europe combines deterrence with reassurance, reinforcing the United States (US) interpretation of regional order while also reassuring China that its core values are not threatened. This middle power approach of trying to ameliorate great power disputes while staying on good terms with both sides contributes to peace and stability in Asia and in relations between the West and China. Hence, Europe provides a positive contribution to an increasingly crisis-prone Asia-Pacific theatre.

Existing debates on power in Asia focus on the US-China relationship and whether they can manage their relationship so as to avoid the use of force as China expands its strategic reach and the US defends its preeminent regional position. Mearsheimer (2014) describes China as a power inevitably seeking military superiority in Asia, not for purposes of conquest but to dictate the boundaries of acceptable behaviour to neighbouring states and to push the US out of Asia. Christensen (2015, 257–266) argues that the US alliance system will continue to face challenges from Chinese coercive diplomacy in the maritime domain, continuing a pattern of assertive and destabilizing behaviour which involves the US and its allies challenging China. Fravel (2011) has described China's maritime strategy as a delaying strategy that seeks to consolidate its claims and deter other states from strengthening their own claims. It is destabilizing if unchecked or unmoderated by the US due to the relative weakness of the Southeast Asian states of the South China Sea littoral.

The few analysts who debate Europe's role in US-Chinese regional strategic competition often describe it as a choice between "bandwagoning" and "balancing". Nordenman (2016) argues that Europe should balance China, emphasizing that Europe can make a difference in US-China strategic competition. Europe is heavily reliant on the global maritime domain and should seek to implement its maritime security strategy more aggressively. By contrast, Duchâtel (2016) argues that Europe cannot significantly influence US-China strategic competition. The US sees Europe as a partner in values that can only make limited contributions to security in the South China Sea.

This chapter places Europe's emerging security role in Asia in the context of US-China relations, investigating whether Europe contributes to deterrence and reassurance, thereby enhancing peace and stability. Europe is depicted as a middle power in between the regional great powers; its military strength, resources and strategic position is such that great powers bid for its support, allowing it to successfully assert its independence. Europe's middle power role facilitates it gradually seeking a significant role in Asia by using its political, economic and military clout to strengthen its alignment with the US, on the basis of common liberal values, without alienating China by crossing Chinese red lines that define its core interests. Europe is operating in a context where both the US and China have become increasingly assertive, advancing their core national interests at the expense of the other, leading to steadily increasing tension levels and risking the use of force. Elements of reassurance have emerged in the form of codes for unplanned encounters to prevent the accidental use of force between their militaries. As a middle power, Europe is increasingly attempting to utilise its attractiveness as a partner of the US and China to support the former's manifestations of right and wrong conduct, while ensuring that European actions are not directed against the latter's core interests. This allows Europe to demonstrate support for core values while ameliorating levels of tension.

In the remainder of the chapter, I first discuss theoretical approaches to middle powers in the context of emerging great power competition, arguing that the English school's approach is useful for understanding Asian power dynamics. Secondly, I focus on the concept of "middle power" as a tool for understanding Europe's role in US-China strategic competition. I argue that Europe is beginning to contribute to a regional order of coexistence involving the accommodation of different understandings of legitimate state conduct to ensure that strategic competition is based on the non-use of force. Thirdly, I conclude by discussing the implications of Europe's middle power role for Asian peace and stability.

Power and US-China strategic competition: how does Europe fit in?

The debate on power and US-China strategic competition is dominated by three theoretical perspectives: realism, constructivism and liberalism. These approaches tend to argue that China is pursuing long-term regional hegemony, and the US is countering these efforts. The few that acknowledge the role of middle powers often see them as losing influence as great power strategic competition grows. Realists argue that China pursues regional hegemony as the balance of power shifts in China's favour. This leads to greater US-China competition. Walt (2018) explains that China will try to reduce the US presence in Asia, leading to an intense competition for allies and influence. Wohlforth (2018) argues that China's rise has facilitated a pugnacious policy of pushback against US pre-eminence in Asia, encouraging the US to double down on its current security commitments. Constructivists tend to argue that the jury is still out, with the possibility of a Sino-centric order emerging out of China's evolving national identity that accompanies its rise. For example,

Callahan (2008) explores the possibility of a Chinese utopia defined by order rather than freedom. This is ultimately a new kind of hegemony where imperial China's hierarchical governance is updated for the 21st century. Liberalism argues that Beijing's hegemonic aspirations are shaped by liberal order even as China seeks greater authority and voice to match its newfound strength. For example, Ikenberry (2014) argues that the resilience of the liberal order encourages China to revise the political hierarchy and enhance its position and status within the global system rather than engaging in revisionist struggles over rival models of modernity or ideologies of international order.

These readings of China's hegemonic aspirations have some merit in highlighting the tension between balancing and accommodating the dynamics between the US and China, particularly in China's Asian neighbourhood. However, they do not conceptualise the role of the many middle-sized powers that form part of the growing strategic competition between the great powers, although their arguments clearly demonstrate that they have a significant bearing on US-China relations. This may be justified by the assessment that middle-sized powers do not behave in accordance with recurring patterns that might allow for a conceptualisation of their role. Instead, their influence may be considered random and, in that sense, without significant impact on world order.

However, when observing developments in Asia, middle-sized powers such as Australia and South Korea seem to play a significant role that cannot easily be ignored. Europe is not typically termed a middle power. Nevertheless, Europe is arguably emerging in an activist role, positioning it strategically in between US-China competition. The activism does not involve a united European Union (EU) acting as a bloc with one voice on all issue areas, such as would be required for Europe to constitute an independent great power pole. The 27 EU Member States have diverse positions across a wide range of policy areas. This makes Europe better positioned to play a middle power role, influencing great power interaction by ameliorating the consequences of strategic rivalry. The EU does this by adopting general policies which are supported by the actions of groups of Member States and individual countries. The security domain is addressed in this chapter because it provides the toughest test of Europe's ability to perform as a middle power. The EU is an economic and normative heavyweight in trade and the promotion of liberal democracy and human rights. However, in the security domain, its influence has traditionally been considered negligible. This chapter seeks to demonstrate that even in this field, Europe plays a middle power role.

For example, because of the internal divisions in the EU on how far to go in criticizing China's behaviour in the South China Sea, European institutions issue general policy commitments which are followed up by a growing number of EU Member States' participation in operations in support of freedom of navigation. This is a good example how, in Asia, the EU designs general policies and leaves it to Member States to implement them in ways that strengthen Europe's Asian footprint.

Concerted European behaviour is not easily explained by means of conventional theories of European integration such as neofunctionalism's focus on integration spill-over (Haas 1958), institutionalism's focus on the importance of Europe-specific institutions for policymaking (Pierson 1996) or multi-level governance's conceptualisation of dispersing authority across multiple levels of political governance (Hooghe and Marks 2001). Today, the intergovernmental European Council consisting of the EU heads of state appears to be key to Europe's concerted action. The challenges of migration into Europe and Brexit have driven home the point that national governments remain the primary actors in decision-making on European integration. The intergovernmental approach (Moravcsik 1998) explains how bargaining, package deals and side payments keep Europe together as an actor; however, it does not show how Europe positions itself *vis-à-vis* other powers. To understand this dynamic, the concept of middle power appears suitable. The usefulness of the middle power concept is discussed in the following section.

Middle power and great power capabilities and values

Liberalism, constructivism and the English school have examined middle powers because these approaches combine a complex understanding of international actors with arguments as to why rules and norms regulating behaviour influence international relations. Liberal and constructivist scholars have investigated middle powers, usually through an institutional-diplomatic lens, seeing them as playing a formative role in international security institutions and exercising influence in international political niches (Emmers 2018; Teo 2018; Efstathopoulos 2018; Cooper et al. 1993). Simon (2018) focuses on the interaction of small and medium-sized Asian powers with great power neighbours and the US to promote their autonomy, prosperity and security. Middle powers rely more on international norms than hard power to constrain great power rivalry. Emmers (2018) has shown how Asian middle powers use multilateral platforms to level the playing field among great and non-great powers, seeking to institutionalise great power relations through forums led by the Association of Southeast Asian Nations (ASEAN) and its norms of procedure by consensus and non-interference.

Simon (2018) and Emmers (2018) observe that existing multilateral structures, such as those provided by ASEAN, cannot stabilise great power relations amid shifts in the regional distribution of power. Does this assessment lead to the conclusion that middle powers have no role to play in the current Asian order, where the US and China are testing the red lines of the other to see how far they can go in manifesting their different preferences for who should play the leading role in regional order?

The English school would argue to the contrary, pointing out that it is precisely in periods of power transition that middle powers play a determining role. The ability of states to ameliorate the dynamics of power politics with societal dynamics encourages middle powers to constrain great power behaviour by means of rules and norms, which determine how much and what kind of order prevails in international relations (Bull 1995).

The English school's conceptualisation of great and middle powers is not merely based on capabilities but also on the ideational element of power. Middle powers are defined by their relationship to great powers. Wight (1978, 30–67) has the most detailed definition of great powers, referring to them as "dominant" powers. Apart from having the capabilities to aspire for dominance, great powers must have designs of international unity and solidarity. Wight's understanding of great powers combines a capabilities argument with a civilisational element based on ideology, religion and historical mythology which invest the great power with policies on right and wrong conduct. In other words, a great power has the capabilities to contemplate war against any other existing single power and ideational power, encouraging it to use its capabilities to implement its version of international order.

Great powers invest efforts in maintaining international order because they have a major stake in designing its key components and because they prefer to preserve peace and stability on their terms to prevent challenges to their great power status. The balance of power ensures that power is distributed in such a way that no single state or entity is able to dominate the remaining states or entities. Relative military and economic power determine the distribution of capabilities and play a central role in determining which states are great powers. Bull's (1995, 97–107) main point is that power balances are contrived, meaning they are based on the conscious actions of states. He argues that states are motivated by the conscious goal of a stable balance. Wight (1966, 104) also attributes the maintenance of the balance of power to conscious policies, emphasizing that stability is not obtained by merely taking into account the distribution of power; adherence to common principles of order, such as the requirement for legitimacy, is equally important.

Does great power competition for economic and military capabilities and ideational influence leave any room for middle power influence? The English school's answer is "yes". The role of middle powers is determined by the degree of stability which great power behaviour brings to the table (Holbraad 1984, 13). Middle powers have little influence on regional order when great power balancing is stable. When international stability is not threatened, the middle powers have little incentive to use their limited resources on order; instead, they will concentrate on other priorities, such as economic development. By contrast, in periods of transition, when international order has not been revised to accommodate changes in the distribution of power and in the values that characterise rising powers, middle powers may be able to obtain influence out of proportion to their resources. Middle powers are keen to be on good terms with all great powers since their strategically advantageous positions depend on good will with them.

The position of a middle power depends on having sufficient capabilities to convince the great powers that it may make a significant contribution to regional stability. Middle powers must have economic capabilities significantly greater than small powers, but smaller than great powers. Military capability is equally important to middle power status, as a middle power must be able to discourage military intervention from great powers (Wight 1978, 65). Political priorities and alliance relations also determine middle power status because these determinants influence military capabilities. Should alliance relations become strained, middle powers must possess sufficient economic and military capacity to assume responsibility for their own defence (Holbraad 1984, 13).

A middle power reveals itself by the successful assertion of independence and by diplomacy. The English school and liberal scholars agree that middle power diplomacy is exercised through entrepreneurship in institutions devising principles of right and wrong international conduct (Cooper and Dal 2016). The role of middle powers is based on such military strength, resources and strategic positioning that, in peacetime, great powers bid for their support and, in wartime, while middle powers cannot win wars against great powers, they must have the capability to inflict costs on great powers out of proportion to what great powers are likely to gain by attacking them (Wight 1978, 64–65).

Middle powers cannot determine or manage security arrangements, but they can contribute to their construction or remodelling. The English school and constructivist scholars agree that middle powers opt for reform and not radical change (Jordaan 2003). Concern for stability is not necessarily the driving force of middle powers. Rather, they may be concerned to maximise their interests, such as maintaining influence. To most unaligned middle powers, the dangers and opportunities engendered by great power competition are too great not to respond to if they are able to exercise influence. States formally aligned with one great power may opt for cooperation with all great powers. The most effective method for middle powers to influence security arrangements is to avoid choosing sides (Holbraad 1984, 127, 144). Middle power behaviour may unintentionally exacerbate great power tensions. However, middle powers may also mediate great power rivalry by facilitating reconciliation. Even middle powers that are allies of a great power can help ameliorate tensions and contribute to stability.

The criteria for identifying a middle power are a medium-sized economic and military capability which allows them to exercise policies independently of great powers and to use diplomatic means to cooperate with all great powers to revise the existing order to better accommodate the interests of great and middle powers. Middle powers have limited influence because their positions are highly dependent on their attractiveness to great powers. This role is usually not accompanied by formal recognition and often goes unnoticed due to the lack of publicity about middle powers. During the Cold War, middle powers had limited leeway because security management was carried out by great powers. By contrast, US-Chinese divergent policies on Asian order in the post-Cold War environment from the 2010s onwards have produced patterns of rivalry that are not constrained by institutionalised security mechanisms. The US and China have not identified each other's red lines regarding their core interests and hence the limits of their willingness to compromise to ensure stability. The great powers vie for allies and partners, allowing middle powers a role in facilitating compromises between different ideas of world order that may help ameliorate rivalry. In the following section, I investigate whether the EU plays the role of middle power, ameliorating US-Chinese rivalry in Asia, and if this entails Europe seeking influence by using its political, economic and military clout to strengthen its alignment with the US, on the basis of liberal values, without alienating China by crossing red lines defining Chinese core interests.

Europe as a middle power in between US-China rivalry: a force for stability?

The EU's economic and military capabilities

The US remains the dominant great power, with the world's largest economy, a military with global reach and an alliance system consisting of more than 30 allies, approximately as many quasi-allies and numerous strategic partners. China is the second largest economy in the world. President Xi Jinping's global economic vision, the Belt and Road Initiative (BRI), puts China at the centre and is already influencing remote areas such as the Arctic. BRI demonstrates that China has the basic great power assets. Militarily, China can project military power outward across the Indian Ocean into the Middle East and, increasingly, in the polar regions.

The English school's understanding of the balance of power as contrived and upheld by great power concern for adhering to common rules of order emphasises the shortcomings of current US-China relations in using the balance of power as an instrument to provide international order. US-China core interests are too far apart to allow for a contrived balance of power that facilitates a common political framework for managing major security and economic issues. Their clashes in the South China Sea demonstrate that the US prioritises freedom of navigation as the basis for defending liberal freedom values against attempts at introducing hierarchy in international relations. US priorities are at odds with China's priority of restoring the Chinese motherland to rectify the alleged violations of Chinese rights by unjust Western and Japanese aggression in the late 19th and early 20th centuries.

Treating Europe as a middle power in between the US and China may seem to assume an unrealistic level of unity similar to that of a unitary state. However, challenges such as Brexit, rising authoritarianism and Russian security challenges have pushed Europe towards more unity than ever because these developments have driven home the point that European countries can only exercise sovereignty in a world of US-China rivalry through common action. I argue that Europe's emerging security role in Asia is that of a middle power, contributing to US deterrence of China while avoiding a challenge to Chinese core values. In political terms, Europe can be understood as a pooled middle power which emerges through institutionalised cooperation aiming at furthering the interests of a group of states more effectively than they could have managed on their own (Odgaard 2007, 64–65). Insofar as such attempts at pooling resources are incomplete, intra-organisational diplomacy must compensate for these deficiencies. For example, EU Member States attempt to negotiate free trade agreements with external powers in unison, although their economies remain separate. Considerable investments in diplomacy to ensure political compromise as a compensation for the absence of unified political authority is necessary for a group of states presenting themselves as a unity to the outside world (Pomorska and Vanhoonacker 2016). Admittedly, within Europe there are exceptions, most notably the United Kingdom (UK), which gravitates towards the US but has little influence on Europe due to Brexit. However, the harsh debates that this decision caused in the UK and the efforts to find a way to maintain links with the EU testify to the attractions of being part of the EU rather than going it alone, even for large European powers. Even if European states do not act as a complete unity across all external issues, there is sufficient common ground between them that they can be termed a middle power in a behavioural sense. EU states have been able to forge a large measure of solidarity in their adoption of common positions towards developments involving external powers and in the Member States' agreement on common principles of conduct.

In terms of economic capabilities, the EU constitutes approximately 28 percent of the global economy. The EU is the second largest economic power in the world after the US in nominal terms and, according to purchasing power parity, after China. The EU's GDP was estimated as US$17 trillion in nominal terms in 2017 (Eurostat 2018a; Trading Economics 2019). Despite being an international economic heavyweight, the EU has faced serious economic challenges in recent years. From 2008, the euro area was faced with a financial crisis and national government debts increased to often unprecedented levels. As a result, taxes have been raised and public services cut, leading to public dissatisfaction in many Member States (European Central Bank 2018). Moreover, economic convergence between European countries that would increase the robustness of the economic union has also stalled, if not reversed, since the global financial crisis. However, considerations from EU-sceptical countries outside the eurozone, such as Denmark, to join the banking union so that national banks enjoy protection from financial distress and can exercise influence demonstrate the continuous attractions of the EU's common institutions (Danmarks Nationalbank 2017).

The EU has traditionally been a civilian power based on primarily economic instruments and cooperation to address issues of international management without significant common military capabilities (Maull 1990). At around 1.3 percent of GDP in 2016, annual EU defence expenditures are about half of US defence spending (Eurostat 2018b). However, the EU is facing traditional and non-traditional threats from regimes and terrorists in Eurasia, the Middle East and Africa, prompting the EU to focus on strengthening defence cooperation and raising defence expenditures. Although the North Atlantic Treaty Organization (NATO) remains the cornerstone of European defence for the foreseeable future, recent initiatives indicate the growing willingness of EU Member States to carry a larger part of the defence burden as a response to growing US unwillingness to pay for European security. The Permanent Structured Cooperation (PESCO), signed by 23 EU Member States on 13 November 2017 and which by 2019 encompassed 25 European states, seeks to develop new military equipment such as tanks and drones and commits the signatory states to regularly increase defence budgets in real terms (Radosavljevic 2017). On 25 June 2018, at France's initiative, nine

EU Member States formalised a plan to create a European military intervention force which, by 2019, encompasses 14 European countries. The UK backed the measure as a way of maintaining strong defence ties with the EU, despite Brexit (EURACTIV.com with AFP 2018).

The EU's Asian middle-power diplomacy

In Asia, Europe operates in a context where the US and China have become increasingly assertive in advancing their core national interests at the expense of the other, leading to steadily increasing tension levels and risk of the use of force. Elements of reassurance have emerged in the form of codes for unplanned encounters to prevent the accidental use of force between militaries in a region characterised by great power rivalry. As a middle power, Europe is increasingly attempting to utilise its attractions as a partner of both the US and China to support US core values while ensuring that European actions are not directed against Chinese core interests. This allows Europe to demonstrate support for core values while ameliorating levels of tension. This ameliorating role is played while Europe asserts its independence from the US, demonstrating that it is not a dependent of the US, and that it pursues interests and values that are, at times, at odds with those of Washington. This approach facilitates Europe's endorsement of Chinese policy initiatives without US approval, as well as European efforts to strengthen links with other Asian middle and small powers in areas of overlapping interests and values.

While Europe supports the continued pre-eminence of the US alliance system, it is concerned to maintain a broad array of connections with Asian countries in view of the diminishing role of the US in Asia and Washington's enhanced focus on US national interests rather than the common interests of allies. In May 2018, the then President of the European Council, Donald Tusk, warned of the capricious actions of US President Trump when EU leaders prepared to discuss their response to the US abandonment of the Iran nuclear deal and the threat of steel and aluminium tariffs. Tusk said that US behaviour demonstrated that the EU had to be prepared to act alone (Khan 2018).

Tusk's critique of the Trump administration is the culmination of a long process of independent policymaking in Europe that started with the decision of 14 EU Member States to join the Chinese-initiated Asian Infrastructure Investment Bank (AIIB). The AIIB was established in 2013 as an alternative to Western-dominated financial institutions such as the World Bank and the International Monetary Fund (European Political Strategy Centre 2015).

Increasingly strained relations between Europe and the US, at a time when European relations with China are marked by conflicts of interest, encourage Europe to seek closer relations with Asian states that are considered compatible with European liberal economic and political values. Two middle powers, the EU and Japan, agreed on an economic partnership agreement in December 2017. This sent a powerful signal against protectionism at a time when Washington was cancelling or renegotiating trade agreements with allies and partners, and Chinese economic policies were undermining European market economic practices. The EU, several ASEAN Member States and ASEAN as a whole are negotiating free trade agreements (FTAs), hoping to profit from the EU's position as the second largest trade partner of ASEAN after China. Similarly, the EU is seeking a FTA with Australia (Scimia 2018). These developments indicate that Europe is becoming more self-reliant in its alliance relations with the US.

Arguably, the most challenging area for Europe in playing a middle power role is extra-regional security issues, simply because issues closer to home—such as migration and Brexit—create pressures for common policies that cannot be ignored. In contrast, Europe's Asian role is much more a policy of choice than necessity. Nevertheless, a flexible cooperation pattern is emerging between the EU institutions which formulate general policies based on common European core interests and values and, due to the different security priorities of European states, a loose and variable configuration of states from Europe that implements the EU's broad policy guidelines. One area where this pattern has emerged is in the South China Sea.

The EU's middle power diplomacy in the South China Sea

Beijing has not clarified China's claim to sovereign territory and maritime zones in the South China Sea. Consequently, the issue of Chinese claims to jurisdiction interfere with Washington's core interest of maintaining freedom of navigation and overflight is also not clarified. This is a US core value and a precondition of the continued effectiveness of the alliance system that forms a basic pillar of global US influence. Equally, this is a European core value. In June 2012, the EU issued guidelines on its foreign and security policy in East Asia. It urged all claimants in the South China Sea to seek peaceful and cooperative solutions in accordance with international law, particularly the United Nations (UN) Convention on the Law of the Sea, while encouraging all parties to clarify the basis of their claims (Council of the European Union 2012).

In the EU's maritime security strategy of 2014, the rule of law and freedom of navigation are listed as its strategic maritime interests (European Commission 2014). The EU's action plan for maritime strategy encompasses promoting the dispute settlement mechanisms of the Law of the Sea, implementing the binding decisions of the International Tribunal for the Law of the Sea and establishing mechanisms for maritime confidence building (Council of the European Union 2014). Because of EU internal divisions on how far to criticise China's behaviour, European institutions do not initiate these types of operations. Instead, general policy commitments are followed up by various EU Member States. In the South China Sea, a growing number of Member States participate in operations in support of freedom of navigation. Since 2016, France has taken the lead in encouraging European operations, deploying naval vessels to sail through the South China Sea annually, with personnel and equipment from other European countries onboard, such as Denmark, the UK and Germany.

The Europeans refrain from sailing within 12 nautical miles from disputed features in the area. Europe thereby avoids direct challenges to the Chinese presence that would result in protests from Beijing that European countries are violating Chinese sovereign rights. In an operation in 2017, a French vessel with personnel from other European countries aboard sailed in support of freedom of navigation in the South and East China Seas, making a port call in Shanghai to demonstrate that its actions were not directed against China. Because the European operation emphasised support for principles of the free movement of military vessels without directing the operation at a particular country, China did not actively protest the actions. However, European operations since 2018 have not included port calls in China. Instead, they regularly include port calls in Vietnam, which has severe maritime disputes with China in the South China Sea. The decision not to visit China demonstrates growing European dissatisfaction with Beijing's continued militarisation of the South China Sea combined with China's negotiation with ASEAN on a code of conduct for the area. China has insisted on restrictions on the free movement of military vessels and aircraft, contributing to concerns that a prospective code of conduct will not be based on the view that the South China Sea is international waters.

In contrast to the US, Europe employs a watered-down version of operations in support of freedom of navigation by keeping at least 12 nautical miles from features occupied by China. Europe thereby avoids challenging Chinese core interests while leaning towards the US policy of demonstrating support for freedom of navigation and overflight for military vessels and aircraft, and supporting the ability of Southeast Asian countries to assert that the South China Sea is not part of the Chinese motherland. Europe's policy is aimed at avoiding a two-power game: it supports the interests of smaller states to advance their entitlement in the area without being bullied by great powers while insisting on the international status of the South China Sea.

At present, neither the US nor China demonstrate willingness to apply compromises to accommodate the core interests and values of the other, resulting in the risk of unplanned encounters between their militaries that may involve the use of force. This risk increases the urgency to negotiate mechanisms to prevent the use of force as a result of such encounters. To lower the risk of such incidents escalating, the member states of the Western Pacific Naval Symposium (WPNS)—of which France is a member and the UK an observer—agreed in 2014 on the Code for Unplanned Encounters at Sea (CUES) (Steinberg and O'Hanlon 2014, 5–14). This agreement has formed the basis of additional US-Chinese agreements for unplanned encounters between the two regional powers. European countries use the WPNS CUES for their operations in the South China Sea.

CUES is an instrument designed to reduce the risk of minor incidents resulting in escalation between states. In the South China Sea, deterrence is complex due to concerns that one opponent intends to damage the other's core interests. This dynamic may lead unplanned encounters to escalate into unsafe and highly provocative incidents in an arena where US and Chinese core interests clash. The 2014 CUES essentially confirms that countries intend to respect ordinary rules for proper conduct at sea and in the air. The communication rules are used by European countries to lower the risk of unplanned encounters spinning out of control due to misunderstandings. When, in April 2017, a French naval vessel encountered a Chinese vessel during its actions to uphold freedom of navigation in the Spratly Islands in the South China Sea, the French vessel used the CUES to avoid an incident. This is merely one example of many of how CUES is used to help prevent incidents. Even countries that are not signatory states to the agreement use them. Thus, in September and October 2017, when a Chinese naval task group visited Europe, not only France but also Denmark conducted drills with the Chinese task group using CUES (Odgaard and Lund 2020, 10–12).

Internal divisions in the EU prevent the union from actively contributing to deter China from advancing its presence and militarizing features in the South China Sea. However, EU Member States form part of the US forward deterrence posture and have contributed to operations supporting freedom of navigation to deter China from conduct that implies that China has sovereign jurisdiction over the area. At the same time, EU Member States are actively promoting CUES in interactions at sea and in the air with China to signal that Europe has no interest in using force against China. Moreover, Europe's decision to refrain from carrying out operations supporting freedom of navigation within 12 nautical miles of Chinese-occupied features confirms to China that Europe is not directly challenging China's presence and status as a South China Sea power.

Conclusion

Relations between the US and China are increasingly characterised by geostrategic rivalry that engenders a revival of mutual deterrence with inadequate reassurance elements—thereby enhancing the risk of the unplanned use of force and, at worst, war. The risk is particularly worrisome in hotspots that involve unplanned incidents between the militaries of the US and China, such as in the South China Sea.

As geostrategic rivalry and mutual deterrence increasingly mar US-Chinese relations, Europe's role as a middle power which attempts to ameliorate tensions without choosing sides between Washington and Beijing has become increasingly important. Europe uses its middle power capabilities to position itself as generally aligned with the US due to their mutual support for liberal values, such as the freedom of the high seas and liberal market economic principles. Values rather than pragmatism form the basis for European middle power diplomacy. Europe is becoming tougher on China by, for example, contributing to US operations supporting freedom of navigation for military vessels and aircraft and criticizing China for its increasingly assertive behaviour towards Southeast Asian states. However, Europe also plays a role in seeking cooperation independently from the US with other Asian states with partially compatible values, such as Singapore, Japan and Australia. It thus promotes a region of many powers that avoids too much reliance on Washington as the latter becomes increasingly focused on protecting its own interests, sometimes at the expense of its allies. In addition, European initiatives in support of the US alliance system, freedom of navigation and forward military presence is less provocative than US actions. Europe tries to avoid challenging Chinese core interests such as China's permanent presence in the South China Sea, while being very active in promoting reassurance measures by engaging in AIIB or using CUES to signal that cooperation is desirable on issues where Europe and China have compatible interests.

It can be argued that Europe's influence is weakened by its inability to combine forces and act in unison. The EU only has very general policies on Asian issues due to its internal divisions. In parts of Eastern Europe, the Balkans and Southern Europe, growing interest in attracting Chinese investments is likely to make nations there less willing to publicly criticise China on Asian security issues because this is often seen as inappropriate interference in domestic affairs by Beijing. The shortcomings of the EU's ability to act means that individual Member States are left to take action. However, at a time when mounting security issues in Europe's neighbourhood in Africa, the Middle East and Russia give rise to equally difficult disagreements about which issues to prioritise, a desirable division of labour may be to let the EU formulate general policies and leave it to individual countries to translate these into practical initiatives. Countries thus have greater freedom of action to work out effective approaches that are pursued in practice.

The French initiative to conduct operations in support of freedom of navigation is a good example of effective middle power diplomacy that positions Europe as an ally of the US in support of core Western values, but from an independent position that involves respect for Chinese core interests to lower Beijing's perceived need to apply deterrence towards European and Asian US allies and partners. Compared to Washington, European states can much better adopt measures of reassurance *vis-à-vis* China because they are not tied to security commitments towards Asian allies. Moreover, Europe is able to support Asian states such as the ASEAN member states, Japan and Australia who find themselves in a similar position to European states, increasingly fearing US abandonment due to enhanced focus on US national interests at the expense of the interests of allies and partners.

The successful use of Europe's potential as a middle power deserves to be pursued across a wider range of security issues in Central, South, Southeast and Northeast Asia as tensions between the US and China continue to grow as they consolidate their relations as strategic opponents with fundamental differences. European partnerships with Asian middle powers help build a coalition that has the potential to prevent the US and China from bilaterally determining the fundamental principles of world order in the coming decades. By strengthening collaboration between middle powers with an interest in preserving values of the liberal world order such as multilateral institutional diplomacy, freedom of navigation and comprehensive free trade, US-China rivalry can be made to serve the interests of middle and small powers.

References

Bull, Hedley. 1995. *The Anarchical Society: A Study of Order in World Politics*, 2nd ed. London: Palgrave Macmillan.

Callahan, William A. 2008. "Chinese Visions of World Order: Post-Hegemonic or a New Hegemony?" *International Studies Review* 10 (4): 749–761.

Christensen, Thomas J. 2015. *The China Challenge: Shaping the Choices of a Rising Power*. New York: W. W. Norton & Company.

Cooper, Andrew F., Richard A. Higgott, and Kim Richard Nossal. 1993. *Relocating Middle Powers: Australia and Canada in a Changing World Order*. Vancouver: UBC Press.

Cooper, Andrew F., and Emel Parlar Dal. 2016. "Positioning the Third Wave of Middle Power Diplomacy: Institutional Elevation, Practice Limitations." *International Journal* 71 (4): 516–528.

Council of the European Union. 2012. "Guidelines on the EU's Foreign and Security Policy in East Asia." No. 11492/12, IV.f., The South China Sea, June 15. http://eeas.europa. eu/archives/docs/asia/docs/guidelines_eu_foreign_sec_pol_east_asia_en.pdf.

Council of the European Union. 2014. "European Union Maritime Security Strategy—Action Plan." No. 17002/14, Para. 1.6, December 16. https://ec.europa.eu/maritimeaffairs/ sites/maritimeaffairs/files/docs/body/20141216-action-plan_en.pdf.

Danmarks Nationalbank. 2017. "The Banking Union—in Brief." www.nationalbanken.dk/ en/publications/themes/Pages/The-banking-union-in-brief.aspx.

Duchâtel, Mathieu. 2016. "Europe and Maritime Security in the South China Sea: Beyond Principled Statements?" *Asia Policy* 21: 54–58.

Efstathopoulos, Charalampos. 2018. "Middle Powers and the Behavioural Model." *Global Society: Journal of Interdisciplinary International Relations* 32 (1): 47–69.

Emmers, Ralf. 2018. "The Role of Middle Powers in Asian Multilateralism." *Asia Policy* 13 (4): 42–47.

EURACTIV.com with AFP. 2018. "Nine European Countries to Formalise EU Defence Force Plan." June 25. www.euractiv.com/section/defence-and-security/news/nine-european-countries-to-formalise-eu-defence-force-plan/.

European Central Bank. 2018. "What Did Forecasters Learn During the European Sovereign Debt Crisis About the Impact of Fiscal Policies on Economic Growth?" *Research Bulletin* 49. www.ecb.europa.eu/pub/economic-research/resbull/2018/html/ ecb.rb180905.en.html.

European Commission. 2014. *European Union Maritime Security Strategy: Responding Together to Global Challenges: A Guide for Stakeholders*. Brussels: Publications Office. https://ec.europa.eu/maritimeaffairs/sites/maritimeaffairs/files/leaflet-european-union-maritime-security-strategy_en.pdf.

European Political Strategy Centre. 2015. "The Asian Infrastructure Investment Bank: A New Multilateral Financial Institution or a Vehicle for China's Geostrategic Goals. European Commission Strategic Notes 1." April 24. https://ec.europa.eu/epsc/publications/ strategic-notes/asian-infrastructure-investment-bank_en.

Eurostat. 2018a. "Tables, Graphs and Maps Interface (TGM) Table." https://ec.europa.eu/ eurostat/tgm/table.do?tab=table&init=1&plugin=1&pcode=sdg_10_10&language=en.

Eurostat. 2018b. "How Much Is Spent on Defence in the EU?" https://ec.europa.eu/ eurostat/web/products-eurostat-news/-/DDN-20180518-1?inheritRedirect=true.

Fravel, M. Taylor. 2011. "China's Strategy in the South China Sea." *Contemporary Southeast Asia* 33 (3): 292–319.

Haas, Ernst. 1958. *The Uniting of Europe: Political, Social, and Economic Forces, 1950–1957*. Notre Dame: University of Notre Dame Press.

Holbraad, Carsten. 1984. *Middle Powers in International Politics*. London: Palgrave Macmillan.

Hooghe, Liesbet, and Gary Marks. 2001. *Multi-level Governance and European Integration*. Oxford: Rowman and Littlefield.

Ikenberry, G. John. 2014. "The Illusion of Geopolitics: The Enduring Power of the Liberal Order." *Foreign Affairs* 93 (3). www.foreignaffairs.com/articles/china/2014-04-17/illusion-geopolitics.

Jordaan, Eduard. 2003. "The Concept of a Middle Power in International Relations: Distinguishing Between Emerging and Traditional Middle Powers." *Politikon* 30 (2): 165–181.

Khan, Mehreen. 2018. "EU's Tusk: With Friends Like Trump, Who Needs enemies?" *Financial Times*, May 16. www.ft.com/content/c3002464-5907-11e8-b8b2-d6ceb45fa9d0.

Maull, Hanns W. 1990. "Germany and Japan: The New Civilian Powers." *Foreign Affairs* 69 (5). www.foreignaffairs.com/articles/asia/1990-12-01/germany-and-japan-new-civilian-powers.

Mearsheimer, John. 2014. "Taiwan's Dire Straits." *The National Interest* 130: 29–39.

Moravcsik, Andrew. 1998. *The Choice of Europe: Social Purpose and State Power from Messina to Maastricht*. New York: Cornell University Press.

Nordenman, Magnus. 2016. "Europe and Its Seas in the Twenty-First Century." *Mediterranean Quarterly* 27 (1): 22–29.

Odgaard, Liselotte. 2007. *The Balance of Power in Asia-Pacific Security: US-China Policies on Regional Order*. Abingdon: Routledge.

Odgaard, Liselotte, and Sune Lund. 2020. *Reducing Russia-NATO Tensions: Codes for Unplanned Encounters at Sea*. Washington, DC: Hudson Institute. https://www.hudson.org/research/16349-reducing-russia-nato-tensions-codes-for-unplanned-encounters-at-sea.

Pierson, Paul. 1996. "The Path to European Integration: A Historical Institutional Analysis." *Comparative Political Studies* 29 (2): 123–163.

Pomorska, Karolina, and Sophie Vanhoonacker. 2016. "Europe as a Global Actor: Searching for a New Strategic Approach." *Journal of Common Market Studies* 54: 204–217.

Radosavljevic, Zoran. 2017. "EU Takes Step Towards Closer Defence Cooperation." *EURACTIV*, November 13. www.euractiv.com/section/defence-policy/news/eu-takes-step-towards-closer-defence-cooperation/.

Scimia, Emanuele. 2018. "EU-Asean Trade: A Counterbalance to US and China." *Asia Times*, March 7. www.asiatimes.com/2018/03/opinion/eu-asean-trade-counterbalance-trump-china/.

Simon, Sheldon. 2018. "Fifty Plus Years of Watching Asia: An American Perspective." *Asia Policy* 13 (4): 74–82.

Steinberg, James and Michael O'Hanlon. 2014. *Strategic Reassurance and Resolve: U.S.-China Relations in the Twenty-First Century*. Princeton, NJ: Princeton University Press.

Teo, Sarah. 2018. "Middle Power Identities of Australia and South Korea: Comparing the Kevin Rudd/Julia Gillard and Lee Myung-bak Administrations." *The Pacific Review* 31 (2): 221–239.

Trading Economics. 2019. "European Union GDP." https://tradingeconomics.com/european-union/gdp.

Walt, Stephen M. 2018. "Rising Powers and the Risks of War: A Realist View of Sino-American Relations." In *Will China's Rise Be Peaceful? Security, Stability, and Legitimacy*, edited by Asle Toje, 13–32. New York: Oxford University Press.

Wight, Martin. 1966. "Western Values in International Relations." In *Diplomatic Investigations: Essays in the Theory of International Politics*, edited by Herbert Butterfield and Martin Wight, 89–131. London: George Allen & Unwin.

Wight, Martin. 1978. *Power Politics*. Leicester: Leicester University Press.

Wohlforth, William C. 2018. "Not Quite the Same as It Ever Was: Power Shifts and Contestation Over the American-Led World Order." In *Will China's Rise Be Peaceful? Security, Stability, and Legitimacy*, edited by Asle Toje, 57–77. New York: Oxford University Press.

4 The subnational dimension of the European Union's relations with China

A solution for tough times?

Tomasz Kamiński and Joanna Ciesielska-Klikowska

Introduction

Subnational units, such as regions, are very internationally active and are attracting increasing attention from scholars, although much less from the general public. Researchers tend to look at regions as non-state actors conducting paradiplomacy and analyse their activities in the context of rising pluralisation in diplomacy. Diplomatic practices, institutions and discourses are thus no longer limited to traditional international diplomacy. This paper takes a slightly different angle by examining regional paradiplomatic activities as a possible instrument of foreign policy by the European Union (EU) and its Member States.

According to our assumption, promoting and maintaining relations at the substate level may be a perfect solution for difficult relations in the triangular relationship between the EU, the United States (US) and China. We assume that these relations are mostly focused on pragmatic cooperation in low politic areas. Nevertheless, they can be an important tool in creating norms and values that are crucial from a European point of view, such as human and labour rights or environmental standards. It can therefore be said that Europe should be guided by the qualities of its international policy and can do so, *inter alia*, by using cities and regions as "transmission belts" to promote its values. Substantially, such economic cooperation may promote principles of democracy, equality and justice, which are core for the European Community.

In the context of growing tensions between China and the West, one may reasonably look for possible ways to mitigate these tensions. We argue that paradiplomatic relations might be part of the solution. At the same time, it seems that, in relation to both global governance problems and regional matters in the Asian region, Europe should wisely choose partners for cooperation. It should remember, however, that the US remains a key partner in maintaining European security. For this reason, the position of the European Union towards the US cannot be confrontational, although it cannot be closed to other global partners. In practice, the norms and values represented by the two transatlantic partners have been built on common foundations. However, modern challenges require openness to cooperation with other states, particularly China. This tripartite cooperation is extremely difficult and is under constant pressure, which may cause crises in international relations. Nevertheless, in the event of a deterioration of connections at the central level, it is the cooperation of cities and regions that can help maintain Western unity, including in the context of competition with China.

The main goal of the chapter is therefore to answer the question of how Europe, identified in our text with the European Union, could benefit from increasing subnational connections with China in an atmosphere of anxiety in the triangular relationship of the US, China and Europe. The authors suggest that, in the possible case of escalating conflict between Beijing and the West, such low-key channels of communication with China might be very useful both for national governments and the EU.

The chapter[1] is structured as follows. Firstly, the phenomenon of fast-growing cooperation on the subnational level between Europe and China is discussed, based on a survey conducted in the five largest EU Member States (Germany, France, Italy, Spain and Poland).[2] Secondly, we present the opportunities and limits of the instrumental use of paradiplomatic ties in foreign policy towards China on the EU level. Finally, in the case of the Federal Republic of Germany (FRG), we try to indicate the possible ways of benefiting from further development of subnational contacts in bilateral relations with the Peoples Republic of China (PRC).

The chapter is based on in-depth literature research, interviews with European External Action Service (EEAS) and European Commission officials, and with representatives of national foreign ministries and sub-state authorities.

EU-China cooperation on the subnational level

The development of the EU's relations with China is characterised by a growing number of interactions on the supranational and interstate, but also on the sub-state, levels. Scholars and experts tend to concentrate on the first two levels, and the academic literature on EU-China relations has been largely reticent on the subnational dimension. Existing studies ignore this phenomenon, even when they note areas where sub-state actors are very active, such as economic relations (Farnell and Crooks 2016; Christiansen and Maher 2017; Zhao 2016) or people-to-people dialogue (Burney et al. 2014).

It is only very recently that the subnational dimension of European relations with China has attracted attention, and a few studies have tried to map this phenomenon on the EU level (Skorupska et al. 2019; Kamiński 2019c; Neves 2018), particularly for Member States (Goette and Gao 2018; Skorupska 2017) or in certain regions (Czapiewski 2015; Kamiński 2019b). There are also some studies on Chinese provinces' foreign activities, particularly in the context of the Belt and Road Initiative (BRI) (Summers 2016; Mierzejewski 2018).

In trying to characterise the picture of subnational links between the EU and China that emerge from the existing research, three things seem to be apparent.

Firstly, the development of sub-state links with People's Republic of China (PRC) has been quite dynamic in recent decades. Different analyses show that the number of bilateral partnerships has been rising steadily. Data from the European

Commission (see Figure 4.1) indicates that, in 2011, the number of partnerships reached almost 500, mainly between cities.

More recent research (Skorupska et al. 2019; Kamiński 2019c) in five EU Member States (Germany, France, Spain, Italy and Poland) has revealed that subnational cooperation with China is very common. Based on data obtained in 2017, nearly 80 percent of the surveyed regions have cooperated with partners from China. The original contacts were launched in the 1980s, particularly by German and French regions. From this time, a few new partnerships have been established almost annually. The dynamic changed in 2014, and the number of new partnerships soared, which can be linked to extended connections under the aegis of the BRI. More than half of existing region-to-region relationships with China commenced in 2014–2016 (see Figure 4.2). Consequently, in

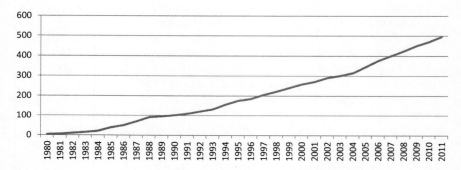

Figure 4.1 Number of partnerships between European and Chinese regions and cities, from 1979 to 2011

Source: Kamiński (2019c).

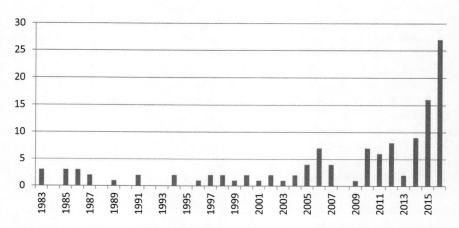

Figure 4.2 Number of established EU-China region-to-region partnerships, 1983–2016

Source: Kamiński (2019c).

many cases, the relations with Chinese partners stem from the earliest stages of development.

Anecdotal evidences also indicates that the number of city-to-city contacts has been rising (Interview with the Project Officer in Eurocities 2019; Interview with the European Commission Official from DG REGIO 2017; Kontinakis et al. 2019); however, there is a lack of comprehensive research regarding this.

Secondly, according to recent research (Kamiński 2019c), the economy seems to be the main area of regional cooperation with China for more than 80 percent of the surveyed European regional officials. Other popular areas of collaboration are higher education (almost 70 percent) and tourism (almost 60 percent). When asked about the motivation for activities with Asian partners, regions usually indicated the promotion of culture and tourism, developing business links and exchange of experiences. Many of them perceive paradiplomatical relations with Chinese regional authorities as important for development in certain areas. For example, the Italian region of Umbria has managed to attract more Chinese tourists, the French region of Auvergne-Rhône-Alpes stresses the importance of academic cooperation with Shanghai and the Polish region of Lodzkie reports rising trade (Skorupska et al. 2019).

These interests have been reflected in the choice of local partners engaged with regional authorities in the process of cooperation with Chinese partners. For many regional authorities, universities and business partners are the closest collaborators. They form an effective cooperation triangle (Skorupska et al. 2019), which is an adaptation of the "triple helix" model of university, industry and local government relations (Etzkowitz and Zhou 2017; Kontinakis et al. 2019). According to this model, academia, business and local/regional governments build a complex network of relationships in which they dynamically cooperate. One of the experts, working as a facilitator of city-to-city links with China, said:

At times, they "take the role of the other" by adopting new, non-traditional roles. For example, companies become educators, the university becomes more entrepreneurial and the local government a business facilitator. In the triple helix model, knowledge does not only flow from university lab to business (the traditional "linear" model of innovation): there are multiple links, flows and backflows between multiple partners that make up a complex tissue of public, private and knowledge actors

(Interview with the Project Officer in Eurocities 2019).

Thirdly, interviews with EU institutions (Interview with the European Commission Official from DG REGIO 2017; Interview with the European Commission Official from DG ENER 2018; Interview with the European External Action Service Officer 2017) show a limited recognition of the phenomenon of subnational collaboration with China. The EU has no monitoring mechanism that could provide its officials with up-to-date figures. There are some activities to encourage cooperation, but they are mainly limited to pilot projects which concentrate on urbanisation dialogue (Kamiński 2019a). All such activities are affected by a lack of funds and human resources as well as by a lack of coordination and strategic vision. The EU has never acknowledged the role of sub-state actors in its foreign policy towards China. Considering the rising number of partnerships with China, this failure might be a serious mistake. In the next section, we will demonstrate that subnational levels of relations affect EU foreign policy and create opportunities to advance European interests, norms and values in China. They should, therefore, not be neglected.

How sub-state activities may affect EU foreign policy

The influence of sub-state activities on EU foreign policy may be examined from two perspectives. The first looks at the rise of regional authority in Europe as a logical consequence of the empowerment of regions (Tatham 2018). It focuses on ways in which sub-state actors exert both informal and formal influence over EU affairs. The second perspective concentrates on the possible methods of employing the paradiplomatic activities of cities and regions within European foreign policy in order to realise the latter's goals more effectively (Kamiński 2019c).

International relations scholars often ignore sub-state actors; they consider nation state the default unit of analysis. This has been called by critics a form of "methodological nationalism" (Wimmer and Glick Schiller 2002; Jeffery and Wincott 2010). The bulk of literature on paradiplomacy (eg. Kuznetsov 2015; Duchacek 1984; Michelmann and Soldatos 1990) was developed in contradiction to these assumptions and is trying to attract attention to the rising role of subnational actors.

The role of sub-state entities in Europe, particularly regions, has grown over time (Marks et al. 2010). Central governments, as well as the EU, must increasingly compromise with sub-state actors throughout the policy cycle, from policy initiation to decision-making and implementation (Tatham 2018). The decentralisation of some competencies by nation states subsequent to their centralisation at the EU level are perceived as main drivers of this trend. It also resulted in increasing overlap, especially in areas such as the environment, transport, agriculture, fisheries, regional economic development and spatial planning (Panara and De Becker 2010). To avoid disempowerment, regions have to "Europeanise" their administration and begin interacting directly with the EU's institutions (Tatham 2016).

Tatham (2018) indicates three ways in which sub-state actors influence the Union.[3] Firstly, they *lobby*, either through their parent state ("intra-state" channels) or directly at the EU level ("extra-state" channels). Supranationally, they act through their staff based in their official offices in Brussels, through activities in the Committee of Regions (CoR) or through international networks of subnational governments. Organisations such as C40 or Eurocities are good examples of this.

Secondly, sub-state actors try to increase their *formal power* on EU issues. Treaty revisions have expanded the role of the CoR over time, adding further areas over which this institution has direct influence on European legislation (Hönnige and Panke 2016). Moreover, they have managed to strengthen the subsidiarity principle, its monitoring and enforcement (Tatham 2018).

Thirdly, regions have formal *veto rights* at the domestic level that may affect the EU policy-making process in even high-political issues such as international trade deals. The most spectacular case is the government of Wallonia, which vetoed the Comprehensive Economic and Trade Agreement (CETA) between the EU and Canada in 2016. The agreement of Wallonia's regional parliament was needed in order to implement CETA; for the first time in its history, the EU Commission had to negotiate directly with a region and introduce changes under pressure from the citizens of a particular region (Magnette 2016).[4]

In the case of EU policy toward China, all three of these elements may play a role. This would be particularly evident in any trade deal with China. Such a deal must be agreed upon not only by Member States' governments and the European Parliament but also by the EU's national parliaments, the seven federal, regional and community parliaments in Belgium, and ten upper chambers, some of which include strong sub-state representations (such as the Italian, Spanish, Austrian or German upper chambers). As Tatham (2018) correctly noted: "The rise of regions not only multiplies institutional dynamics in Europe, it also visibly complicates the political dynamics of policy negotiations". One can easily imagine that particular regions (as veto players) might be targeted by foreign powers in order to influence, delay or even block the process.

In this context, subnational links may create a channel for the Chinese to further undermine European cohesion. China may use its relationship with particular regions to convince their authorities to act as agents of Chinese interests. Attaching political influence to China's economic presence is not unusual at the level of Member States. There are examples where European countries were reluctant to support the EU's "anti-Chinese" political actions (e.g. in 2017, Greece blocked an EU statement at the United Nations (UN) Human Rights Council condemning China's human rights violations). The same mechanism of influence may potentially be adopted at the subnational level.

The case of EU-China relations also indicates that, in addition to the three previous ways in which sub-state actors affect EU policy, we can add another element: *direct actions*. Regions and cities take autonomous actions that impact national and European relations with China. To illustrate this point, we consider several cases.

After backing away under Chinese pressure from plans to give the Dalai Lama honorary citizenship in 2012 (Alpert 2012), Milan's authorities did so four years later. This provoked official reaction from the Chinese Foreign Ministry condemning the Italian city (Barry 2016). The situation complicated *post factum* talks between the European Commission and China on the project of "EU-China Tourism Year 2018". Milan had to be excluded from the list of places officially engaged in this venture (Interview with the European External Action Service officer 2017).

A similar case occurred in 2017, when the city of Weimar awarded a human rights prize for Ilham Tohti, a Uyghur dissident. Beijing had protested to Berlin through diplomatic channels (Interview with German diplomat 2019) and the official website of the city of Weimar was attacked by hackers who deleted all content related to the prize (China Change 2017).

A recent example comes from Prague, where liberal mayor Zdenek Hrib withdrew the city from a twin cities agreement with Beijing that explicitly recognised the "one China policy", under which the PRC claims sovereignty over Taiwan. Moreover, the mayor met the head of Tibet's government-in-exile, Lobsang Sangay, and restored the practice of flying the Tibetan flag from Prague's town hall (Tait 2019). In response, Beijing cancelled a tour in China by the Prague Philharmonic Orchestra, which had spent two and a half years in preparation and lost nearly US$ 200,000 on the cancelled visit. Czech President Milos Zeman wrote to Xi Jinping distancing himself from Prague's policy (Schmitz 2019).

These incidents show that autonomous actions taken by sub-state actors can potentially impact not only national relations with China but sometimes also European-level policy. In the next part of this chapter, we will examine how the EU, using the example of Germany, can potentially make use of sub-state relations with the PRC.

Theoretically, paradiplomacy may positively influence state and international policies because it brings extra rationalisation to the decision-making process. The external relations of sub-state actors can contribute to the foreign policy of states and even make it more efficient (Soldatos 1990; Kuznetsov 2015). In the context of European policy, we can point out two ways in which EU foreign policy might benefit: by fostering the implementation of some policy goals, and by creating alternative political channels of communication with foreign partners. The latter might be even more important than the former.

The EU's China strategy (European Commission and High Representative of the Union for Foreign Affairs and Security Policy 2016) does not stress the importance of subnational actors' activities to achieve its goals, a seemingly major omission. The sub-state level is appropriate for tackling many important problems presented in the document and plays a crucial role in reaching some of its objectives (Kamiński 2019c).

Firstly, the EU aspires to promote a more open, sustainable and inclusive growth model in China by supporting and encouraging economic, environmental and social reforms in the PRC. Contacts on the sub-state level can enable the direct transfer of knowledge and best practice where they are needed—to local communities. In by-passing highly politicised dialogues on the state level, cities and regions can offer more channels for influencing Chinese society.

Secondly, the EU aims to attract "productive Chinese investment in Europe". Regional authorities play a crucial role in negotiating foreign direct investment (FDI) deals. Big Chinese investments in particular are accompanied by political agreements between local or regional authorities (Mierzejewski 2018). Even establishing train connections which facilitate and promote bilateral trade are politicised and engage regional authorities on both sides. The development of the Lodz-Chengdu cargo train link may serve as a good example of such a connection (Kamiński 2019b).

Thirdly, the strategy says that the EU will strengthen cooperation with China on research and innovation. Skorupska et al. (2019) show that universities closely cooperate with regions in their activities with China. Consequently, the EU's science diplomacy should acknowledge sub-state authorities as important stakeholders and partners for collaboration.

Finally, the EU hopes to strengthen people-to-people (P2P) links by attracting more Chinese students and tourists who "would contribute to fostering intercultural dialogue and promoting cultural diversity and civil society participation" (European Commission and High Representative of the Union for Foreign Affairs and Security Policy 2016). The development of subnational links creates a network necessary to implementing this policy goal. Moreover, cultural and educational exchange, not to mention tourism promotion, are on the list of priorities in regions' relations with Chinese partners. A community of interest between the EU and sub-state actors is also quite clear in this regard. This should lay a good foundation for closer cooperation with China, but there are even more strategic reasons why the EU should promote sub-state contacts.

Hence, interconnections between regions and cities create new channels of political communication with China, which might prove very useful in cases of deteriorating relations at the intergovernmental level. Rising tensions between the US and China might force Europe to be involved in the diplomatic conflict, most probably on the American side—voluntarily or under US pressure. Europeans, however, are also looking for their own, third path of cooperation between the powers. An example of this is a reaction to Trump's withdrawal from the Paris Agreement, an illustration of the significance of sub-state relations in mitigating crises on the diplomatic level. Despite a political impasse between Washington and Beijing, many local and regional authorities in the US have declared their continued cooperation on climate, clean energy or low-carbon development. China has acknowledged this, and president Xi Jinping even met in person with the governor of California, Jerry Brown (Hernández and Nagourney 2017).

Subnational interactions with China: case study of Germany

In these considerations, Germany (FRG) is a special case of a country that conducts intensive three-tier international cooperation—at the *macro-level* of the EU, at the *medium-level* of its Member States, as well as at the *micro-level* of region-to-region cooperation.

At the *macro-level*, Germany is an economically and politically leading country in Europe and an actor which masterfully plays the game between EU, US and China. Today, the FRG is trying to find its own place on the global stage, somehow denying the well-known saying of Henry Kissinger that it is "too big for Europe, but too small for the world" (Ash 1993). Thus, as Habermas (2011) indicates, by going through a series of difficult crises in the EU with a defensive hand, Germany has facilitated the "Germanisation" of European politics and transformed itself into a European leader which can impose on Europe to realise German policy (Bulmer and Paterson 2018; Schoeller 2019). At a *medium—level*, the FRG values close relations with neighbouring or partner states—with Western ones since the 1950s, especially France (Ciesielska-Klikowska 2017) and the US (Gatzke 1980; Trommler and Shore 2001) and, since its 1970s turn to *Ostpolitik*, with the Eastern states (Hofmann 2007). However, German political activity is also intensive at the *micro-level*. The 16 German *Länder* conduct rigorous, multifaceted and multidimensional *quasi*-foreign policies, thus complementing the possibilities of pursuing interests in foreign policy conducted at the central level. The issue of making use of paradiplomatic cooperation is broadly anchored in the German federal system, described in the Constitution from 1949 and supported in practice by additional laws (Sturm 2013; Plöhn and Steffani 1994).

According to jurisprudence and the prevailing view of law, German *Länder* have original state power, are parliamentary republics and, thus, have the quality of states. As legal institutions, they conduct economic, social and cultural policies, maintain contacts with regions in other countries, establish foreign representations, become members of international organisations and associations, and sign international agreements, as confirmed in the Lindau Agreement of 1957 (Bundesratsdrucksache 1992; Leonardy 1999; Jeffery 1999). They also make use of paradiplomatic tools within the framework of EU—since the mid-1980s, the *Länder* have had representative offices in Brussels (Nagel 2010). They have participated in European politics through the legal provisions of the "European Article" (Art. 23), the Act on Co-operation between the Federation and the Federal States in Matters Concerning the EU, and the Agreement between the Federation and the Federal States; moreover, the upper chamber of the FRG's legislature, the *Bundesrat*, has extensive competence to speak on European matters (Jeffery 2007).

There are three levels in which the German federal states participate in European politics, depending on the extent to which the competence of *Länder* or the *Bundesrat* applies: i) in the case of EU matters concerning political areas in which the *Bundesrat* was previously entitled to participate, the *Länder* have the right to participate in deliberations which determine the position of the federal government; ii) when the essential interests of the *Länder* are at stake, the *Bundesrat* has the right to appoint representatives who, together with the competent federal ministry, can participate in negotiations in the EU Council; iii) a representative of the *Länder* may also be the only representative of Germany in the Council convening EU applications solely regarding *Länder* authority. It should also be emphasised that, in cases where the federal government has legislative powers, it must take into account the position taken by the *Bundesrat* in determining the German negotiating position. The consent of the *Bundesrat* is also required to change and amend EU treaties. Thus, *vis-à-vis* the above-mentioned Tatham study (2018), the *Bundesrat*, as representative of all *Länder*, may implement its competencies on European policy through *lobbying, formal powers* or *veto rights*.

It can therefore be assumed that the *Länder* assist the implementation of the foreign policy objectives of the entire federation by supporting the execution of certain policy goals through the *Bundesrat*, the federal government or at the EU level, and by creating an alternative political channel of communication with foreign partners.

The latter is realised in practice in a number of ways. One is sustaining political relations with other regions and countries by signing international agreements and partnerships and by carrying out international visits. A second is establishing offices as representations in regions of third-party countries. A third is by activities carried out in cooperation with partner regions (joint fairs, exhibitions, conferences or academic collaboration). A fourth is that the *Länder* create alternative political channels of communication with foreign partners by the exchange of good practices in public administration. Germany thus increases the benefits of bilateral and multilateral international cooperation at the sub-state level.

However, as Neves (2018) observes, these relationships have completely different characteristics to *macro-* and *medium-level* relations for several reasons: they are based on the multidisciplinary and holistic approach of economic, social, environmental, educational and cultural ties, which are demonstrably more vivid than those at higher levels; they bind representatives of regional governmental, private and non-governmental sector; they are founded on strong interpersonal relations; and they are oriented to the long-term, which makes them generally very stable.

Given the high effectiveness of German policy implemented by regions in the European and American contexts—described many times (Roose 2010; Statz and Wohlfarth 2010; Gorzelak et al. 2004; Cziomer 2005; Kiwerska 2013)—it is worth investigating the less researched contacts of *Länder* with Chinese provinces through lenses mentioned above.

1. The first Sino-German sub-state contacts were based on the political decisions of central and regional authorities from both sides, which were related to the desire to develop economic relations and were founded on bilateral visits and the signing of partnerships between regions and cities. The first region-to-region cooperation was established in 1982 (Baden-Württemberg with Liaoning), as was the earliest city-to-city relation (Duisburg-Wuhan). There are today 23 regional and 141 city partnerships—their number has increased over 40 years, but the upward trend does not reflect that characterizing regional cooperation with the PRC for the entire EU (see Table 4.1, compare to Figures 4.1 and 4.2).

The main driving forces behind establishing region-to-region relationships were the changing economic conditions and China's increasing opening to the world. However, it cannot be forgotten that deepened cooperation was also supplemented by central governments in Berlin and Beijing—a particularly significant development of regional cooperation followed the signing of the Strategic Partnership in Global Responsibility in 2004, the implementation of Sino-German governmental consultations in 2011 and the upgrading of strategic partnership into the Comprehensive Strategic Partnership in 2014 (Presse- und Informationsamt der Bundesregierung 2014). In contrast to other European countries, the BRI did not fuel the building of regional cooperation (Interview with German diplomat 2019) (see Figure 4.3).

2. The *Länder* remain significant actors on the global arena, thus proving their high activity in international affairs by establishing their own representative

Table 4.1 Regional partnerships with China

German Land	*Chinese Province*		
Baden-Württemberg	Liaoning (1982)	Jiangsu (1984)	
Bayern	Shandong (1987)	Guandong (2004)	
Brandenburg	Hebei (2015)		
Bremen	City of Dalian (1985)	Guandong (2004)*	
Federal State of Berlin	Beijing (1994)		
Hamburg	Shanghai (1986)		
Hessen	Jangxi (1985)	Hunan (1985)*	
Mecklenburg-Vorpommern			
Niedersachsen	Anhui (1984)		
Nordrhein-Westfalen	Jiangsu (1986)	Shanxi (1984)	Sichuan (1988)
Rheinland-Pfalz	Fujian (1989)		
Saarland	Hunan (2006)*	Hubei (1996)	
Sachsen-Anhalt	Shanghai (2017)	Heilongjiang (2003)*	
Sachsen	Hubei (2007)		
Schleswig-Holstein	Zhejiang (1986)		
Thüringen	Shaanxi (1997)*		

* Non-active or probably non-active partnerships (pointed out as non-active by regional officers in the survey or no information about any form of activity in recent years found)
Source: own elaboration on the basis of the survey (2016/2017) among all regional offices responsible for cooperation with China (see footnote 2), combined with Goette and Gao (2018) and followed by review of official websites of German *Länder*.

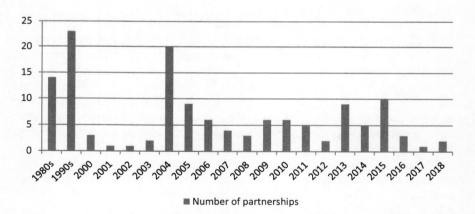

■ Number of partnerships

Figure 4.3 The number of established links between German and Chinese cities
Source: own elaboration based on Goette and Gao (2018).

offices to pursue their interests in the partner region. Such offices are not necessary, but certainly desirable, for an active international policy. Western and southern federal states (Baden-Württemberg, Bayern, Nordrhein-Westfalen, Rheinland-Pfalz or Saarland) are especially vigorous in global affairs, although their potential to develop their foreign activities is not the same due to differences in populations and the relative size of their economies (Statistische Ämter des Bundes und der Länder 2019; Eurostat 2019). The importance of international offices can be confirmed by the example of Hamburg, a city with *Land*-status, the largest seaport in Germany and a huge industrial and financial centre; its authorities have placed great emphasis on internationalisation. For many years, relations with China have been fostered by Hamburg's office in Shanghai, together with its Chamber of Commerce, Port of Hamburg and Hamburg Travel. These efforts have had measurable effects: China is today the second most important trade partner for the Hamburg agglomeration (Goette and Gao 2018).

3. Regions actively cooperate in the organisation of joint trade fairs, trade missions, exhibitions, conferences and academic cooperation. In fact, by conducting regional cooperation with China, German *Länder* and cities have achieved numerous goals, mostly focused on five issues: business and trade, tourism, academic exchange and educational and cultural cooperation (Federal Ministry of Education and Research 2015). One of the regions particularly determined to cooperate with China is Nordrhein-Westfalen. The city of Duisburg, located there, can boast the largest dry port in Europe, which is a great flywheel for the German economy, and regional contacts with the PRC. This hinterland hub, two-thirds owned by the *Land* and one-third by the city, drives the relationship on a *macro* and *micro* scale. Duisburg receives 40 cargo trains from Chongqing every week and has over 80 Chinese companies actively participating in its economy, while the University of Duisburg-Essen has one of the most important research centres dealing with China and Asia in general—the Institute of East Asian Studies—which fuels discussion about the Middle Kingdom throughout the region (Interview in In-East 2019). Partners organise, *inter alia*, the Chinese Spring Festival—sponsored jointly by GFW Duisburg, the Confucius Institute Metropole Ruhr and the University of Duisburg-Essen—and arrange support for Chinese students and graduates (GFW Duisburg 2019).

Nevertheless, the benefits associated with cooperation with China are also available to smaller urban centres. Economically weak Magdeburg (the capital city of Sachsen-Anhalt) has been implementing a dynamic partnership with Harbin since 2008; Sachsen-Anhalt also has an office in Shanghai. Magdeburg and Harbin actively support cooperation projects in business, training and education, as well as cultural projects. Examples of this are the Ice and Snow Festival, the Harbin Fair or more local *Buntes China in Magdeburg* (Eng. Colourful China in Magdeburg). Considering the fact that Magdeburg and the wider *Land* do not have a broadly developed industry that would be a driving force in contacts with China but do have high schools and colleges that specialise in exact sciences, they focus on maintaining broad contacts in the educational sector through, for example, Otto-von-Guericke University or the Magdeburg-Stendal University of Applied Sciences (Interview with Dr. G. Henkel 2018).

4. The regions and cities share good practice in the field of public administration. Taxes, construction, administration management, natural environment and municipal waste management remain themes that connect all cities. Therefore, Sino-German relations feature a vital exchange of knowledge and experience

related to waste management, urban transport, caring for municipal greenery or building smart cities (Münchner Kreis 2013). Green management is one of the crucial working areas between Baden-Württemberg, Jiangsu and Liaoning (Baden-Württemberg 2015). Germans give environmental protection the priority among contemporary social challenges, so collaboration with China on the latest technology and environmental monitoring is extremely important (Forschungs- gruppe Wahlen 2019). In light of the withdrawal of President Trump from the Paris Agreement, the search for an international partner in pro-environmental change is fundamental for Germany—so China can take its place as Germany's main partner in this matter. The framework of regional cooperation has a long history; hence, the experience can be easily moved to the central level, which is already happening through the German and Chinese ministries responsible for the environment and for urban and rural development (GIZ 2020).

Generalizing the research results, it should be stated that regions may use bilat- eral relations with other sub-state actors to build a strong political position in their own country, to promote themselves in the international arena, to eliminate investment risk, to build a regional/city brand attractive for foreign direct invest- ments, to benefit from social and information networks and to support *diasporas*, especially students and employees (Düben 2019).

Given the dynamics of change on the world stage and current growing ten- sions, especially in the EU-US-China triangle, these *micro-level* relationships can also be used firstly to safeguard relations at the central level, which are today in a difficult position due to the ongoing US trade war with the PRC. The US and China are among the largest export markets for German and European companies outside the EU. A crisis between these two would therefore directly damage Euro- pean economies, including the budgets of individual companies (mainly in the automotive and high-tech industry), and thus also the funds of local governments. Great risks to the EU associated with escalating trade tensions and increased global protectionism could also arise. This could lead, in turn, to uncertainties in global trade, potentially reducing future investment and trade growth and jeopard- izing the credibility of the World Trade Organization. Trade misunderstandings between the two major powers would therefore brutally affect the export-oriented German and European economy. A return to bilateralism, protectionism and global trade uncertainty would thus be tough for Germany and for the EU as a whole (Schmucker 2018). It seems that, in this situation, individual states and regions may lobby for a return to open and multidimensional international cooperation, which will be profitable at the *macro-*, *medium-* and *micro-levels*.

Independent communication channels at the subnational level might make many areas of cooperation with China and the US more resilient through diplo- matic storms. Such a detachment of low-policy issues from high-politics may be very beneficial, especially in the case of tensions that make political communica- tion more difficult or even impossible.

This can be illustrated by the example of Bayern, which, despite the arms embargo on the PRC since the early 1990s, maintains military cooperation with China. The current Interior Minister Horst Seehofer, as Prime Minister of Bayern in 2008–2018, pursued a policy of dynamic cooperation with the PRC, primarily with the partner province of Shantung. This resulted in a sales contract worth EUR 1 billion for 1,000 helicopters manufactured in Bavarian plants, which afterwards allowed the construction of a combat helicopter factory in Qingdao in 2019—a joint venture of Airbus Helicopters and the Chinese UGAC (Hegmann and Wüpper 2019). Seehofer today, as a member of the federal government and a known opponent of the Foreign Minister Heiko Maas—for whom issues of protecting human rights and resolving armed conflicts are crucial—would find lobbying for military cooperation with PRC at the inter-state level rather difficult, if not impossible. However, the previously created opportunities for regional cooperation and lobbying in Berlin and Beijing have brought measurable profits. The steps taken by Seehofer have not led to tensions with the Americans, although the US Army Garrison Bavaria, with over 40,000 soldiers and civilians, are stationed in this *Land*. In fact, Germany's limited expenditure on defence policy is to blame for the turbulence in German-US relations, not their military cooperation with China (Fischer and Winterer 2019).

The aspect of personal animosities, ideological differences or the ambitions of individual politicians are also significant for the implementation, pace and quality of regional connections. The human factor—involvement or the lack thereof from specific members of political circles, of the economic milieu and increasingly from academic circles (the "triple helix" scheme)—also seems a key feature of cooperation. Undoubtedly, use of the sub-state channel via particular people can be observed as an alternative or counteraction to activities undertaken at the central level. This may lead to controversy in internal policy but, at the same time, make it possible to encapsulate interstate relations with additional opportunities at a lower level.

Conclusion

The research in this chapter leads to the conclusion that the development of sub-state relations between Europe and China can be beneficial for both the national governments and the entire EU. Firstly, in the event of expanding international anxiety, subnational channels of communication with China might be used to mitigate tensions and secure continued cooperation in many areas, despite political storms. Moreover, by utilising this *micro-level*, the EU may transmit democratic values and good practice, thus influencing consciousness changes in China while avoiding unnecessary animosities in the US-China-EU triangle.

Secondly, the closer coordination of activities with China at all levels of contact (supranational, national and subnational) may help implement European policy goals. In fact, the cooperation of cities and regions, due to the intensive involvement of the political, economic and social milieus of all sides, is a potentially useful tool for transferring norms and values significant for the EU. The interviews and data analysis we conducted show that the EU and its Member States can stand on the side of decent values and ensure their compliance at the central level, while focusing on pragmatic cooperation in low-political areas at the regional level.

This channel often seems to be "depoliticised" and rather non-confrontational because economic matters are the driving force for cooperation. This method may thus prove a solution during tough times as it does not cause international controversy nor adversely affect interstate cooperation.

Thirdly, given that the world is rapidly moving towards bipolarity, Europe must look for a third path for itself. Realizing that European security relies heavily on US involvement, Brussels cannot afford open political conflict with Washington. Therefore, the strategic partnership of both entities seems crucial to EU interests. Nevertheless, the Union can and should look for partners in areas beyond the transatlantic axis. The Asian direction, including towards China, thus seems natural because China is the second most important economic partner of the EU (after the US).

Nevertheless, confronted with rising US and PRC influence or increasing competition between them (even in the form of a trade war), the EU position will be difficult. Assuming that the issue of maintaining the unity of the West is a prerequisite for maintaining European security, Europe's task should be to seek channels of cooperation that do not cause political controversy but do not entail directly advocating either side. Thus, the EU should lead change in international policy with the help of paradiplomatic tools which can indirectly serve the pursuit of high policy interests. Sub-state actions, if uncoordinated with the national and the EU levels, may provoke tensions as well. Consequently, strengthening political dialogue on China between the EU's institutions, national states and regional authorities would be desirable.

Notes

1 This chapter is the result of a three-year project entitled "The Role of Regions in the European Union Policy towards China", which was financed by the Polish National Science Centre (number: 2015/19/B/HS5/02534).
2 In total, the data is from 75 regions in the five countries (91percent of all the regions in these countries). The survey, which has not been published, was conducted in December 2016 and in the first half of 2017 by researchers from the University of Lodz and the Polish Institute of International Affairs.
3 He concentrates on regions only; however, in our opinion, some of methods described (e.g., lobbying) apply to cities as well.
4 It agreed that CETA should be accompanied by a legally binding interpretative instrument that clarifies and completes the treaty on key issues.

References

Alpert, Emily. 2012. "Italian City Pulls Back from Making Dalai Lama a Honorary Citizen." *LA Times Blogs: World Now*, Blog, June 21. https://latimesblogs.latimes.com/world_now/2012/06/hold-tibet.html.

Ash, Timothy Garton. 1993. *In Europe's Name: Germany and the Divided Continent*. New York: Random House.

Baden-Württemberg. 2015. "Weitere Vertiefung der Zusammenarbeit mit chinesischen Partnerprovinzen." October 22. www.baden-wuerttemberg.de/de/service/presse/pressemitteilung/pid/weitere-vertiefung-der-zusammenarbeit-mit-jiangsu/.

Barry, Colleen. 2016. "Milan Honors Dalai Lama as Citizen Over China's Objections." *AP News*, October 20. https://apnews.com/fabaa18bef2a4038b6778eed4583e0dc.

Bulmer, Simon, and William E. Paterson. 2018. *Germany and the European Union: Europe's Reluctant Hegemon?* Basingstoke: Palgrave Macmillan.

Bundesratsdrucksache. 1992. "Stellungnahme des Bundesrates zum Entwurf eines Gesetzes zu dem Abkommen vom 2. Mai 1992 über den Europäischen Wirtschaftsraum (EWR-Abkommen)." Beschluss Nr. 368. https://dipbt.bundestag.de/doc/brd/1992/D368+92.pdf.

Burney, Matthieu, Joelle Hivonnet, and Kolja Raube. 2014. "'Soft Diplomacy' and People-to-People Dialogue Between the EU and the PRC." *European Foreign Affairs Review* 19 (Special Issue): 35–56.

China Change. 2017. "The City of Weimar in Germany Saw Its Website Attacked for Giving Human Rights Prize to Uighur Professor Ilham Tohti." November 8. https://chinachange.org/2017/11/08/the-city-of-weimar-in-germany-saw-its-website-attacked-for-giving-human-rights-prize-to-uighur-professor-ilham-tohti/.

Christiansen, Thomas, and Richard Maher. 2017. "The Rise of China—Challenges and Opportunities for the European Union." *Asia Europe Journal* 15 (2): 121–131.

Ciesielska-Klikowska, Joanna. 2017. *Francja i Niemcy w procesie integracji europejskiej w latach 1992–2007*. Łódź: Wydawnictwo Uniwersytetu Łódzkiego.

Czapiewski, Tomasz. 2015. "The (Para)Diplomacy of Scotland Towards Asian Countries." *Zeszyty Naukowe Uniwersytetu Szczecińskiego Acta Politica* 31: 59–76.

Cziomer, Erhard. 2005. *Polityka zagraniczna Niemiec: kontynuacja i zmiany po zjednoczeniu, ze szczególnym uwzględnieniem polityki europejskiej i transatlantyckiej*. Warszawa: "Politeja" Fundacja Promocji Wiedzy o Polityce.

Düben, Björn Alexander. 2019. "Are the Gloves Coming Off in China-Germany Economic Relations?" *The Diplomat*, May 3. https://thediplomat.com/2019/05/are-the-gloves-coming-off-in-china-germany-economic-relations/.

Duchacek, Ivo D. 1984. "The International Dimension of Subnational Self-Government." *Publius: The Journal of Federalism* 14 (4): 5–31.

Etzkowitz, Henry, and Chunyan Zhou. 2017. *The Triple Helix: University—Industry—Government Innovation and Entrepreneurship*. London: Routledge.

European Commission and High Representative of the Union for Foreign Affairs and Security Policy. 2016. *Joint Communication to the European Parliament and the Council: Elements for a New EU Strategy on China*. Brussels: European Commission, June 22.

Eurostat. 2019. "GDP at Current Market Prices by NUTS 2 Regions." https://appsso.eurostat.ec.europa.eu/nui/show.do?dataset=nama_10r_2gdp&lang=en.

Farnell, John, and Paul Irwin Crooks. 2016. *The Politics of EU-China Economic Relations: An Uneasy Partnership*. Basingstoke: Palgrave Macmillan.

Federal Ministry of Education and Research. 2015. "China Strategy 2015–2020: Strategic Framework for Cooperation with China in Research, Science and Education." www.bmbf.de/pub/China_Strategy_Longversion.pdf.

Fischer, Michael, and Paul Winterer. 2019. "US Threats to Withdraw Troops Cause Stir Among German Politicians." www.dpa-international.com/topic/us-threats-withdraw-troops-cause-stir-among-german-urn%3Anewsml%3Adpa.com%3A20090101%3A190809-99-407600.

Forschungsgruppe Wahlen. 2019. "Wichtige Probleme in Deutschland seit 01/2000." http://www.forschungsgruppe.de/Umfragen/Politbarometer/Langzeitentwicklung_-_Themen_im_Ueberblick/Politik_II/#Prob11.

Gatzke, Hans W. 1980. *Germany and the United States: A "Special Relationship?"* Cambridge: Harvard University Press.

GFW Duisburg. 2019. "Zusammenarbeit zwischen Duisburg und China: Aktivitäten, Status quo und Perspektiven." www.gfw-duisburg.de/aktuelles/presse/detail/ zusammenarbeit-zwischen-duisburg-und-china-aktivitaeten-status-quo-und-perspektiven/.

GIZ. 2020. "Sino-German Urbanisation Partnership." www.giz.de/en/worldwide/41623. html.

Goette, Anja, and Qianlan Gao. 2018. *Deutsch-Chinesische Kommunalbeziehungen*. Bonn: Servicestelle Kommunen in der Einen Welt.

Gorzelak, Grzegorz, John Bachtler, and Mariusz Kasprzyk, eds. 2004. *Współpraca transgraniczna Unii Europejskiej: Doświadczenia Polski i Niemiec*. Warszawa: Wydawnictwo Naukowe Scholar.

Habermas, Jürgen. 2011. "Pakt dla Europy czy przeciw Europie?" *Gazeta Wyborcza*, April 11.

Hegmann, Gerhard, and Gesche Wüpper. 2019. "Mega-Order der Militärs verschaffen der Hubschrauber-Sparte einen Schub." *Die Welt*, January 24.

Hernández, Javier C., and Adam Nagourney. 2017. "As Trump Steps Back, Jerry Brown Talks Climate Change in China." *The New York Times*, June 6. www.nytimes. com/2017/06/06/world/asia/xi-jinping-china-jerry-brown-california-climate.html.

Hofmann, Arne. 2007. *The Emergence of Détente in Europe: Brandt, Kennedy and the Formation of Ostpolitik*. London and New York: Routledge.

Hönnige, Christoph, and Diana Panke. 2016. "Is Anybody Listening? The Committee of the Regions and the European Economic and Social Committee and Their Quest for Awareness." *Journal of European Public Policy* 23 (4): 624–642.

Interview in In-East (University of Duisburg-Essen). 2019. Duisburg, December 3.

Interview with Dr. G. Henkel. 2018. Magdeburg, June 20.

Interview with the European Commission Official from DG ENER. 2018. Brussels, January 17.

Interview with the European Commission Official from DG REGIO. 2017. Brussels, November 17.

Interview with the European External Action Service Officer. 2017. Brussels, November 15.

Interview with German Diplomat. 2019. Berlin, April 17.

Interview with the Project Officer in Eurocities. 2019. Brussels, January 30.

Jeffery, Charlie. 1999. *Recasting German Federalism: The Legacies of Unification*. London and New York: Pinter.

Jeffery, Charlie. 2007. "Towards a New Understanding of Multi-Level Governance in Germany? The Federalism Reform Debate and European Integration." *Politische Vierteljahresschrift* 48 (1): 17–27.

Jeffery, Charlie, and Daniel Wincott. 2010. "The Challenge of Territorial Politics: Beyond Methodological Nationalism." In *New Directions in Political Science: Responding to the Challenges of an Interdependent World*, edited by Colin Hay, 167–188. Basingstoke: Palgrave Macmillan.

Kamiński, Tomasz. 2019a. "The Urbanisation Dialogue Between the EU and China: Reality Check." *EU-China Observer* 2: 9–13.

Kamiński, Tomasz. 2019b. "What Are the Factors Behind the Successful EU-China Cooperation on the Subnational Level? Case Study of the Lodzkie Region in Poland." *Asia Europe Journal* 17 (2): 227–242.

Kamiński, Tomasz. 2019c. "The Sub-State Dimension of the European Union Relations with China." *European Foreign Affairs Review* 24 (3): 367–385.

Kiwerska, Jadwiga. 2013. *Rozchodzenie się dwóch światów? Stany Zjednoczone i relacje transatlantyckie 1989–2012*. Poznań: Wydawnictwo Naukowe i Innowacje.

Kontinakis, Nicolaos, Yue Liu, Baige Huo, Yun Li, and Jinjing Zhang. 2019. *Cooperation Plans and Guidelines*. Brussels: URBAN-EU-CHINA Innovation Platform on Sustainable Urbanisation.

Kuznetsov, Alexander. 2015. *Theory and Practice of Paradiplomacy: Subnational Governments in International Affairs*. London and New York: Routledge.

Leonardy, Uwe. 1999. "The Institutional Structures of German Federalism." Electronic Edition. http://library.fes.de/fulltext/bueros/london/00538007.htm#E10E15.

Magnette, Paul. 2016. "Wallonia Blocked a Harmful EU Trade Deal—but We Don't Share Trump's Dreams." *The Guardian*, November 14. www.theguardian.com/commentisfree/2016/nov/14/wallonia-ceta-ttip-eu-trade-belgium.

Marks, Gary, Lisabet Hooghe, and Arjan Schakel. 2010. *The Rise of Regional Authority: A Comparative Study of 42 Democracies (1950–2006)*. London: Routledge.

Michelmann, Hans J., and Panayotis Soldatos, eds. 1990. *Federalism and International Relations: The Role of Subnational Units*. Oxford: Oxford University Press.

Mierzejewski, Dominik. 2018. "The Role of Local Governments in the New Silk Road." In *China's New Silk Road: An Emerging World Order*, edited by Carmen Mendes, 135–151. London and New York: Routledge.

Münchner Kreis. 2013. "Smart Cities: China und Deutschland lernen voneinander." *Pressemitteilung*, September 18. www.muenchner-kreis.de/fileadmin/üdokumente/Pressemitteilungen/130918_PM_SmartCities.pdf.

Nagel, Klaus-Jürgen. 2010. "Foreign Policy: The Case of the German Lander." In *Foreign Policy of Constituents Units at the Beginning of 21st Century*, edited by Ferran Requejo, 121–141. Barcelona: Generalitat de Catalunya, Institut d'Estudis Autonòmics.

Neves, Miguel Santos. 2018. "The Paradiplomacy Region-to-Region Dimension in EU-China Relations." Electronic Edition. www.academia.edu/41155179/The_Paradiplomacy_Region_to_Region_Dimension_of_EU_China_relations.

Panara, Carlo, and Alexander de Becker, eds. 2010. *The Role of the Regions in EU Governance*. Heidelberg: Springer Science & Business Media.

Plöhn, Jürgen, and Winfried Steffani. 1994. "Bund und Länder in der Bundesrepublik Deutschland." In *Handbuch der deutschen Bundesländer*, edited by Jürgen Hartmann, 2nd ed. Bonn: Bundeszentrale für politische Bildung.

Presse- und Informationsamt der Bundesregierung. 2014. "Joint Declaration Between Germany and China." March 28. https://archiv.bundesregierung.de/archiv-de/meta/startseite/joint-declaration-between-germany-and-china-460244.

Roose, Jochen. 2010. *Vergesellschaftung an Europas Binnengrenzen: Eine vergleichende Studie zu den Bedingungen sozialer Integration*. Wiesbaden: Springer VS.

Schmitz, Rob. 2019. "Czech-Chinese Ties Strained as Prague Stands Up to Beijing." *NPR. org*, October 30. www.npr.org/2019/10/30/774054035/czech-chinese-ties-are-affected-as-prague-stands-up-to-beijing.

Schmucker, Claudia. 2018. "US-China Trade War: Why Germany Should Support the EU." *ISPI*, May 31. www.ispionline.it/it/pubblicazione/us-china-trade-war-why-germany-should-support-eu-20678.

Schoeller, Magnus G. 2019. *Leadership in the Eurozone: The Role of Germany and EU Institutions*. Basingstoke: Palgrave Macmillian.

Skorupska, Adriana. 2017. "Paradyplomacja Polska—Chiny: Współpraca Polskich Województw z Chińskimi Prowincjami." *Sprawy Międzynarodowe* 2: 131–140.

Skorupska, Adriana, Justyna Szczudlik, and Tomasz Kamiński. 2019. *The Subnational Dimension of EU-China Relations*. Warsaw: Polski Instytut Spraw Międzynarodowych.

Soldatos, Panayotis. 1990. "An Explanatory Framework for the Study of Federal States as Foreign-Policy Actors." In *Federalism and International Relations*, edited by Hans J. Michelmann and Panayotis Soldatos. Oxford: Oxford University Press.

Statistische Ämter des Bundes und der Länder. 2019. "Fläche und Bevölkerung nach Ländern." www.statistikportal.de/de/bevoelkerung/flaeche-und-bevoelkerung.

Statz, Albert, and Charlotte Wohlfarth. 2010. "Kommunale Partnerschaften und Netzwerke: Ein Beitrag zu einer transnationalen Politik der Nachhaltigkeit." In *Schriften zur Demokratie*, vol. 20. Berlin: Heinrich-Böll-Stiftung.

Sturm, Roland. 2013. "Demokratie als 'Leitgedanke' des deutschen Föderalismus." *Informationen zur politischen Bildung* 318: 3–5.

Summers, Tim. 2016. "China's 'New Silk Roads': Sub-National Regions and Networks of Global Political Economy." *Third World Quarterly* 37 (9): 1628–1643.

Tait, Robert. 2019. "Zdeněk Hřib: The Czech Mayor Who Defied China." *The Guardian*, July 3. www.theguardian.com/cities/2019/jul/03/zdenek-hrib-the-czech-mayor-who-defied-china-taiwan.

Tatham, Michaël. 2016. *With, Without, or Against the State? How European Regions Play the Brussels Game*. Oxford: Oxford University Press.

Tatham, Michaël. 2018. "The Rise of Regional Influence in the EU—From Soft Policy Lobbying to Hard Vetoing." *Journal of Common Market Studies* 56 (3): 672–686. https://doi.org/10.1111/jcms.12714.

Trommler, Frank, and Elliott Shore, eds. 2001. *The German-American Encounter: Conflict and Cooperation Between Two Cultures, 1800–2000*. New York: Berghahn Books.

Wimmer, Andreas, and Nina Glick Schiller. 2002. "Methodological Nationalism and Beyond: Nation-State Building, Migration and the Social Sciences." *Global Networks* 2 (4): 301–334.

Zhao, Minghao. 2016. "The Belt and Road Initiative and Its Implications for China-Europe Relations." *The International Spectator* 51 (4): 109–118.

Part II
Geostrategic issues and Europe's security

5 The EU's Asia security policy and the US factor

Challenges and opportunities

Emil Kirchner

Introduction

Historically, the United States (US) has played a leading role in Asian security politics, backed by a substantial economic and military presence and a number of bilateral defence treaties with individual Asian countries. In contrast, the European Union's (EU) security role in Asia[1] has been more mundane, based primarily on economic links and its considerable support of US Asian policy. The introduction of former President Trump's "America First" policy has not only brought about a more nationalistic US but has also had huge repercussions for multilateralism and global governance. In addition, it has spiked Sino-US rivalry. As a consequence, we are witnessing both an escalation in power competition between China, Russia and the US and a joint attack by these powers on the EU's principles of shared sovereignty and the liberal model of democracy (Laidi 2019). This constellation of factors has put the EU in the crossfire between these competing powers (Otero-Iglesias and Esteban 2020). To what extent can the EU safeguard its own interest in such a power game? Can it play a brokering role, for example, between China and the US by trying to maintain a balance between its economic and security interests, or is it advisable, partly because it lacks military muscle and partly because of existing defence ties, to align with the US? These choices, if ever truly valid, have been overshadowed by the onslaught of the coronavirus pandemic. The fallout from that pandemic is likely to not only have geopolitical implications in the Sino-US context (Campbell and Doshi 2020) but ensuing economic problems are also likely to undermine EU cohesion, erode its geopolitical influence and make it vulnerable to Chinese influences (Techau 2020). Furthermore, it puts fears of Russia military adventurism and concerns over the reliability of the US as a security partner more firmly on the EU security agenda, as well as efforts to establish "strategic autonomy". What then are the implications for the EU's Asia security policy? Two likely contrasting developments can be envisaged.

A weakening of the EU's Asia security policy is likely in the event of open Sino-US military hostilities, in which the EU would most likely support the US position and hence again play a subservient role. But its Asia security policy may also be affected by becoming a victim of ongoing US trade deals with China and other Asian countries, or from a negative US stance on the Chinese Belt and Road

Initiative (BRI). In the absence of a Sino-US military conflict, a strengthening of the EU's Asia security policy could occur through the establishment of an EU "strategic autonomy", which could enhance perceptions in Asia that it is a security actor in its own right rather than a mere military extension of the US. However, with the EU's strategic autonomy still in its infancy, the core engagement of EU security policy in Asia is likely to remain non-traditional security fields, such as combatting terrorism, cyber-crime and espionage, climate change and energy policy. These efforts are likely to be enhanced by, for example, the 2018 EU Connectivity Strategy to Asia (EEAS 2018), a flurry of free trade agreements (FTAs) with Asian countries and the pursuit of peace diplomacy. In all these instances, the EU would need to develop a cohesive and coherent security strategy for Asia, translate hostilities—at least to some extent—into cooperation with Russia and ensure that the US will tolerate a more independently-minded EU-Asia security policy. Moreover, given the high value the EU places on effective multilateral order, derived partly from its export dependency, its strategy should be to garner support for this from any willing state with similar policy aims.

This chapter explores these matters in more detail. Its focus will be the EU rather than individual EU Member States. However, this does not deny the hybrid nature or co-existence of European and national foreign policies. Consequently, this chapter focuses predominantly on the EU level as the main level of analysis, while incorporating the role of Member States where appropriate into the examination of various security aspects. An attempt is thus made to explore the challenges and opportunities that the EU is likely to encounter in forging its future Asia security policy. Before doing so, a brief review of the nature of EU-Asia security relations is provided.

The context of EU-Asia relations

The absence of a distinct EU military presence in Asia diminishes the EU's attractiveness as a security actor. Lacking a sufficiently distinct security profile with respect to the US, the EU can therefore be too easily dismissed by Asian countries— especially China—as lacking independence, relevance and trust (Kirchner 2019). The lack of an EU military presence in Asia makes it look impotent in terms of potential conflicts arising from the Taiwan Straits or Chinese assertiveness in the East and South China Seas (of which China is staking claim to roughly 80 percent) or upholding freedom of navigation in that region. This lack of credibility is furthered by the EU's absence from the Six-Party Talks concerning the North Korean nuclear arms programme. In seeking to be taken seriously as a (hard) security actor in East Asia, the EU finds itself torn between, on the one hand, the potential irrelevance that comes with having no assets of its own in the region and, on the other hand, losing its potential as a neutral player due to its close association with the US (Christiansen et al. 2016). In addition, with few exceptions (e.g., climate change), the EU lacks coherence in its security policy towards Asia as it is unable to effectively coordinate security policy among the various national interests and the parallel attempts of Member States to conduct their own policies with Asian countries (Duke and Wong 2016; Wissenbach 2007). Moreover, insofar as the EU has an Asia policy, it is accused by such actors as Japan as being too China-centric.[2] However, as the COVID-19 outbreak causes substantial disruption in EU-China trade, the quest for supply chains independent of China must go further and deeper.

Nonetheless, despite drawbacks for the EU in projecting an Asia security policy, there are areas in which the EU has established a presence in Asia and in which fruitful cooperation with Asian states has taken place and is likely to expand. This is clearly the case with matters of economic security (Kirchner et al. 2016). Security cooperation is further enhanced through the EU aid programme for Asia, which is the largest in the region (Casarini 2013), through bilateral and multilateral efforts on climate change objectives and through collaboration by China, Japan and South Korea in the EU's anti-piracy naval escort missions in the Gulf of Aden. There is also cooperation in the field of international terrorism, especially on combatting its financing, and with regard to civil protection, such as on disaster emergency management. In addition, the EU shares with ASEAN the "commitment to regional integration—as a means of fostering stability and prosperity— and to multilateralism—as a way to constrain unilateral and hegemonic attitudes" (Casarini 2012, 4). The EU became a signatory to the ASEAN Treaty of Amity and Cooperation in 2012. The ASEAN Regional Forum, in which the EU, rather than its Member States, holds membership, provides an additional channel for security cooperation with Asian and North American states, as well as with Russia. The EU, together with its Member States, participates in the Asia Europe Meeting. However, it has failed to obtain membership of the ASEAN Defence Minister Plus process and the East Asia Summit.

Moreover, the EU has established, or is in the process of introducing, FTAs with a number of Asian countries,[3] some of which, such as those with Japan and South Korea, carry specific security cooperation arrangements. For example, a crisis management agreement was ratified by South Korea in December 2016, making it the first Asia-Pacific state to have a formal security cooperation arrangement with the EU.

On the maritime dispute in the South China Sea, the EU has issued a statement supporting the 2016 Hague Court ruling on peaceful resolutions and has supported ASEAN endeavours to reach agreement on a code of conduct in that sea. The EU has also upgraded its economic and political relations with China's rival claimants there, such as Vietnam and the Philippines. Arguably, the EU's emphasis on non-military security matters in its dealings with Asia reflects the absence of a manifest EU military capacity or, in contrast, highlights its longstanding emphasis on portraying itself as either a civilian or normative power (Manners 2002). Nevertheless, in a series of tangible steps since 2015, the EU is signalling that it seeks to improve its security and defence capacity and its role as a security actor. Russia's annexation of the Crimea in 2014, the growing power of China, the decision of the United Kingdom (UK) to leave the EU (Brexit) in 2016 and the policies introduced by former President Trump have resulted in steps by the EU to implement and/or to reinforce the Lisbon provisions with security and defence provisions. These efforts include the introduction of the EU Military Planning and Conduct Capability, a European Defence Fund to support EU defence research and capability development, and an expressed commitment to enhance security activities. Nonetheless, it will probably be a long time, if at all, before these steps will become building blocks towards "strategic autonomy" in security and defence, "credible military defence capabilities" or a European army, as advocated by some European leaders. Yet, this is not to deny that a certain sense of "realism" is creeping into EU security and defence strategy and, hence, a departure from the long-held, dominant "normative power" position.

Future perspective on the EU's Asia security policy

While military affairs, such as a potential Sino-US military confrontation, are a constant concern in the international arena, much of the interstate competition since 2016 has been fought through economic—or, more specifically, geo-economic—matters. While this competition is primarily protectionist in nature, as in the case of former President Trump's "America First" policy, it is predominantly geared to expand international influence in the case of China. Both developments have had a significant impact on how the EU should respond, especially with regard to its Asia security policy, given the trade and investment importance of Asia for the EU and the vulnerability of sea-borne trade transit through the Indo-Pacific. It is therefore unsurprising to find that the EU's Global Strategy declares the security interests of Asia and Europe to be intertwined. However, in the pursuit of this recognition, there is also a danger that the EU will be forced to take sides, either voluntarily or involuntarily, between the US and China in the case of escalating military confrontation. In the meantime, one of the most pressing challenges for the EU is how to deal with the BRI and with Chinese investments in or acquisitions of critical infrastructure in the EU.

The Chinese belt and road initiative: challenges and opportunities

The introduction of the BRI bears both economic benefits and political/security risks for the EU. Economic opportunities arise from the road component of the BRI that will traverse Central Asia. This will provide synergies between Chinese investment plans in infrastructure and connectivity and the EU's (Juncker Plan) investment programme, as well as through the services of the European Bank for Reconstruction and Development and the European Investment Bank, the extended Trans-European Transport Networks and the EU-China Connectivity Platform. EU-China cooperation could also be enhanced through the EU's new Central Asia Strategy, which was adopted on 15 May 2019 (Council of the EU 2019), and the 2018 EU Connectivity Strategy to Asia (EEAS 2018).[4] This latter strategy seeks to ensure that tender processes will be open and transparent to promote good governance and a level playing field (rules-based). It also insists that the infrastructure networks to be built are coherent and interoperable, as well as financially and environmentally sustainable. Adherence to these stipulations will become an important criterion of whether the EU Connectivity Strategy to Asia will become a partner rather than a competitor of the BRI.

There are political and security concerns that relate to the apparent debt-trap associated with Chinese investments abroad, whereby countries involved are unable to repay loans, or where consequent political concessions are extracted. Examples have already been cited where Greece, Hungary and Poland (all major recipients of Chinese investments) have not supported EU decisions on issues dealing with Chinese maritime activities in the East and South China Seas and on human rights (Fallon 2016; Klose et al. 2017). Not surprisingly, it is also those EU countries with substantial Chinese investments that are willing to engage with the BRI project and hence split ranks within the EU. This is further exacerbated by the 17 + 1 arrangement that China has with Central and East European states, including Greece, which has been described by some observers as a Chinese "divide and rule" tactic (Kratz et al. 2016). There is an additional danger from the economic fallout of the coronavirus pandemic that debt-ridden EU states or individual companies in those states will be susceptible to Chinese support or acquisition and therefore willing to make trade-offs between cash and political influence, or between cash and security concerns, such as concerning the role of Huawei. Already, the EU Commissioner for Competition, Margarethe Vestager, has warned that China could go on a big coronavirus-induced shopping spree, buying out hundreds of cash-strapped European companies (The Economist 2020). On the other hand, a substantial number of EU states have become members of the Asian Infrastructure and Investment Bank (AIIB), the financial arm of the BRI. See also the chapter on the Belt and Road Initiative in this volume (Chapter 10).

Moreover, Chinese infrastructure investment in Central Asia, in addition to carrying the danger of supporting authoritarian regimes in that region and hence undermining EU democratic reform efforts among Central Asian states, also invokes the spectre of geo-economic and potential political dominance in that region. In other words, there is a danger that Chinese investment in Central Asian states will make that region dependent on Chinese capital and increasingly bound by Chinese rules governing everything from trade to cybersecurity. Kaplan (2018) goes as far as to argue that China's BRI uses infrastructure as a weapon of neo-colonial domination. Similarly, Small (2018) sees the BRI as representing the groundwork for a Sinocentric global order. Similar concerns also exist about Chinese efforts to establish a military base in Djibouti and a naval installation in Gwadar, Pakistan. The US' withdrawal from the Transpacific Partnership (TPP) risks some Asian countries being sucked closer into China's orbit. For their part, the Chinese are eager to woo South Asian nations that want to hedge against India, Central Asian governments that want to keep Russia at bay and countries on the EU's southern and eastern fringes that are tired of nagging or cold-shouldering from Brussels (The Economist 2018a).

In view of these challenging operational, political and geopolitical factors, the EU needs to give serious consideration to the extent and nature (as an equal or subservient partner) of its BRI engagement. The extent and nature of BRI engagement also affects its relations with other Asian countries, the US and Russia. Not only is the US opposed to the BRI, but it also has urged EU members not to engage with it. In addition, it has undertaken measures to circumvent the BRI, such as the 2018 Better Utilization of Investment Leading to Development (BUILD) Act and the new International Development Finance Corporation (IDFC), which began operating in 2019. However, the IDFC will have about US$60 billion in capital, whereas the BRI is a trillion US dollar effort (Kapstein and Shapiro 2019). The US has also explored the possible establishment of a rival joint regional infrastructure scheme with Japan, India and Australia. These discussions have, in turn, given rise to Chinese anxiety about the birth or rebirth of the "Quad" as a polarising alliance dedicated to China's containment (Ujvari 2019). This in turn places the issue of the BRI, especially its maritime component, into the context of Chinese assertive, if not aggressive, maritime behaviour in the East and South China Seas. The EU has steered clear of this issue and has tried in the past to maintain neutrality in this territorial dispute. This EU line will come under stress as Sino-US rivalry escalates; it may force the EU to support the position of either China or the US, with the latter appearing the most likely outcome. The following section will shed further light on EU and US approaches to Asian security.

EU-Asia security relations in the context of EU-US and Sino-US security relations

Until the inauguration of former President Trump, it was generally assumed that, in order to compensate for its lack of hard power projection in the Asia region, the EU would support the US military presence there (Keohane 2012). This view is explicitly advocated in the June 2012 EU Guidelines on Foreign and Security in East Asia, which state that the EU should "remain sensitive" to the US role in East Asian security and that the "credibility of US defence guarantees in the region is essential for the region" (Council of the EU 2012, 15). However, there have also been lingering differences in approach between the EU and the US. Whereas the EU perceives China as a partner—albeit a systemic rival in regard to global governance matters—the US sees China more as an enemy and has adopted a more aggressive policy towards it[5]—described as "containment" or "balance of power". Moreover, by 2018 there was a prevailing mood in the US that they and China were either entering a new Cold War (Blackwill and Tellis 2019) or were locked in the "Thucydides Trap", in which a rising power challenges the ruling hegemon and the two slide into a major war (Allison 2017). US efforts to stymie Chinese geopolitical expansion include imposing steep tariffs on Chinese goods, gutting the State Department to free up funds for the military, inserting US forces into East Asian territorial disputes and planning to hit China early and hard in the event of war (Beckley 2018).

This scenario of a potential Sino-US conflict has exacerbated pre-existing European fears that closer alignment with US strategic initiatives relating to China could: draw the EU into regional conflicts or security hotspots in East Asia;

complicate EU-China relations; affect its ability to act as a more or less neutral player in Asia-Pacific affairs (Casarini 2012; van der Putten 2013); prevent it from having an active voice for reconciliation in Asia; undermine its ability to pursue its own political relationships with governments in the region—especially with its formal strategic partners China, India, Japan and South Korea (Keohane 2012); and lose credibility in the region. On the other hand, there is an ongoing EU-US Dialogue for the Asia-Pacific Region which also deals with European concerns that American preoccupation with the rise of China may have supplanted traditional US policy interests in Europe (Pollack 2012).

Undoubtedly, former President Trump's introduction of the "America First" policy has exacerbated tensions in transatlantic and transpacific security relations, as evidenced by the US withdrawal from the TPP, Transatlantic Trade and Investment Partnership (TTIP), the Iranian nuclear deal, and the Paris Climate Accord, bypassing WTO rules, questioning US commitments to the North Atlantic Treaty Organization (NATO) and suspending joint US-South Korean military manoeuvres. Moreover, Trump fatuously accused the EU of being "set up to take advantage of the US" and chastised it for unfair trade (The Economist 2018b). He also branded the European partners of NATO as delinquent because of underpayments and treated them not as partners but as quasi-enemies of the US.

Single European states and the EU have variously reacted to Trump's measures and tactics. For example, Chancellor Merkel has insisted that Europe can no longer rely on the US. President Macron has demanded EU "strategic autonomy" on defence in a time when the US had "turned its back" on its old ally (quoted in Rettman 2018), and declared NATO "brain dead". Donald Tusk has stated that former President Trump "is on a mission against what we stand for" (Waterfield and Sage 2018). Of course, it is also the case that, already under President Obama, US foreign policy realigned priorities such that Asia moved to the top of the agenda (Binnendijk 2014), diverting attention and resources away from Europe. Additionally, former President Trump's "America First" policy might be an aberration in the development of US foreign policy, though it seems that Trump's policies are part of a wider, and therefore more lasting, process of change in US foreign policy.

While the EU is concerned with the US position on China and on Asia generally, it is also sensitive to Sino-Russian relations. It is interesting in this context that while the EU most fears Russia, the US most fears China.

EU-Asia security relations in the context of Sino-Russian relations

It comes as a no surprise to note that Russia and China have strategic interests in Central Asia. While Russian efforts to maintain stability in the Eurasia region seek to preserve its sphere of influence (Lo and Hill 2013; Diesen 2018), these efforts are also important for China because of security concerns linked to its fears that political instability in Central Asia (e.g., the spread of ISIS to Central Asia) could spill over into China's restive northwestern Xinjiang province. Similarly, both Russia and China have been wary of any American presence in the region, share a disdain for "colour revolutions" and are determined to overturn the US-led global order (Maçães 2019). For Gabuey, "the deepening of military ties between these two former rivals is real, and a stronger strategic partnership between Beijing and Moscow could, given time, upend a half century of U.S. military planning and strategy" (Gabuey 2018, 4). Besides their mutual strategic interests, it is also worth noting that there is a considerable amount of mistrust between China and Russia, reflecting past conflicts and border disputes (Aron 2019). In line with this lack of trust, China does not want to be dragged into a military confrontation with the US as a result of belligerent or unintentional Russian missteps in the Middle East or Europe. By the same token, Russia does not want to be forced to take sides if China clashes with other strategic Russian economic partners such as Vietnam or India.

Despite these misgivings, there is agreement between Russia and China to pursue convergence between the BRI and the European Economic Union (EEU), as confirmed in a joint statement by President Putin and President Xi in May 2015 (Aron 2019). Given this constellation, and as the three main integration projects in the Eurasian landmass—the EU, the EEU and the BRI—geographically overlap, there might be an opportunity for them to work together to avoid conflict and look for synergies between their objectives. However, the EU is rightly suspicious that the EEU is more of a Russian geopolitical project than a genuine economic union between its members (Bond 2017), in part aimed to dilute or prevent EU encroachment into Eastern Europe or Central Asia.

The annexation of the Crimea, the conflict in Eastern Ukraine (the Donbas region) and hybrid subversive activities have left deep scars about Russia in the minds of EU institutions. Therefore, significant changes on the part of Russia's foreign policy would need to occur before the EU should engage in a trilateral strategic dialogue with both China and Russia. However, the growing power of China has made President Macron believe that the time has come for greater *détente* with Russia, seeing it as one of the big geostrategic players that cannot be kept away from the table (Gottemoeller 2019). But not all NATO allies agree, particularly Poland and the Baltic states.

This is not to imply that collaboration with China and Russia is straightforward: important economic, political and security issues stand in the way. In the case of China, there are critical issues about its political and economic openness and whether it supports the liberal international order. Not only has China effectively resisted liberal reforms on issues of democracy and the rule of law, but it has also effectively maintained control over foreign investment in China. As a consequence, the EU agrees with the substance of America's complaints about China's forced transfer of technology, uneven protection of intellectual property and state subsidies for its firms that have caused gluts in the supply of commodities such as steel. There is hence a strong EU desire for a reform of the existing WTO rules, as expressed in the European Commission's document "EU-China: A Strategic Outlook" (European Commission 2019). However, the EU disagrees with the tactic of sanctions that former President Trump introduced in pursuit of these aims and with his threat to close down the WTO.[6]

With respect to global governance, China is a "selective stakeholder", picking and choosing which responsibilities to assume based on a narrow cost-benefit analysis (Campbell and Ratner 2018; Christiansen et al. 2019). This selectivity or lack of reliability is, according to the EU High Representative, particularly noticeable in times of crisis, such as COVID-19, and indicates that China has "a different understanding of the international order" (Guillott 2020). China has set out to build its own set of regional and international institutions, such as the New Development Bank or the AIIB, rather than deepening its commitment to existing ones. It is for this reason that the European Commission's 2019 paper on China describes it as "a systemic rival promoting alternative models of governance" (European Commission 2019, 1). However, there are areas where the EU and China are more on the same page than with the US, such as climate change, the maintenance of the Iranian Joint Comprehensive Plan for Action (JCPOA) and preserving the United Nations (UN) system. In 2019, China was the second-largest UN contributor after the US, both to the general budget and to peacekeeping (The Economist 2019).

Prospects for an EU-Asia security policy

As the foregoing analysis demonstrates, EU security activities in Asia intersect with the interests of China and the US and/or are affected by the policies of these two countries, as well as by the rivalry between these two competing powers. The effects are both external and internal. Externally, it challenges EU efforts to sustain multilateral and liberal international governance principles. In addition, the EU needs to guard against increasing Sino-US military rivalry and avoid becoming a collateral victim of Sino-US trade deals. Internally, US policies on the Iranian nuclear deal affect the cohesion of the EU, and increased US-Chinese economic, technological and geopolitical rivalry entails significant risks for the EU's interests, "leading to political fragmentation as highlighted by the lack of common positions on Huawei's role in European 5G networks, Chinese inward investments, the South China Sea disputes or the endorsement of the Belt and Road initiative" (Otero-Iglesias and Esteban 2020, 19). "Split tactics" or divide-and-rule manoeuvres by both the US and China, co-joined by Russia, are further challenges to EU integration. Evidence for these tactics can be found in US policy under Trump to support Brexit and a preference for bilateral over multilateral relationships. On the Chinese side, evidence is the establishment of the 17+1 arrangement, which, as indicated above, might become an even stronger divisive factor as a consequence of COVID-19.

The EU has a number of policy options to meet these challenges that are both external and internal in nature. The external option involves deciding what position to adopt in dealing with China and the US, on the one hand, and with other Asian countries and ASEAN, on the other. Internally, an important factor will be how the EU establishes "strategic autonomy" and associated security and defence capacity. In terms of relations with China and the US, the EU should try to be friends with both and maintain an ambivalent position that may even evolve into a distinct role (Noesselt 2016). Although there is some uncertainty about how long such an approach might last, especially if the US were to press harder on EU alignment (Otero-Iglesias and Esteban 2020), it would appear worthwhile for the EU to pursue it and engage along the following lines. With regard to China, the EU should collaborate in the BRI and on other global measures (e.g., trade and climate change) by, for example, insisting on the standard principles outlined in the EU Connectivity Strategy to Asia, pressing China on the issue of reciprocity and demanding China engage in tangible WTO reforms that tackle distortions caused by China's industrial subsidies—a change also demanded by the US.

However, the question of how the EU should deal with China's increasingly assertive, if not threatening, maritime policy in the East and South China Seas remains largely unresolved. The EU has slim prospects of involvement in the maritime issues of the South China Sea or Indo Pacific, where the Quad (Australia, India, Japan and the US) is becoming the main forum for discussion. Hence, a repeat of the exclusion it encountered regarding the Six-Party Talks over North Korea's nuclear programme is likely.

With regard to its relations with the US, the EU should keep channels open to the US administration and minimise, if not counteract, negative fallout from the US domestic and foreign policy. However, maintaining open channels or pursuing a business-as-usual approach with the US might not be easy if Trump's US domestic and foreign policy were to continue, especially as some of these policy decisions could have detrimental consequences for the EU in economic (trade), political, security and public diplomacy terms (environment, developmental/aid programmes, human rights). On the other hand, negative US policy decisions or withdrawal from the global scene (abandoning multilateralism in most of its forms) could give the EU the chance to become more influential in global trade, climate and humanitarian issues. However, this would require wider EU international collaboration. In this context, Daalder and Lindsay suggest that, in order to safeguard the multilateral system, the EU should link efforts with other multilaterally minded countries, such as Australia, Canada, Japan and South Korea (Daalder and Lindsay 2018). The success of such efforts would be subject to the trade-offs these countries are prepared to make in respect to US political ties, especially if that country decides to discriminate against these states either economically or politically. On the other hand, with the election of President Biden, US foreign policy may return to some of the long-held principles of multilateralism.

In terms of future actions, the EU could strengthen its involvement with the ASEAN-led regional security architecture and other forms of multilateral security cooperation in Asia, including the ASEAN Defence Ministers Meeting Plus process[7] and the East Asia Summit. Like the ARF, the ADMM-Plus is designed both as a mechanism for multilateral security dialogue and consultation as well as a framework for non-traditional security cooperation. To date, seven areas— maritime security, humanitarian assistance and disaster relief (HADR), counter-terrorism, peacekeeping operations, military medicine, humanitarian mine action (or demining) and cyber security—each with its own dedicated experts' working group (EWG), have been mandated by the ADMM-Plus as areas for practical collaboration by its member countries. The EU has already launched plans for increased cooperation with five pilot countries—India, Indonesia, Japan, South Korea and Vietnam—in the areas of counterterrorism, cybersecurity, maritime security and crisis management. Noteworthy also are the dialogues that the EU conducts directly with 11 Asian countries on a military-to-military level and the gradual deployment of military advisers in several EU delegations across Asia, starting with the EU delegation to ASEAN in Jakarta. Moreover, the EU and India started a military-to-military dialogue in 2019 to expand their maritime security partnership in the Indian Ocean, building on the EU's role in fighting piracy in the Gulf of Aden through the EU NAVFOR Operation Atalanta.

In addition, the EU should seek to establish synergies or partnerships between its Connectivity Strategy to Asia and similar Asian counterparts, some of which already exist. For example, the so-called EU-Japan connectivity partnership will cover sectors from transport to digital industries as part of a wider effort to revive multilateral cooperation. In line with the principles laid down in the EU's Connectivity Strategy, the EU-Japan agreement calls for transparent procurement practices, ensuring debt sustainability and high standards of economic, fiscal, financial, social and environmental sustainability (Geeraerts 2019). This agreement could be seen as a riposte to China's growing assertiveness in shaping the regional and global order.

A similar EU link could involve ASEAN's Master Plan on ASEAN Connectivity 2025, which addresses problems of transnational organised crime and any kind of illicit smuggling and trafficking, cybersecurity and attacks on transport and energy security. The EU Connectivity Strategy to Asia can also benefit from the Council Conclusions on Enhanced EU Security Cooperation in and with Asia of 18 May 2018. It identified as key areas for deeper security engagement maritime security, cyber security, counter-terrorism, hybrid threats, conflict prevention, the proliferation of chemical, biological, radiological and nuclear weapons, and the development of regional cooperation (Council of the EU 2018).

The EU should also enhance the role of FTAs with Asian countries by establishing a security component in existing and future FTAs along the lines of the existing FTA with South Korea, which contains crisis management formal security cooperation with the EU. The EU should also seek a Euro-Pacific agreement with countries that form the Comprehensive and Progressive Agreement for Trans-Pacific Partnership to sustain and protect the multilateral system (Laidi 2019).

Conclusion

As the EU is in the crossfire between competing powers—China, Russia and the US—(Otero-Iglesias and Esteban 2020) and as it experiences attacks on its core values—such as the maintenance of a liberal global order and effective multilateralism—how should the EU respond to these and/or develop a coherent and effective Asia security policy? The EU's response will have to carefully balance the interests it has with China and the US. As found in a study of 18 EU states, "all considered the US the most important ally and they all depend on the military protection, but they also want to do as much business with China as possible" (Esteban et al. 2020, 15). Hence, barring a major Sino-US military confrontation, which would align the EU with the US, the EU's Asia security policy should engage in partnerships with Asia-Pacific countries based predominately, but not exclusively, on non-military aspects. These should involve strengthening EU peace diplomatic activities and support negotiations, de-escalation of tensions and eventual enhancement of trust in such places as Myanmar, the Philippines, Afghanistan and Kashmir.

It should also involve, potentially in conjunction with ASEAN, a brokering role between China and the US regarding maritime territorial issues in the South China Sea. Collaboration with Asian counterparts should be intensified on aspects of non-proliferation, climate change, cyber security, economic security and natural disaster management. The safeguarding of the multilateral order should be another priority, which may also require a brokering role between the US and China but would need support from other states such as Australia, Canada, Japan and South Korea. Given the large export dependency of EU states, the EU's need to defend the multilateral order is guided primarily by economic interests and complemented by norms and value considerations.

Non-military efforts should be aided by the EU Connectivity Strategy to Asia, which, as Geeraerts suggests, also "resonates with a wider EU push to transform itself into a true strategic player—to better use the bloc's economic heft in trade, aid and investment to achieve strategic foreign policy goals" (Geeraerts 2019, 4). Already, the participation by a number of Asian states in the anti-piracy naval operation in the Gulf of Aden indicates that military factors are not excluded from the EU's security toolbox. This type of cooperation could be strengthened if the EU were to build a credible security and defence architecture which can live up to the Lisbon Treaty's aim of establishing an "autonomous" CSDP and CFSP. However, building up a credible CSDP or CFSP faces challenges from Member States who jealously guard their national sovereignty, frictions over neutral versus more military-oriented states, small versus large states and eastern versus western Member States. On the other hand, progress in this field would further promote collaboration on peacekeeping operations with Asian partners and greatly improve the image of the EU as a responsible stakeholder in regional and global security matters and as an actor that can deliver greater defence expenditure (satisfying US demands). It would also convince countries like China and Japan that it is not merely an economic power but increasingly also a security partner. It remains to be seen whether the build-up of an enhanced EU military capacity would eliminate US fears that creating a duplicate military structure[8] could sap NATO's own resources. President Macron, although steadfast in his claim that European defence is not an alternative to NATO, but "an indispensable complement", has called for a "new architecture of confidence and security" which relies less on US power and includes Russia (Montaz 2020). Much forward thinking will depend on the impact of the COVID-19 crisis on the big international actors such as China, the EU, Russia and the US. Some observers see the EU, because of its lack of cohesion and political drive, as the big geopolitical loser from the coronavirus pandemic (Techau 2020). There are, hence, interesting times ahead in the development of EU relations with key external powers such as China, Russia and the US, and how this will, in turn, affect the EU's Asia security policy.

Notes

1 For the purpose of this chapter, Asia will be regarded primarily as key players such as China, India, Japan and South Korea—who have strategic partnerships with the EU—and ASEAN. These Asian actors are also singled out as being key in the Council's Conclusions on Asia of May 2018 (Council of the European Union 2018).
2 EU-China relations do have high-level institutional ties not found elsewhere in Asia. Among these are the High-Level EU Economic and Trade Dialogue, the High-Level Strategic Dialogue together with the High-Level People-to-People Dialogue. In addition, in 2014 the two partners introduced the China-EU 2020 Strategic Agenda for Cooperation.
3 By 2018, Partnership and Cooperation Agreements had been signed with Asian countries such as Indonesia, Malaysia, Mongolia, the Philippines, Singapore, Thailand and Vietnam. The EU has a Framework Agreement and a Free Trade Agreement with the Republic of Korea, which both have been ratified. Additionally, in 2018 the EU and Japan established an Economic Partnership Agreement and a Strategic Partnership Agreement.
4 However, the allocation of €60 billion for the 2021–2027 budgetary period from EU and other public and private sources combined seems rather meagre when compared with the various € trillions earmarked for the BRI.
5 The US takes a different and more assertive line than the EU on a number of US-China issues (for example, on Taiwan, Tibet and the South China Sea). This difference also surfaced in the ruling by the Arbitration Tribunal of the United Nations Convention on the Law of the Sea that had been submitted by the Philippines against China with regard to territorial disputes in the South China Sea. Whereas the US strongly condemned China for not accepting the ruling, the EU only expressed lukewarm support for it.
6 The US administration blocked nominations to seats on the WTO appellate board, which left it in crisis from December 2019.
7 These include the ten ASEAN states and eight of its dialogue partners: Australia, China, India, Japan, New Zealand, Russia, South Korea and the US.
8 One is reminded of the three "dont's" expressed by then US Secretary of State, Madeleine Albright, in 1998 with regard to a European Security Identity, who stated that the key to a successful initiative is to focus on practical military capabilities. Any initiative must avoid pre-empting Alliance decision-making by *de-linking* European Security Defence Identity (ESDI) from NATO, avoid *duplicating* existing efforts, and avoid *discriminating* against non-EU members. See the text of Secretary Albright's remarks to the North Atlantic Council ministerial meeting, Brussels, 8 December 1998 (NATO 1998).

References

Allison, Graham. 2017. *Destined for War: Can America and China Escape Thucydides' Trap?* Boston: Houghton Mifflin Hartcourt.

Aron, Leon. 2019. "Are Russia and China Really Forming an Alliance? The Evidence Is Less Than Impressive." *Foreign Affairs*, April 4. www.foreignaffairs.com/articles/china/2019-04-04/are-russia-and-china-really-forming-alliance.

Beckley, Michael. 2018. "Stop Obsessing About China: Why Beijing Will Not Imperil U.S. Hegemony." *Foreign Affairs*, September 21. www.foreignaffairs.com/articles/china/2018-09-21/stop-obsessing-about-china.

Binnendijk, Hans. 2014. *A Transatlantic Pivot to Asia: Towards New Trilateral Partnerships*, edited by Hans Binnendijk. Washington, DC: Center for Transatlantic Relations.

Blackwill, Robert, and Ashley J. Tellis. 2019. "The India Dividend: New Delhi Remains Washington's Best Hope in Asia." *Foreign Affairs*, September–October. www.foreignaf fairs.com/articles/india/2019-08-12/india-dividend.

Bond, Ian. 2017. *The EU, the Eurasian Economic Union and One Belt, One Road: Can They Work Together?* Centre for European Reform, March 16. https://www.cer.eu/publications/archive/policy-brief/2017/eu-eurasian-economic-union-and-one-belt-one-road-can-they.

Campbell, Kurt M., and Rush Doshi. 2020. "The Coronavirus Could Reshape Global Order: China Is Maneuvering for International Leadership as the United States Falters." *Foreign Affairs*, March 18. www.foreignaffairs.com/articles/china/2020-03-18/coronavirus-could-reshape-global-order.

Campbell, Kurt M., and Ely Ratner. 2018. "The China Reckoning: How Beijing Defied American Expectations." *Foreign Affairs*, March–April. www.foreignaffairs.com/articles/china/2018-02-13/china-reckoning.

Casarini, Nicola. 2012. *EU Foreign Policy in the Asia Pacific: Striking the Right Balance Between the US, China and ASEAN*. Brussels: European Institute for Security Studies, Analysis, September.

Casarini, Nicola. 2013. *The European 'Pivot'*. Brussels: European Institute for Security Studies, ISSU Alert, March.

Christiansen, Thomas, Emil Kirchner, and Han Dorussen. 2016. "Against the Odds: (Considerable) Convergence and (Limited) Cooperation in EU-China Security Relations." In *Security Relations Between China and the European Union: From Convergence to Cooperation?* edited by Emil Kirchner, Thomas Christiansen, and Han Dorussen, 229–247. Cambridge: Cambridge University Press.

Christiansen, Thomas, Emil Kirchner, and Uwe Wissenbach. 2019. *The European Union and China*. London: Red Globe Press, Palgrave Macmillan.

Council of the European Union. 2012. "Guidelines on the EU's Foreign and Security Policy in East Asia (11492/12)." Brussels, June 15. http://eeas.europa.eu/asia/docs/guidelines_eu_foreign_sec_pol_east_asia_en.pdf.

Council of the European Union. 2018. "Enhanced EU Security Cooperation in and with Asia—Council Conclusions (28 May 2018) (9265/18)." Brussels, May 28. www.consilium.europa.eu//media/35379/st09265-en18.pdf.

Council of the European Union. 2019. *Central Asia: Council Adopts a New EU Strategy for the Region*. Brussels: Council of the European Union, June 17. www.consilium.europa.eu/en/press/press-releases/2019/06/17/central-asia-council-adopts-a-new-eu-strategy-for-the-region/.

Daalder, Ivo H., and James M. Lindsay. 2018. "The Committee to Save the World Order: America's Allies Must Step Up as America Steps Down." *Foreign Affairs*, November–December. www.foreignaffairs.com/articles/2018-09-30/committee-save-world-order.

Diesen, Glenn. 2018. *Russia's Geoeconomic Strategy for a Greater Eurasia*. London: Routledge.

Duke, Simon, and Reuben Wong. 2016. "Chinese and EU Views of Military Security: Crafting Cooperation." In *Security Relations Between China and the European Union: From Convergence to Cooperation?* edited by Emil J. Kirchner, Thomas Christiansen, and Han Dorussen, 19–41. Cambridge: Cambridge University Press.

The Economist. 2018a. "Briefing: China's Belt and Road Initiative." *The Economist*, July 28.

The Economist. 2018b. "The Western Alliance is in Trouble: That Should Worry Europe, America and the World." *The Economist*, July 7.

The Economist. 2019. "China and the United Nations: A New Battle Ground." *The Economist*, December 7.

The Economist. 2020. "Is China Winning?" *The Economist*, April 18.

EEAS. 2018. *Connecting Europe and Asia—Building Blocks for an EU Strategy*. Brussels: EEAS, September 19. https://eeas.europa.eu/headquarters/headquarters-homepage/50708/connecting-europe-and-asia-building-blocks-eu-strategy_en.

Esteban, Mario, Miguel Otero-Iglesias, Una Aleksandra Bērziņa-Čerenkova, Alice Ekman, Lucrezia Poggetti, Björn Jerdén, John Seaman, Tim Summers, and Justyna Szczudlik, eds. 2020. "Europe in the Face of US-China Rivalry." European Think-Tank Network on China Report, January. www.egmontinstitute.be/content/uploads/2020/01/200122-Final-ETNC-report-Europe-in-the-Face-of-US-China-Rivalry.pdf.

European Commission. 2019. *EU-China—A Strategic Outlook*. Strasbourg: European Commission, March 12. https://ec.europa.eu/commission/sites/beta-political/files/communication-eu-china-a-strategic-outlook.pdf.

Fallon, Theresa. 2016. "The EU, the South China Sea, and China's Successful Wedge Strategy." *Center for Strategic and International Studies, Asia Maritime Transparency Initiative*, October 13. https://amti.csis.org/eu-south-china-sea-chinas-successful-wedge-strategy/.

Gabuey, Alexander. 2018. "Why Russia and China Are Strengthening Security Ties: Is the U.S. Driving Them Closer Together?" *Foreign Affairs*, September 24. www.foreignaffairs.com/articles/china/2018-09-24/why-russia-and-china-are-strengthening-security-ties.

Geeraerts, Gustaaf. 2019. "Europe and China's Belt and Road Initiative: Growing Concerns, More Strategy." Egmont Security Policy Brief No. 118. www.egmontinstitute.be/content/uploads/2019/11/SPB118.pdf.

Gottemoeller, Rose. 2019. "NATO Is Not Brain Dead: The Alliance Is Transforming Faster Than Most People Think." *Foreign Affairs*, December 19. www.foreignaffairs.com/articles/united-states/2019-12-19/nato-not-brain-dead.

Guillot, Louise. 2020. "Europe Has Been 'Naïve' About China Says Josep Borrell." *Politico*, March 5. www.politico.eu/article/europe-has-been-naive-about-china-josep-borrell/.

Kaplan, Robert D. 2018. *The Return of Marco Polo's World: War, Strategy, and American Interests in the Twenty-First Century*. New York: Random House Trade.

Kapstein, Ethan B., and Jacob N. Shapiro. 2019. "Catching China by the Belt (and Road): How Washington Can Beat Beijing's Global Influence Campaign." *Foreign Policy*, April 20. https://foreignpolicy.com/2019/04/20/catching-china-by-the-belt-and-road-international-development-finance-corp-beijing-united-states/.

Keohane, Daniel. 2012. "The EU's Role in East Asian Security." In *Look East, Act East: Transatlantic Agendas in Asia Pacific*, edited by Patryk Pawlak, 45–50. European Union Institute for Security Studies, ISS Report 13. www.iss.europa.eu/sites/default/files/EUISSFiles/Final_Report_13LEAE_1.pdf.

Kirchner, Emil. 2019. "China and the European Union." In *Oxford Research Encyclopedias: Politics*. https://oxfordre.com/politics/view/10.1093/acrefore/9780190228637.001.0001/acrefore-9780190228637-e-1131.

Kirchner, Emil, Thomas Christiansen, and Han Dorussen. 2016. "EU-China Security Cooperation in Context." In *Security Relations Between China and the European Union: From Convergence to Cooperation?* edited by Emil Kirchner, Thomas Christiansen, and Han Dorussen, 1–18. Cambridge: Cambridge University Press.

Klose, Stephan, Astrid Pepermans, and Leia Wang. 2017. "An Uphill Struggle: Towards a Coordinated EU Engagement with China's Belt and Road Initiative." *European Policy Brief*, November 21. www.egmontinstitute.be/content/uploads/2017/11/EPB-48.pdf.

Kratz, Agatha, Dragan Pavlićević, Angela Stanzel and Justyna Szczudlik. 2016. *China's Investment in Influence: The Future of 16 + 1 Cooperation*. London: European Council on Foreign Relations, December 14. www.ecfr.eu/publications/summary/chinas_investment_in_influence_the_future_of_161_cooperation7204.

Laidi, Zaki. 2019. "Can Europe Learn to Play Power Politics. Centre for European Reform." November 28. www.cer.eu/publications/archive/essay/2019/can-europe-learn-play-power-politics.

Lo, Bobo, and Fiona Hill. 2013. *Putin's Pivot: Why Russia Is Looking East*. Washington, DC: Brookings Institution Press, July 31. www.brookings.edu/research/opinions/2013/07/31-russia-china-pacific-pivot-hill.

Maçães, Bruno. 2019. "The Coming Wars. Russia to China: Together We Can Rule the World. Only Europe Can Prevent an Eastern Bloc." *Politico*, February 17. www.politico.eu/blogs/the-coming-wars/2019/02/russia-china-alliance-rule-the-world/.

Manners, Ian. 2002. "Normative Power Europe: A Contradiction in Terms?" *Journal of Common Market Studies* 40 (2): 235–258.

Montaz, Rym. 2020. "Macron Torn Between Poland and Putin." *Politico*, February 5. www.politico.eu/article/emmanuel-macron-poland-russia-moscow-policy/.

NATO. 1998. *Foreign Ministers Meetings*. Brussels: NATO HQ, December 8–9. www.nato.int/docu/comm/1998/9812-hq/08-09.htm.

Noesselt, Nele. 2016. "The European Union and China's Multidimensional Diplomacy: Strategic Triangulation?" *European Foreign Affairs Review* 21 (3): 11–28.

Otero-Iglesias, Miguel, and Mario Esteban. 2020. "Introduction." In *Europe in the Face of US-China Rivalry*, edited by Mario Esteban, Miguel Otero-Iglesias, Una Aleksandra Bērziņa-Čerenkova, Alice Ekman, Lucrezia Poggetti, Björn Jerdén, John Seaman, Tim Summers, and Justyna Szczudlik. European Think Tank Network on China Report, January. www.egmontinstitute.be/content/uploads/2020/01/200122-Final-ETNC-report-Europe-in-the-Face-of-US-China-Rivalry.pdf?type=pdf.

Pollack, Jonathan D. 2012. "China's Rise and US Strategy in Asia." In *Look East, Act East: Transatlantic Agendas in Asia Pacific*, edited by Patryk Pawlak, 51–58. European Union Institute for Security Studies, ISS Report 13. www.iss.europa.eu/sites/default/files/EUISSFiles/Final_Report_13LEAE_1.pdf.

Rettman, Andrew. 2018. "EU Needs to Stand Apart from US, France and Germany Say." *EUobserver*, August 28. https://euobserver.com/foreign/142668.

Small, Andrew. 2018. "The Backlash to Belt and Road: A South Asian Battle Over Chinese Economic Power." *Foreign Affairs*, February 16. www.foreignaffairs.com/articles/china/2018-02-16/backlash-belt-and-road.

Techau, Jan. 2020. "Saving Europe from Corona's Nasty Geopolitics." *EUobserver*, April 15. https://euobserver.com/opinion/148057.

Ujvari, Balazs. 2019. "The Belt and Road Initiative—the ASEAN Perspective." Egmont Security Policy Brief 107, March. www.egmontinstitute.be/content/uploads/2019/03/SPB107.pdf.

van der Putten, Frans-Paul. 2013. "The Security Dimension in EU-China Relations." In *Brussels-Beijing: Changing the Game?* edited by Nicola Casarini, 53–58. Brussels: European Union Institute for Security Studies, ISS Report 14.

Waterfield, Bruno, and Adam Sage. 2018. "President Trump's War on western world order." *The Times*, June 30. www.thetimes.co.uk/article/president-trumps-war-on-western-world-order-h6pshskjs.

Wissenbach, Uwe. 2007. *The EU's Effective Multilateralism—But with Whom? Functional Multilateralism and the Rise of China.* Berlin: Internationale Politikanalyse, Friedrich-Ebert-Stiftung, Mai. http://library.fes.de/pdf-files/id/04469.pdf.

6 Europe and the South China Sea

Challenges, constraints and options

Michael Paul

Introduction

Roughly 80 percent of global trade by volume and 70 percent by value is transported by sea and is handled by ports worldwide (UNCTAD 2018). Of that volume, 60 percent of maritime trade passes through Asia, with the South China Sea (SCS) carrying an estimated one-third of global shipping. Its waters are of critical importance for China, Taiwan, Japan and South Korea, all of which rely on the Malacca straits "chokepoint", which connects the SCS and, by extension, the Pacific Ocean with the Indian Ocean and Persian Gulf. The three crude oil importers with the largest volumes passing through the SCS—China, Japan and South Korea—collectively account for 80 percent of total crude oil volume transiting the SCS in 2016 (EIA 2018); an estimated \$3.4 trillion in trade passed through it in that year. According to data presented by "China Power" (CSIS 2016), Germany had the biggest such share of the European countries, followed by the United Kingdom (UK) and France. In 2018, the sea accounted for just over half of all goods traded between the EU-28 and the rest of the world. The value of goods carried by sea was twice that recorded for goods transported by air and more than thrice that for goods transported by road (Eurostat 2018).

In the new international security environment, the SCS has emerged as an arena of United States (US)-China strategic competition, forming an element of the Trump administration's more confrontational approach toward China. Rivalry among states is growing over access to strategically relevant areas, such as the Arctic or Asia-Pacific. This has profound implications for Europe, too. To understand these stakes, this chapter analyses the challenges, constraints and options for the European Union (EU) and European countries with respect to maritime security in the SCS. It argues that the challenges posed to established rules in the maritime domain call for a reinforcement of multilateral dialogue in order to promote stability. A close look at the issues will show that the EU and individual European states can and should play a limited but valuable role in this regard by promoting norms of good governance, by actively supporting the creation of regional codes of conduct, by boosting transatlantic talks on challenges related to China and by increasing their own naval presence.

The South China Sea dispute

Because of its favourable monsoon winds, the South China Sea[1] was already an important trade route in ancient times. It is as vitally important to Asia as the Mediterranean Sea is to Europe; as with the Mediterranean, domination of the SCS must be understood as an attempt to control the region's most important sea routes. As a Pacific Rim sea, it was already being used for the exchange of goods between Southeast Asia's coastal states when the largely jungle-covered inland made overland trade impossible. The SCS thus became the joint hub and pivot of a region characterised by diversity, be it political, economic, cultural or religious. As a security space, it has been subject to contests for geopolitical supremacy between regional kingdoms for over a millennium and between regional and extra-regional European colonial powers for many centuries (Paul 2016).

In the 21st century, the SCS provides the main trade route for the prospering East Asian economies. Whoever controls this nexus for regional and global economic activity controls an important part of the global economy. Over 60,000 ships transporting goods valued at over US$3.4 trillion passed through the sea in 2016. This corresponded to 21 percent of global trade. Five countries rely on the SCS for more than 50 percent of their total trade: Vietnam (86 percent), Indonesia (85 percent), Thailand (74 percent), Singapore (66 percent) and Malaysia (58 percent). The SCS ensures the supply of Northeast and Southeast Asian states with energy and raw materials and itself has large offshore gas and oil fields. Furthermore, about 10 percent of the world's catch of edible fish are provided by its abundant fishing grounds (CSIS 2016; Panda 2017; Paul 2017).

Its exceptional importance as a sea line of communication (SLOC) and a reservoir of resources has made the SCS and its four groups of islands (Pratas, Paracel, Spratly and Scarborough) the object of overlapping regional territorial claims by China and Taiwan, the Philippines, Malaysia, Brunei and Vietnam. In some cases, this has already led to military confrontations and violent nationalist clashes. With the exception of Brunei, all the claimant states have erected various buildings and installations on islands and reefs. Many of the reefs or rocks are underwater at high tide and are not suitable for human settlement. Only the largest natural island in the Spratly group, Itu Aba (Taiping), occupied by Taiwan, is an "island" under the 1982 United Nations Convention on the Law of the Sea (UNCLOS): it has all the required characteristics of a "naturally formed area of land, surrounded by water, which is above water at high tide" (UNCLOS 1982, Art. 121, Para. 1).

In accordance with UNCLOS, states can claim as their exclusive economic zone (EEZ) an area that stretches out to sea from their coast for up to 200 nautical miles (370 kilometres), measured from the baseline along the coast (*ibid.*, Art. 55 and 57). The EEZ remains a part of the high seas, but the coastal state is entitled to exploit its natural resources, including fishing, and is granted individual sovereignty rights (*ibid.*, Art. 56). China is laying claim to an area of the SCS that is more than 540 nautical miles (1,000 kilometres) from its coast, a claim justified on historical grounds (Gao and Jia 2013; Mitter 2015). The Chinese Nationalist Kuomintang government produced a map of China in 1947 that shows all the islands to which China now lays claim—including the fishing, navigation and resource rights associated with them. According to this map, more than 80 percent of the SCS falls under Chinese jurisdiction (Gao and Jia 2013; Kraska 2015; Raine and Le Mière 2013).

In May 2009, China's Permanent Representation to the United Nations (UN) sent two *notes verbales* to the UN General Secretariat. They contained a map roughly based on the 1947 version and showing a U-shaped nine-dash line (NDL), as well as a declaration that China had "indisputable sovereignty" over the islands enclosed by the NDL and their territorial waters. Vietnam, Malaysia and the Philippines asserted their own, mutually competing claims and also sent the UN *notes verbales*. The catalyst for this diplomatic flurry was a problematic deadline: submissions on continental shelf areas had to be made to the UN by May 2009.[2] Since 2009, however, Beijing has done much in the way of assertive diplomacy: in March of that year, Chinese ships prevented the USNS *Impeccable* from continuing its passage near the island province of Hainan and ordered it to leave the EEZ. Again in 2009, Beijing exerted pressure on foreign oil companies to stop exploration in disputed waters. In another note in April 2011, China added that Chinese sovereignty and its resulting claims were well founded in history and the law. The burden of proof for such historical claims lies with the claimant and is quite difficult: none of the territorial claims are well substantiated for they all rest on assertions that some isles or reefs have been known since ancient times to peoples living in areas belonging to today's sovereign states (Stanzel 2016).

The disputes thus trace back to before 1982, when UNCLOS was established. China has therefore taken a different approach. It focuses on extending the area of the applicability of Chinese legislation (for instance, in a law to protect the marine environment) beyond zones defined under maritime law—such as territorial waters (UNCLOS 1982, Art. 3), EEZ (*ibid.*, Art. 55) or continental shelf (*ibid.*, Art. 76)—to include "any other sea areas under the jurisdiction of the People's Republic of China". In other words, China is attempting to fill a perceived legal vacuum by using national legislation. Such "gap-filling", however, is questionable under international law. Ultimately, the practical significance of the nine-dash line remains unclear, although this ambiguity seems to be deliberate, affording China a certain latitude in the claims it puts forward and making it more difficult for other parties to refute them.

The US has urged a peaceful resolution to the territorial conflicts in the SCS but has not taken a position on the various claims made. Nevertheless, the US State Department has examined China's territorial claims and has criticised the *notes verbales* for not specifying whether they concern only ownership of the islands (which are not named individually) or maritime zones as well. US diplomats have thus called on China to clarify its position unambiguously and bring it into line with maritime law. Furthermore, the geographical data is insufficient to clearly define the area. In a move likely to aggravate matters, Chinese maps published since 2014 show a vertical "line" east of Taiwan, thereby virtually uniting the Republic of China with the People's Republic by the stroke of a pen (Bader 2014; O'Rourke 2015; Paul 2016; U.S. Department of State 2014).

This already complicated situation concerning maritime law became even more politically charged in July 2010 when then US Secretary of State Hillary Clinton declared freedom of navigation in the SCS to be in the national interest of the US. China saw its traditional territorial claims under threat; it now routinely refers to these as China's "core national interests", placing them in a category similar to Taiwan. A particularly problematic legal point between Washington and Beijing is whether military activities by third states are prohibited in EEZs, as they are in territorial waters (as part of the "right to innocent passage" provisions contained in UNCLOS 1982, Art. 17). China is demanding that the US stop such activities in its EEZ, which have repeatedly led to incidents in Chinese airspace and at sea. The US follows a broad interpretation, under which the same rights obtain in an EEZ as on the high seas (O'Rourke 2015). China takes a more restricted view. To some extent, the controversy between the two powers resembles the historical dispute of *mare liberum* versus *mare clausum* (Paul 2017).

These interpretations of maritime law—freedom of navigation versus exclusive maritime zones—are incompatible and collide heavily in the case of the land features in the South China Sea claimed by China. Washington's conduct, however, is also ambiguous. On the one hand, the US argues, in accordance with UNCLOS,[3] that claims to maritime zones are valid only if they emanate from a recognised coastal state. On the other hand, it wants to apply a broad interpretation of maritime law in Washington's favour so that the same military activities are allowed in any EEZ as on the high seas. Both arguments are certainly plausible. EEZs cover over 30 percent of the world's seas. If the US renounced its military activities in all of these, it could hardly maintain maritime superiority (as suggested by the 2018 US Navy design), thus losing its dominant position characterised by its extensive ability to exert influence or project power on a global scale. Consequently, the US stresses the freedom of navigation (and overflight) as a guiding principle the world over—just as France declared the "[f]reedom of maritime and air navigation" as "a fundamental principle of international relations" (Ministère des Armées 2019).

Challenges: the South China Sea dispute

The Spratly Archipelago (called Nansha in Chinese) lies at the heart of China's territorial claims in the SCS. It extends over more than 540 nautical miles (1,000 kilometres) and consists of about 120 scattered rocks, coral reefs and other low-tide elevations. The majority of these are not islands under maritime law (UNCLOS 1982, Art. 121) since they are mostly covered by water, and a low-tide elevation that is submerged at high tides has no territorial sea of its own. In 1998, China used national legislation to grant itself jurisdiction over a 200 nautical mile (370 kilometres) zone for all its claimed territories. Among these, it counts the entire Spratly Archipelago. In 2011, it applied to the UN for an EEZ of 200 nautical miles (370 kilometres) for each of the reefs it occupies. Using national legislation and state practice, China has thus laid claim to almost the entire South China Sea, largely corresponding to the NDL. In 2014, before the controversy could be settled either diplomatically or by arbitration, China created new facts on the ground by reclaiming land. Every area used by China for reclaiming land—such as the Fiery Cross, Mischief and Subi Reefs—is also claimed by at least one other state. Three, including the Mischief Reef, are inside the EEZ claimed by the Philippines.

In 2013–15, seven new artificial islands in the South China Sea were created by China ahead of an international tribunal assessing the merits of competing national claims in this body of ocean. Some of these outposts now host significant military capabilities,[4] helping to propel China's historical claim to virtually all of this sea space. Substantial expansion was carried out on Woody Island in the northern Paracel Archipelago as well as on the Fiery Cross, Subi and Mischief Reefs in the Spratly Archipelago, on which large installations and concrete runways have been built. Their length allows fighter aircraft and even long-range bombers to be deployed. Chinese outposts have changed the strategic situation in the region: the newly created "islands" all over the sea (functioning as stationary aircraft carriers and air-defense platforms) will make freedom of navigation (and overflight) at some point dependent on China's goodwill (Paul 2017). The bases substantially improve the operating range and thus the deployment possibilities of China´s armed forces, coast guard and maritime militias. Like military bases on the mainland, the SCS outposts are integrated into a larger Chinese joint force system-of-systems that supports evolving PLA strategies (Dahm 2020).

The Permanent Court of Arbitration (PCA) in The Hague decided on 12 July 2016 in the case *Philippines v. China* on all 15 applications except one according to the terms advocated by Manila. The tribunal found that the historical claims of the nine-dash-line are not, as claimed by Beijing, consistent with the Convention and are therefore legally invalid. Distinguishing between islands, rocks and tide elevations, the Court came to the conclusion that none of the outstanding high-tide elevations in the area of the Spratly Islands are "islands" according to maritime law and thus have no exclusive economic zone. Moreover, it was noted that China has prevented the Philippines from exercising the exploration of oil and gas deposits and fishing in its EEZ since 2010 and, through measures for land reclamation, has further violated more articles of the Convention and the sovereign rights of the Philippines (PCA 2016).

China as a signatory to UNCLOS is bound by the PCA ruling, despite boycotting the proceedings. Legally, all the claims made by China and other littoral states concerning the SCS are invalid. All can claim only possession of waters according to other criteria provided by the Law of the Sea. The Court has opened a wide space for compromise—provided the claimants want it. However, the first reaction of China's foreign ministry was that "the award is null and void and has no binding force. China neither accepts nor recognizes it" (PRC 2016).

Washington has long ignored the implications of China's behaviour in the South China Sea. The 2015 passage of the USS *Lassen* was the first freedom of navigation operation (FONOP) in the area since 2012 and was intended to demonstrate that the US would not accept any restrictions on its freedom of navigation in this region. The USS *Lassen* operation was intended to emphasise that

China's base-building activities had not altered the *status quo*. Consequently, the Americans treated the outpost erected on a "low-tide elevation" as an artificial island, which may have a security zone of 0.23 nautical miles (500 metres) but no territorial sea (Glaser and Dutton 2015; Kraska 2015). China requires foreign military vessels to either ask permission or provide advance notice before sailing through territorial seas. However, under UNCLOS, a foreign warship can pass within 12 nautical miles (22 kilometres) of a territorial claim as long as it takes a direct route and conducts no military operations. Accordingly, USS *Montgomery* conducted the first 2020 FONOP through waters near the Spratly Islands that are claimed by China.

At its core, the SCS dispute is a regional conflict about an important shipping lane, territorial claims and rich resources that primarily involve Southeast Asian nations and China. But it also has global repercussions. Firstly, it concerns a superhighway of the seas. An impediment to the shipping traffic would have a direct impact on world trade in general but particularly on China, Taiwan, Japan and South Korea. Second, the SCS has become a site of great power competition between Beijing and Washington; important allies and partners of the US are also involved in the dispute about China's territorial claims. China desperately wants control of the "three seas" (South China Sea, East China Sea, Yellow Sea) for its national security to make use of them as room to maneuver, to deter enemies and to project power. But exclusive Chinese sea control would mean an end to the US alliance system in the Asia-Pacific (and was, therefore, an important reason for rebalancing US forces under President Obama).[5] Thirdly, it is a conflict about international norms and laws that calls into question a fundamental principle of the liberal world order: the "freedom of the seas" versus exclusive maritime zones.

A new era of great power naval competition has begun in which Washington can no longer take for granted its ability to access, let alone dominate, the littorals of rival states like China and Russia. In East Asia, China's growing military capabilities for anti-access and area denial (A2/AD) increasingly complicate US operational planning assumptions and would inflict serious costs on US armed forces if they access China's maritime littoral in the case of conflict. The strategy is clear: air-sea denial of US forces, which may seek to sustain large-scale military operations in support of Taiwan, of its partners in the SCS as well as in the East China Sea. China's overall political-military strategy is also clear: to cause doubt in the minds of decision makers and any future US administration as to the "winnability" of an armed conflict against Chinese forces within the first island chain and, ultimately, to undermine America's role as a regional security provider (Poling 2020; Rudd 2018).

A key element of US national strategy is to prevent the emergence of a regional hegemon in one part of Eurasia or another on the grounds that such a hegemon could represent a concentration of power strong enough to threaten core US interests. Although American policymakers have not often stated this national strategic goal explicitly, US military (and diplomatic) operations in recent decades can be viewed as having been carried out in no small part in support of this key goal.

"China is now capable of controlling the SCS in all scenarios, short of war with the United States", US Admiral Philip S. Davidson said during a 2018 Senate confirmation hearing ahead of his appointment as commander of the US Pacific Command (Power 2020). Nevertheless, short of a conflict, Chinese domination over or control of its near-seas like the SCS could help it to: control fishing operations and oil and gas exploration activities; coerce, intimidate or put political pressure on countries bordering the SCS; enforce a maritime exclusion zone (i.e., a blockade) around Taiwan; facilitate the projection of Chinese military power and political influence further into the Western Pacific; and achieve the broader goal of becoming a regional hegemon in Eurasia (CRS 2019). US-bound commerce is marginally reliant on Southeast Asian waterways; US interest in the SCS is thus dominated by geopolitics while EU's interest is shaped by economics.

Constraints

Asia accounts for 35 percent of EU exports (€618bn) and 45 percent of its imports (European Commission 2018). EU-Asia trade depends on stable and secure sea lines and, therefore, on a solution to the problem of divergent claimant states in the SCS—especially China's NDL claim. There have not, however, been many opportunities for EU leaders to discuss China. Chancellor Angela Merkel has urged Europeans to take China, and not just the US and Russia, into account when discussing global affairs and to consider Beijing's ambitions and economic might. "No matter how diligent, no matter how great we can be—with a population of 80 million, we will not be able to resist if China decides that it no longer wants good relations with Germany", Merkel said at the 2019 Munich Security Conference. But the big question will be, Merkel said, "Do we stick to the principle of multilateralism . . . even if multilateralism is not always great, but is difficult, slow, complicated?" (Eder 2019).

What would the EU's (preferably common) approach to China and the rising great power competition on the global stage look like? Europe alone cannot significantly influence the developing world conflict between the US and China. However, according to Peter Rudolf (2020), "Its consequences might be dramatic if the economic interdependence between the United States and China dissolved, economic blocs or closed economic spaces emerged and a process of economic de-globalization began" (also see Lake 2018). In China's maritime domain, this could include a process towards a sphere of influence, which would mean a shift towards a *mare clausum* in which Beijing would decide the rules of the sea routes crossing the SCS—although such a sphere of influence would not be a stable system with other major powers in the region, thus constraining China's power projection.

EU countries must balance conflicting interests—the need to economically cooperate with China and, at the same time, protect the Western-shaped international order from Chinese challenges. While France claims to defend its freedom of navigation, it has also chosen to stay outside territorial waters claimed by China in the SCS, reducing the risk of incidents with Chinese naval forces. Nevertheless,

Paris did practically show its will and intent of keeping the law of the sea. Berlin is still looking for a whole-of-government approach but is willing to send a frigate in the Indo-Pacific region as soon as its ruling coalition can agree on the message that this should send. Thus, while China is constrained by rivals in the region, European countries prefer self-constraints which do no harm to both norms and business.

Europeans and Asians do not want a permanent confrontation between two great powers in their neighbourhood—Russia and China. Europe needs more cooperation with Moscow, and Asia must look for a new arrangement with a more powerful Beijing. But European countries, acting in concert with Asian partners (and a post-Trump administration in Washington)[6] can make a difference.

Options

European countries, as industrialised trading nations with an extensive socio-economic exchange with East Asia, depend on maintaining the freedom of navigation. Subsequent G7 statements of 2015 and 2016 confirmed the joint reaction to China's assertiveness in the SCS (Stanzel 2016), as did a joint statement by France, Germany and the UK on the situation in the SCS from August 2019. The European Commission declared in its 2019 EU-China Outlook that "China's maritime claims in the South China Sea and the refusal to accept the binding arbitration rulings . . . affect the international legal order and make it harder to resolve tensions affecting sea-lanes of communication vital to the EU's economic interests" (European Commission 2019). Thus, today, as a key challenge to the EU, China has become,

> simultaneously, in different policy areas, a cooperation partner with whom the EU has closely aligned objectives, a negotiating partner with whom the EU needs to find a balance of interests, an economic competitor in the pursuit of technological leadership, and a systemic rival promoting alternative models of governance.
>
> (*ibid.*, 1)

The EU should therefore continue to promote stability and respect for good governance in partnership with Southeast Asian countries.

The maritime dispute in the SCS cannot be resolved on the basis of legal considerations alone. Such considerations will only be helpful once there is political will to resolve the conflict. But efforts to resolve the issues by diplomacy have repeatedly failed. Several attempts were made to initiate multilateral conflict resolution in which China refused to participate, insisting on the principle of bilateral discussion. Negotiations on a code of conduct (COC), agreed in principle in 2002,[7] have failed to make headway. In February 2018, China agreed to start negotiating the details of the COC with ASEAN but, to date, there is no clarity on whether the outcome document will be "legally binding" as originally envisioned. This lack of clarity is due to the difficulty of establishing verification and enforcement mechanisms between parties with such highly asymmetric power capabilities as China and ASEAN Member States. In August 2018, a single draft negotiating text was first put forward with an agreement reached by China and ASEAN to finalise the COC within three years, starting from 2019. Having faced frequent tensions in the SCS, the agreement demonstrates that a diplomatic mechanism to manage the dispute is possible. However, according to Nguyen Minh Quang (2019), there are still significant hurdles that reflect differences among the parties. These include the undefined geographic scope of the SCS, disagreement on dispute settlement mechanisms, different approaches to conflict management and the undefined legal status of the COC. According to Cronin and Neuhard (2020, 28), China wants to establish regional rules that favour Beijing:

> In particular, Beijing wants to build a dispute settlement system that does not include the UNCLOS dispute arbitration mechanism. It also wants to create a rule prohibiting joint military exercises with countries outside the region (i.e., the United States) unless prior approval is provided by all parties to the agreement. Similarly, Beijing wants to establish a rule prohibiting resource development with countries outside the region.

China could thus avoid another arbitration case, veto the participation of ASEAN countries in future US exercises and reduce competition over the resources of the SCS.

Europe will have to shoulder more responsibility in protecting the global commons. The 2014 EU Maritime Security Strategy (EUMSS) encouraged Member States' armed forces to

> play a strategic role at sea and from the sea and provide global reach, flexibility and access that enable the EU and its Member States to contribute to the full spectrum of maritime responsibilities. Their sustained presence needs to support freedom of navigation and contribute to good governance by deterring, preventing and countering unlawful and illicit activities within the global maritime domain.
>
> (EUMSS 2014)

However, the challenges are great and Europe's naval forces are constrained by decades of decline. French Defence Minister Jean-Yves Le Drian told attendees of the 2016 Shangri-La dialogue that France would encourage the EU to undertake "regular and visible" patrols in the SCS area (Panda 2016). Since then, both France and the UK have sent ships to the SCS. Britain's HMS *Albion* conducted a freedom of navigation patrol in waters near the Paracel Islands in late August 2018. The *Albion's* patrol was a traditional assertion of freedom of navigation on the high seas, unlike the freedom of navigation operations of the US Navy that are designed to challenge what Washington views as excessive maritime claims—for example, in the context of Chinese artificial "islands". The patrol by the British warship demonstrated the UK's intention to engage in the Southeast Asian region and signaled that the Royal Navy is likely to be a regular party patrolling the SCS. As usual, Beijing only made official comments after Western media cited British defence sources about the *Albion* naval patrol. Like US FONOPs, which have expanded under Trump in both frequency and complexity (Cronin and Neuhard), China reacted by sending vocal warnings, its warship and fighter jets to shadow the HMS *Albion*. The *Albion* indeed contributed to the external powers' endeavor to uphold the right of free access to the waterways (and airways) in the SCS.

In another relevant operation, France and the UK conducted a joint FON patrol through Mischief, Subi and Fiery Cross Reefs in the Spratly Islands in late June 2018 (Luc 2018). President Emmanuel Macron of France did not publicly raise objections to Chinese policy in the SCS during his 2019 trip to Shanghai and Beijing, and the French declaration released at the end of his meeting with Chinese President Xi Jinping on November 6 made no mention of the contested waters (Scimia 2019). But Paris has toughened rhetoric against China's behaviour in the SCS in recent years, and the French navy deploys assets in the SCS on an average three or four times per annum. Minister of the Armies Florence Parly stated in the 2019 document "France and Security in the Indo-Pacific", with clear reference to China:

> In the South China Sea, the large-scale land reclamation activities and the militarisation of contested archipelagos have changed the status quo and increased tensions. The potential consequences of this crisis have a global impact . . . Such a case highlights how multilateralism is questioned by asser-tive policies which are threatening the stability of the whole region.
>
> (Ministère des Armées 2019)

France considers itself a resident power in the Indo-Pacific, where it has over-seas dependencies and vast exclusive economic zones. It regularly exercises its right of maritime navigation. It also organises multilateral exercises in the Indian and Pacific Oceans. In 2019, Admiral Christophe Prazuck, chief-of-staff of the French navy, proposed joint patrols in Indo-Pacific waters between the navies of France and Australia (Scimia 2019). Thus, in the future, Australian warships could contribute to escorting the carrier *Charles de Gaulle*, while French frigates could escort Australian amphibious ships. European powers do not want to coun-ter China's military power, which is growing in accordance with the gradual shift from "offshore waters defense" to a combination of "offshore waters defense" and "open seas protection" (McDevitt 2016). Europe could, though, help build an effective and shared maritime domain awareness (MDA).[8] As a "maritime secu-rity provider", enhancing MDA globally has been one of the EU's main capacity-building activities and contributions to maritime security (Pejsova 2019).

Conclusion

Looking for enduring solutions, like strengthening norms of behavior, means building another set of codes of conduct to govern the seas of the Indo-Pacific.

There are currently no agreements on norms or an institution that brings together Indo-Pacific Member States like ASEAN. India and Indonesia could play a constructive role in the Indo-Pacific; both have great legitimacy as non-US allies and traditionally non-aligned states. Strengthening areas of shared concern, such as illegal fishing and piracy through coastguard cooperation, could be a starting point, followed by navy-to-navy activities. According to Ghiasy et al. (2018), the EU can play an instrumental role in a COC by establishing a two-track platform and could assist in mitigating some of the imbalances.[9]

Multilateralism is key for bringing countries together to counter threats confronting the region. Joint initiatives, such as the Sulu Sea Trilateral Patrol[10] and the Malacca Straits Patrol (MSP),[11] demonstrate that countries must collaborate to solve common security threats. According to Anderson (2016), the development of the MSP network is promising, creating greater modes of information sharing and closer coordination.

Encouraging China to participate in providing security as a global public good is one side of the coin. On the other, "China's increasing military capabilities coupled with its comprehensive vision and ambition to have the technologically most advanced armed forces by 2050 present security issues for the EU, already in a short to mid-term perspective" (European Commission 2019).

Should Europe seek a more ambitious role in a more tense Indo-Pacific to uphold or shape the regional order? Clearly, a militarisation of the EU's Asia policy is neither possible nor plausible (Stanzel 2016), although there is little doubt that China would like to achieve military primacy in and around the SCS. More recently, the question of how to deal with China has also found its way into North Atlantic Treaty Organization (NATO) debates, both as a result of US references to the country as a strategic competitor and by European worries about joint naval manoeuvres by China and Russia in the Mediterranean and Baltic Seas (see Paul 2019). An informal trilateral EU–US–NATO dialogue on China was therefore proposed (Simón 2019). Such a dialogue would not only help bring together the economic, technological and security aspects relating to China's rise but would also help bridge differences between the EU and the US.

Brussels should examine the possibility of a stronger security policy engagement and concern itself more urgently with questions of maritime security in the region. Given its limited ability to project military force, it is unrealistic to assume that the EU will play a significant security role in Asia, but it should play a larger role in reinforcing international legal norms. EU and European countries can help ASEAN develop common norms for policing its maritime zone and sharing maritime domain awareness. This could result in codes of conduct that respect international maritime law and the freedom of navigation, thus enhancing maritime safety and security in the SCS and the Indo-Pacific region. Nevertheless, European countries like France and the UK have concluded that it is necessary to adopt a more formal and transparent freedom of navigation policy to help uphold the law of the sea and dissuade revisionists from hostile, illegal and/or excessive activities. John Hemmings and James Rogers (2019) argued "that the Royal Navy is not only bolstered to meet the growing challenge from the PRC and other revisionist states, but also that it maintains a persistent, if not permanent, naval presence in the Indo-Pacific region, and Southeast Asia and the South China Sea in particular". Germany should both establish a presence at the Information Fusion Centre (IFC) in Singapore[12] and send a frigate to the Indo-Pacific, signaling a clear intention to protect the rules-based system.

The EU's new, more hard-nosed approach toward China is likely to set the tone in the 2020s. But will it last? New leadership is keen to deliver on the EU's global role. The tougher line allows weaker and more vulnerable Member States to stay the course with China—concerning both freedom of navigation in the SCS and protection of human rights—without facing retribution from Beijing. However, European political unity will be under stress from post-Brexit repercussions, illiberal triumphs across Europe and COVID-19. The political impact of the new coronavirus, a pandemic that started in China and spread through a highly integrated global economy with shattering speed, is as of yet unknown. Nevertheless, China benefits from a near-peer strategic position: "In an ironic twist, an epidemic that started in China may end by increasing Beijing's international reach" (Mead 2020). These are tough times for the EU.

Notes

1 The name "South China Sea" has become established in the English-speaking world and thus also as the commonly used international designation. In Asia it is known neutrally by the direction in which it lies, as seen from the respective country. Thus, the Chinese call it the "South Sea" and the Vietnamese the "East Sea".
2 Submissions were received by the Commission on the Limits of the Continental Shelf (CLCS).
3 While the US is not a party to UNCLOS, it adheres to it as a matter of customary law.
4 According to Cronin and Neuhard (2020), the primary purpose of these bases in the Spratly Islands is not to support general conventional military power but to facilitate information superiority in keeping with China's informationised warfare operational concepts. During peacetime, it helps the country's maritime forces to more effectively track and harass foreign vessels which operate in the SCS.
5 Government officials and scholars around the world have switched their labels for Asia from "Asia Pacific" to "Indo-Pacific" after President Donald Trump popularised the latter during his first Asia trip in November 2017.
6 As Henry Kissinger puts it, "The United States, if separated from Europe in politics, economics and defense, would become geopolitically an island off the shores of Eurasia" (Kissinger 2014).
7 The 2002 ASEAN-China Declaration on the Conduct of Parties in the South China Sea has not yet been fully implemented.
8 Maritime domain awareness involves surveillance, intelligence and information collection about ships through human reports and automated systems and subsequent fusion and sharing of this data among all relevant stakeholders. It is an essential tool in maritime security used for law enforcement and incident management.
9 Until 2021, the EU will co-chair the ASEAN Regional Forum (ARF) Inter-Sessional Meeting on Maritime Security, in which it tries to promote cooperation on non-traditional maritime security issues, including port security, IUU fishing and law enforcement.
10 A trilateral cooperation mechanism for managing a range of transnational challenges in the Sulu Sea between Indonesia, Malaysia and the Philippines.

11 The Malacca Straits Patrol is a set of practical cooperative measures undertaken by Indonesia, Malaysia, Singapore and Thailand to ensure the security of the Straits of Malacca and Singapore (Singapore Government 2015).
12 The Information Fusion Centre (IFC) is a regional Maritime Security (MARSEC) centre situated at the Changi Command and Control Centre (CC2C) and hosted by the Republic of Singapore Navy.

References

Anderson, Megan. 2016. "The Malacca Strait Patrol: A Maritime Security Network Analysis." Leiden University Working Paper, February. www.researchgate.net/publication/295907874_The_Malacca_Strait_Patrol_A_Maritime_Security_Network_Analysis.

Bader, Jeffrey A. 2014. *The U.S. and China's Nine-Dash Line: Ending the Ambiguity*. Washington, DC: Brookings Institution Press.

Center for Strategic and International Studies (CSIS). 2016. "How Much Trade Transits the South China Sea?" https://chinapower.csis.org/much-trade-transits-south-china-sea/.

Congressional Research Service (CRS). 2019. *U.S.-China Strategic Competition in South and East China Seas: Background and Issues for Congress*. CRS Report R42784, December 20. Washington, DC: Congressional Research Service.

Council of the European Union. 2014, June 24. *European Maritime Security Strategy (EUMSS)*. Brussels: General Secretariat of the Council.

Cronin, Patrick M. and Ryan Neuhard. 2020. *Total Competition: China's Challenge in the South China Sea*. Washington, DC: Center for a New American.

Dahm, J. Michael. 2020. "Beyond 'Conventional Wisdom': Evaluating the PLA's South China Sea Bases in Operational Context." *War on the Rocks*, March 17. https://warontherocks.com/2020/03/beyond-conventional-wisdom-evaluating-the-plas-south-china-sea-bases-in-operational-context/.

Eder, Florian. 2019. "Brussels Playbook: Orbán Splits the EPP—China Finally on Europe's Agenda—Decisions and Consequences." *Politico*, February 20. www.politico.eu/newsletter/brussels-playbook/politico-brussels-playbook-orban-splits-the-epp-china-finally-on-europes-agenda-decisions-and-consequences/.

European Commission. 2018. "Connecting Europe and Asia -Building Blocks for an EU Strategy." Brussels JOIN (2018) 31 final, September 19. https://eeas.europa.eu/sites/eeas/files/joint_communication_-_connecting_europe_and_asia_-_building_blocks_for_an_eu_strategy_2018-09-19.pdf.

European Commission. 2019. "EU-China—A Strategic Outlook." Strasbourg, March 12. https://ec.europa.eu/commission/sites/beta-political/files/communication-eu-china-a-strategic-outlook.pdf.

Eurostat. 2018. "International Trade in Goods by Mode of Transport." https://ec.europa.eu/eurostat/statistics-explained/index.php/International_trade_in_goods_by_mode_of_transport.

Gao, Zhiguo, and Bingbing Jia. 2013. "The Nine-Dash Line in the South China Sea: History, Status, and Implications." *The American Journal of International Law* 107 (1): 98–124.

Ghiasy, Richard, Fei Su and Lora Saalman. 2018. *The 21st Century Maritime Silk Road: Security Implications and Ways Forward for the European Union*. Solna: SIPRI.

Glaser, Bonnie S., and Peter A. Dutton. 2015. "The U.S. Navy's Freedom of Navigation Operation around Subi Reef: Deciphering U.S. Signaling." *The National Interest*,

November 6. https://nationalinterest.org/feature/the-us-navy%E2%80%99s-freedom-navigation-operation-around-subi-reef-14272.

Hemmings, John and James Rogers. 2019. *The South China Sea: Why It Matters to "Global Britain".* London: The Henry Jackson Society. https://henryjacksonsociety.org/publications/the-south-china-sea-why-it-matters-to-global-britain/.

Kissinger, Henry. 2014. *World Order.* New York: Penguin Press.

Kraska, James. 2015. "The Nine Ironies of the South China Sea Mess." *The Diplomat,* September 17. https://thediplomat.com/2015/09/the-nine-ironies-of-the-south-china-sea-mess/.

Lake, David A. 2018. "Economic Openness and Great Power Competition: Lessons for China and the United States." *The Chinese Journal of International Politics* 11 (3): 237–270.

Luc, Tuan Anh. 2018. "Are France and the UK Here to Stay in the South China Sea?" *The Diplomat,* September 14. https://thediplomat.com/2018/09/are-france-and-the-uk-here-to-stay-in-the-south-china-sea/.

McDevitt, Michael. 2016. *China's Far Sea's Navy: The Implications of the "Open Seas Protection" Mission.* A Paper for the "China as a Maritime Power" Conference. Arlington, VA. www.cna.org/cna_files/pdf/China-Far-Seas-Navy.pdf.

Mead, Walter Russell. 2020. "China's Coronavirus Opportunity." *Wall Street Journal,* March 17.

Ministère des Armées. 2019. *France and Security in the Indo-Pacific.* Paris: Directorate General for International Relations and Strategy.

Mitter, Rana. 2015. "The End of the Second World War and the Shaping of Geopolitics in East Asia." *RUSI Journal* 160 (4): 14–17.

O'Rourke, Ronald. 2015. *Maritime Territorial and Exclusive Economic Zone (EEZ) Disputes Involving China: Issues for Congress.* CRS Report R42784. Washington, DC: Congressional Research Service, December 22.

Panda, Ankit. 2016. "French Defense Minister to Urge EU South China Sea Patrols." *The Diplomat,* June 6. https://thediplomat.com/2016/06/french-defense-minister-to-urge-eu-south-china-sea-patrols/.

Panda, Ankit. 2017. "How Much Trade Transits the South China Sea? Not $5.3 Trillion a Year." *The Diplomat,* August 7. https://thediplomat.com/2017/08/how-much-trade-transits-the-south-china-sea-not-5-3-trillion-a-year/.

Paul, Michael. 2016. *A "Great Wall of Sand" in the South China Sea? Political, Legal and Military Aspects of the Island Dispute.* Berlin: Stiftung Wissenschaft und Politik.

Paul, Michael. 2017. *Kriegsgefahr im Pazifik? Die maritime Bedeutung der sino-amerikanischen Rivalität.* Baden-Baden: Nomos.

Paul, Michael. 2019. *Partnership on the High Seas? China und Russia's Joint Naval Manoeuvres.* Berlin: Stiftung Wissenschaft und Politik.

Pejsova, Eva. 2019. *The EU as a Maritime Security Provider.* Brussels: European Union Institute for Security Studies. www.iss.europa.eu/content/eu-maritime-security-provider.

People's Republic of China (PRC). 2016. "Statement of the Ministry of Foreign Affairs of the People's Republic of China on the Award of 12 July 2016 of the Arbitral Tribunal in the South China Sea Arbitration Established at the Request of the Republic of the Philippines." July 12. https://academic.oup.com/chinesejil/article-abstract/15/4/905/2765120?redirectedFrom=fulltext.

Permanent Court of Arbitration (PCA). 2016. "PCA Case N° 2013–19 in the Matter of the South China Sea Arbitration Before an Arbitral Tribunal Constituted Under Annex VII to the 1982 United Nations Convention on the Law of the Sea Between the Republic of the Philippines and the People's Republic of China, Award." July 12. www.pcacases.com/pcadocs/PH-CN%20-%2020160712%20-%20Award.pdf.

Poling, Gregory B. 2020. "The Conventional Wisdom on China's Island Bases Is Dangerously Wrong." *War on the Rocks*, January 10. https://warontherocks.com/2020/01/the-conventional-wisdom-on-chinas-island-bases-is-dangerously-wrong/.

Power, John. 2020. "Has the US Already Lost the Battle for the South China Sea?" *South China Morning Post*, January 18. www.scmp.com/week-asia/politics/article/3046619/has-us-already-lost-battle-south-china-sea.

Quang, Nguyen Minh. 2019. "Negotiating an Effective China—ASEAN South China Sea Code of Conduct." *East Asia Forum*, July 31. www.eastasiaforum.org/2019/07/31/negotiating-an-effective-china-asean-south-china-sea-code-of-conduct/.

Raine, Sarah, and Christian Le Mière. 2013. *Regional Disorder: The South China Sea Disputes*. London: International Institute for Strategic Studies.

Rudd, Kevin. 2018. "Understanding China's Rise Under Xi Jinping. Address to Cadets: United States Military Academy, West Point." March 5. https://asiasociety.org/sites/default/files/2019-01/Understanding%20China%27s%20Rise%20Under%20Xi%20Jinping_1.pdf.

Rudolf, Peter. 2020. *The Sino-American World Conflict*. SWP Research Paper 2020/RP 03. Berlin: Stiftung Wissenschaft und Politik.

Scimia, Emanuele. 2019. "To Gauge France's South China Sea Intentions, Look at What It Does, Not What It Does Not Say." *South China Morning Post*, November 11.

Simón, Luis. 2019. *EU-NATO Cooperation in an Era of Great-Power Competition*. Washington, DC: German Marshall Fund of the United States (GMF).

Singapore Government. 2015. *Fact Sheet: The Malacca Straits Patrol*. Singapore: MINDEF, April 21. www.mindef.gov.sg/web/portal/mindef/news-and-events/latest-releases/article-detail/2016/april/2016apr21-news-releases-00134/.

Stanzel, Volker. 2016. "Need Disputes Turn into Armed Conflicts? East Asia's Maritime Conflicts in a New Environment: Consequences for the European Union." *European Foreign Affairs Review* 21 (3/1): 65–80.

United Nations Conference on Trade and Development (UNCTAD). 2018. "Review of Maritime Transport 2018." https://unctad.org/en/PublicationsLibrary/rmt2018_en.pdf.

United Nations Convention on the Law of the Sea (UNCLOS). 1982, December 10. "United Nations Treaty Series, Vol. 1833 (1994)." https://treaties.un.org/doc/Publication/UNTS/Volume%201833/volume-1833-A-31363-English.pdf.

U.S. Department of State. 2014. *Limits in the Seas. No. 143. China: Maritime Claims in the South China Sea*. Washington, DC: U.S. Department of State.

U.S. Energy Information Administration (EIA). 2018. "More Than 30% of Global Maritime Crude Oil Trade Moves Through the South China Sea." August 27. www.eia.gov/todayinenergy/detail.php?id=36952.

7   Europe and the North Korea conundrum

Navigating the China–South Korea–United States triangle

Ramon Pacheco Pardo

Introduction

"We have no eternal allies, and we have no perpetual enemies. Our interests are eternal and perpetual, and those interests it is our duty to follow" (House of Commons Debates 1848). This quote from Henry John Temple, better known as Lord Palmerston—twice prime minister and three times foreign secretary of the United Kingdom (UK) between 1830 and 1865—holds true across time and space. It highlights one of the core tenets of the Westphalian world order, at least from a realist perspective: self-interested states living in an anarchical international system ought to maximise their power and wealth. Sometimes, this can be done through alliances with other states with similar interests. However, these alliances will disintegrate once they lose their purpose.

The post-Westphalian, liberal international order based on international organisations pooling the resources of groups of states is meant to have put an end to this self-interested approach to international relations. States bring their resources together and self-interest is diluted, replaced by the common good. The European Union (EU) is considered the greatest expression of the post-Westphalian world order. This has led to the argument that the EU will project its model to the rest of the world and behave differently in international affairs. In its most popular conception, the EU is a normative power exporting its values to the rest of the world. These values, including democracy, human rights and the rule of law, put the individual rather than the state at the centre of foreign policy (Manners 2002). Self-interest is replaced by a post-Westphalian common good of supposedly universal values.

Except that the world remains Westphalian. Self-interest still rules, with international institutions unable to promote the common good when the core interests of a particular state are at stake. Neither the United States (US) nor China, the two greatest contemporary powers, will sacrifice their core interests for the sake of the common good. As their relationship fluctuates between bilateral summits with specific practical outcomes and ongoing ideological and trade wars, international organisations demonstrate their inability to govern the international system.

In this context, the EU has decided to put its interests at the core of its foreign policy. As EU High Representative for Foreign Affairs and Security Policy Josep

Borrell (2020) has put it, Europe must embrace its power, "deal with the world as it is" and "devise credible approaches to dealing with today's global strategic actors: the US, China, and Russia". This does not preclude using international organisations when necessary or working together with, or against, the US and China when it suits Brussels' interests.

This chapter analyses the policy of the EU towards one of the most pressing global challenges in this era of China-US competition: North Korea's nuclear conundrum. It will do so by positioning the EU's interests in the context of its turn towards a realist (in the international relations sense) policy but also in the context of a realistic policy towards an issue in which not only China and the US but also South Korea have a central role. Therefore, the chapter actually positions the EU in the China–South Korea–US triangle which its North Korea policy must navigate. This chapter thus shows why and how the EU's policy towards North Korea, rooted in its own interests rather than any claims about common values, can lead to either cooperation or competition with China and the US.

Building on the three guiding questions that inform this volume, this chapter argues that the EU should: 1) take a pragmatic approach to the North Korean nuclear conundrum, avoiding merely symbolic gestures so as to be considered a serious actor in Asia-Pacific security affairs; 2) implement a policy informed but not determined by norms and values, as befits a realist power; and 3) avoid taking sides between China and the US, which is feasible considering that both support the denuclearisation of North Korea.

The chapter is divided as follows. In the following section, I outline the EU's permanent interests by examining its main foreign policy strategy documents. I then place these interests in the context of the North Korea nuclear conundrum. This is followed by a section analysing these interests with reference to the China–South Korea–US triangle or, perhaps, the EU–China–South Korea–US quadrangle. In the concluding section, I summarise my findings.

The EU's global strategy: evolution, not revolution

Throughout its post-Maastricht Treaty history, the foreign policy of the EU is said to be based on liberal values. The European Security Strategy (ESS) "A Secure Europe in a Better World" emphasised building an international order based on multilateralism and cooperation with partners as core elements of the EU's foreign policy (Council of the European Union 2003). This was reinforced by the ESS implementation report, which called for "partnerships for effective multilateralism" (Council of the European Union 2008).

In 2016, the Global Strategy for the EU's Foreign and Security Policy (Global Strategy), "Shared Vision, Common Action: A Stronger Europe", replaced the ESS. The Global Strategy reinforces the EU's commitment to both multilateralism and its partners. Multilateralism and the EU's strategic partnerships are seen as mutually reinforcing. Indeed, the Global Strategy calls for flexibility in the form of global governance on a case-by-case basis. Depending on the threat, multilateral institutions may take a leading role; alternatively, partnerships may be as important as multilateralism (European Union 2016).

However, the behaviour of the EU while President Barack Obama was in power suggested that it was willing to take a realist approach to foreign policy when its core interests were at stake. Most notably, Brussels and Washington publicly sparred during negotiations on the Transatlantic Trade and Investment Partnership (TTIP) as they sought to maximise (realist-inspired) relative gains at the expense of (liberal-inspired) absolute gains. Although the EU and the US have fairly similar economies, differences on issues such as labour standards, investor-state dispute settlement provisions or (alleged) healthcare privatisation derailed the negotiations (Aggarwal and Evenett 2017). As a result, TTIP negotiations ultimately failed.

Interestingly, the Global Strategy did not specifically mention China as a partner (European Union 2016). Indeed, High Representative Federica Mogherini presented a separate China strategy almost in parallel to the Global Strategy. The "Elements for a New EU Strategy on China" communiqué took a decidedly realist approach towards Beijing. Brussels made it clear that it wanted mutual benefits in its relationship with Beijing, and that it sought to promote the rule of law in this bilateral relationship (European Commission 2016), with the implicit assumption that this had not been the case before. The China strategy put the EU's own interests at the centre of its relationship with Beijing.

This realist approach to international relations has strengthened as a new European Commission took over in December 2019. President Ursula von der Leyen (2019) has called for the EU to "learn the language of power". High Representative Borrell (2019) has vowed to make a "Geopolitical Commission". The message is clear: in an era of "America First", Chinese assertiveness and Sino-American competition, the EU must use all the tools at its disposal to be an actor of significance within global affairs. Brussels must also put its interests first; traditionally liberal tactics and goals might be pursued when necessary, but self-interest and the use of all of Europe's power tools must be prioritised.

In summary, the foreign policy of the EU has remained fairly stable since the ESS was adopted in 2003. The Global Strategy adopted in 2016 does not deviate significantly from the ESS. Partnerships and multilateralism in particular are cornerstones of the EU's foreign policy. Since the ESS implementation report adopted in 2008, both these cornerstones have been linked to each other. At the same time, however, the EU has been realist when necessary. Its relationship with the US, even during the "good years" of the Obama administration, as well as with China, shows this to be the case. Furthermore, even multilateralism and partnerships have a place in a realist foreign policy—as shown below in the case of North Korea.

The EU and the North Korea conundrum

North Korea's nuclear programme is one of the EU's main security concerns in Asia. China's rise aside, it is arguably the top one. Indeed, North Korea was named in the 2003 and 2008 ESS implementation reports by specific reference to its weapons of mass destruction (WMD); non-proliferation in the Korean Peninsula is mentioned in the 2016 Global Strategy. North Korea's nuclear weapons and missile programs have thus been a concern for the EU from the outset of its security strategy, a period of almost two decades.

Zooming in on the EU's Asia-specific security concerns, the "Enhanced EU Security Cooperation in and with Asia" (Asia Security Strategy) conclusions adopted by the Council of the European Union in 2018 prioritise the proliferation of chemical, biological, radiological and *nuclear* (CBRN; emphasis added) weapons as a top concern for the EU (Council of the European Union 2018). North Korea is not mentioned as a threat by name; however, no country is. Nevertheless, North Korea is the main proliferation concern in Asia. Therefore, it is a top security worry on the Asian continent according to the EU's first-ever Asia Security Strategy.

Under its "critical engagement" policy, in place since the mid-2000s, the main goal of the EU when it comes to the North Korean nuclear conundrum has been clear: non-proliferation of nuclear weapons (European External Action Service 2016). Other goals include stability on the Korean Peninsula and improvement of the human rights situation of ordinary North Koreans. However, the main objective is to prevent Pyongyang from illegally selling and transporting its nuclear technology to third parties.[1] This underscores the realism underpinning the EU's North Korea policy as well as its pragmatism. The normative goal of improving the human rights situation of ordinary North Koreans is secondary to the EU's own security, in the form of the non-proliferation of nuclear weapons.

Why does a realist EU prioritise North Korea's nuclear proliferation activities? Above all, it is due to Pyongyang's proliferation efforts in the Middle East (Pacheco Pardo 2018). Several of its past, present and would-be nuclear weapons and technology clients are based there. The region is sufficiently unstable without declared nuclear powers: the emergence of a declared nuclear power in the Middle East could lead to a domino effect whereby its enemies would seek to follow the same route. That would be very dangerous for Europe as it borders the region.

A related, key concern is the threat that North Korea's nuclear technology could fall into the hands of jihadist terrorist groups, leading to the explosion of a dirty bomb in a European city (Pacheco Pardo 2018). Terrorism is one of the key security concerns for the EU, as evidenced in the ESS, the ESS implementation report and the Global Strategy, as well as the Asia Security Strategy. Indeed, several EU Member States have suffered jihadist terrorist attacks for decades now (Europol 2019). If a dirty bomb were to explode in Europe, there is a high probability that nuclear or other materials would have been smuggled from the Middle East.

North Korea's nuclear proliferation and its programme in general is also perceived as a threat by the EU due to the example that it sets for other would-be nuclear powers (Pacheco Pardo 2018). The case of North Korea shows that the international community has little if any means of preventing would-be nuclear powers from developing their own weapons programs. Sanctions, diplomatic pressure or negotiations have all proved insufficient to prevent Pyongyang from developing its nuclear program. Certainly, North Korea has a more developed programme than Iran or Syria ever had. However, these programs were even less developed in the past, while Pyongyang has been able to develop its own over the decades.

Finally, the EU is also concerned about North Korea's proliferation activities because they pose a general threat to international law. In particular, there is a challenge to the nuclear non-proliferation regime (*ibid.*). North Korea (in)famously left the Non-Proliferation Treaty (NPT) that underpins the regime in 2003 without any significant consequence (Hur 2018). This sets a particularly negative example since the NPT has long been hailed as a success story.

In other words, the EU takes a realist approach towards North Korea's nuclear programs. Its main concerns relate directly to self-preservation, instability in its immediate neighbourhood and a terrorist attack on its soil. Preservation of the non-proliferation regime matters insofar as it relates to the EU's own security, including preventing North Korea being an example for other would-be nuclear powers that could also undermine the regime.

In terms of tactics, the ESS, ESS implementation report and Global Strategy all emphasise the use of partnerships. These include both China and the US, which, as we will see in the next section, share the EU's concerns about North Korea's nuclear program. Indeed, the North Korea nuclear issue is a rare example in which the US and China have shared the same goal from the outset of the second nuclear crisis in 2002 (Funabashi 2007; Hur 2018; Pacheco Pardo 2019). EU partners on this matter also include South Korea, the other main player in Korean Peninsula affairs. These nations are three of only eleven EU strategic partners (Ferreira-Pereira and Guedes Vieira 2016). In practice, cooperation includes dialogue and meetings, support for partners' non-proliferation policies or information and expertise exchange.

Brussels also prioritises multilateralism. The EU was disappointed with its exclusion from the Six-Party Talks (6PT) to solve the North Korean nuclear issue (Lee 2017). Convened between 2003 and 2008, the 6PT were the main multilateral forum involving North Korea and could conceivably make a return in the future (*ibid.*). Indeed, the EU sees a role for regional organisations to address security risks in East Asia (Council of the European Union 2018). Interestingly for the EU, the Northeast Asia Plus Community of Responsibility (NAPCR) launched by President Moon Jae-in in 2017 reserves a seat at the table for the EU (Ministry of Foreign Affairs of the Republic of Korea 2017). This shows that the EU can credibly ask for a role in future North Korea security discussions.

Arguably, under its "critical engagement" policy, sanctions have been the main tool for the EU to address the North Korea nuclear conundrum in recent years. Brussels has one of the most comprehensive North Korea sanctions regimes in the world. EU sanctions are based on a transposition of United Nations (UN) Security Council resolutions, but they include autonomous sanctions that go beyond what the UN requires (European External Action Service 2016). There is an agreement among EU Member States that sanctions should remain in place

unless and until North Korea starts taking meaningful steps towards denuclearisation (*ibid.*).

Direct dialogue with North Korea, another component of its "critical engagement policy", is another tool for the EU to address the North Korean nuclear issue.
However, the dialogue was last held in 2015 (European External Action Service
2015). This contrasts greatly with the use of sanctions, which has increased since
2016. The EU has thus withheld dialogue from North Korea as the country accelerated the development of its nuclear weapons program, including the development of ICBM capabilities.

While partnerships, multilateralism, (potential) dialogue and even sanctions—
as opposed to war—suggest that the EU's tactics to address the North Korean
nuclear conundrum are underpinned by liberal ideas, the reality is different. As
realist thinkers dating back to Morgenthau's seminal work have argued, states
should use multilateralism and dialogue out of self-interest if they can thus maintain or strengthen their relative power (Morgenthau 2006). As for sanctions, they
ultimately affect the general population, so there are questions as to whether they
can actually be considered a liberal tool. Indeed, realists claim that sanctions are
ultimately based on gaining relative power (Mearsheimer 2001). Also, the forceful interdiction of North Korea's nuclear and WMD shipments shows that the EU
is willing to use military means to deal with Pyongyang.

Indeed, the EU and its Member States are part of the Proliferation Security Initiative (PSI). This counter-proliferation initiative was launched by the US in 2003
(U.S. Department of State 2020). As then US Under Secretary for Arms Control and
International Security Affairs John Bolton (2007) stated, North Korea was the main
target of PSI. The legality of PSI has been challenged since it interferes with the
right of innocent passage and freedom of navigation (Logan 2005). However, the
EU's embrace of this tool from its outset proves that, ultimately, the EU will follow
the realist principle of using all tools at its disposal to guarantee its own security.

Sparring vertices, converging interests: the China–South Korea–US triangle and North Korea

The North Korea nuclear issue has been a top concern for China, the United Sates
and Pyongyang's southern neighbour, South Korea, at least since—if not before—
the first North Korea nuclear crisis of 1993–94. Focusing on the second nuclear
crisis of 2002 onwards and its aftermath, North Korea's nuclear programme has
remained a top concern for all three countries. Indeed, the 6PT set up in 2003 to
address the second crisis was the first instance of sustained Sino-American cooperation to deal with a hard security issue since at least the end of the Cold War
(Funabashi 2007). In other words, this issue had an impact beyond the "narrow"
focus of dealing with North Korea's nuclear programme and actually needs to be
placed in the context of broader US–China dynamics.

Despite the ideological differences and geopolitical interests across successive
American, Chinese and South Korean administrations, all of them have shared
at least one common goal: North Korea's denuclearisation.[2] Furthermore, it can

be said that all their leaders have shared one main approach to try to achieve this goal: engagement and diplomacy (Pacheco Pardo 2019). Certainly, there are differences in policy among these administrations. China has consistently argued for diplomacy and a step-by-step approach, whereas the US and South Korea take confidence-building measures in parallel as their way to deal with North Korea. George W. Bush, in the case of the US, and Roh Moo-hyun and Moon, in the case of South Korea, have supported this approach. However, broadly speaking, the US' Barack Obama and Donald Trump and South Korea's Lee Myung-bak and Park Geun-hye believed that North Korea should denuclearise—or at least take substantial steps in this direction—before diplomacy can start in earnest and before economic engagement with the US, South Korea and the international community at large can be implemented (*ibid.*). Nevertheless, the fundamental approach of denuclearisation through engagement and diplomacy has remained remarkably unchanged since 2003.

This matters for the EU insofar Brussels has consistently argued that engagement and diplomacy are necessary for dealing with North Korea. Indeed, the fact that the term "engagement" has been part of the EU's North Korea policy since the mid-2000s suggests that Brussels does believe in the benefits of this approach (Kim and Choi 2020). As a non-central actor in the North Korean nuclear issue, it would be difficult for Brussels to press for a different approach if China, South Korea and the United Stated opposed it.[3] But the EU's approach aligns with that of the three key actors in dealing with the North Korean nuclear issue. In this case, the EU's self-interest in the choice of this particular tactic creates an opportunity for cooperation with the US and China, showing that a realist EU can nonetheless use a liberal tool when it suits its self-interest and aligns with the interests of Beijing and Washington.

North Korea's development of its nuclear programme has led to an increase in the number and scope of sanctions. Especially since Kim Jong-un came to power, Pyongyang has dramatically accelerated its nuclear and missile test programme (CSIS 2020). Sanctions have consequently increased in parallel, especially in 2016–17, when North Korea accelerated the development of its nuclear and missile test programme until it successfully tested two ICBMs and conducted its sixth nuclear test.[4] As of 2020, North Korea is subject to a comprehensive sanctions regime that goes beyond the country's nuclear and missile programme and targets the country's economy and general population.

Bush, Hu Jintao and Roh prioritised engagement over sanctions.[5] These three were in power when Pyongyang's nuclear programme was still underdeveloped—or at least its level of development was relatively unknown. Indeed, Pyongyang's first nuclear test in 2006 came towards the end of the Bush and Roh presidencies, as well as towards the end of Hu's first term in office (Pacheco Pardo 2019). UN Security Council sanctions were imposed following the nuclear test and a missile test earlier, in July 2016, but there was still a preference for diplomacy and engagement over sanctions (Hur 2018).

The situation changed when Lee came to power in 2008 and Obama one year later. From the outset, Lee made it clear that his administration would take a tougher approach towards Pyongyang. This included implementing sanctions as well as the imposition of South Korea's own autonomous sanctions following the ROKS *Cheonan* sinking and the shelling of Yeonpyeong Island. Both of them were North Korean attacks on South Korea in 2010, resulting in South Korean casualties (Cha and Katz 2011). Park also followed a tougher approach towards North Korea and the South Korean National Assembly passed a North Korean Human Rights Act allowing sanctions to also be imposed on human rights grounds (Pacheco Pardo 2019). Both leaders left the door open to engagement, but only after North Korea had decided to take steps towards denuclearisation.

Obama was the first US president to prioritise sanctions over engagement to deal with North Korea. Washington made use of the UN Security Council to gradually increase sanctions on Pyongyang and also reinforced sanctions on human rights grounds (*ibid.*), a policy also followed by Trump. Even though Trump held two summits and another meeting with Kim Jong-un, the US leveraged the UN Security Council and unilateral sanctions on North Korea as well (*ibid.*). In contrast, Hu and later Xi Jinping have continued to advocate engagement over sanctions to deal with Pyongyang. Xi did allow the 2016–17 rounds of sanctions to dramatically escalate pressure on North Korea. But China started to call for their removal shortly after Trump and Kim held their first summit in June 2018. Similarly, Moon did continue with sanctions implementation after he came to power in 2017 but also called for sanctions relief as diplomacy took hold on the Korean Peninsula (*ibid.*).

Faced with a clear split between the US and China, especially from 2018, the EU decided to take sides. From 2016, Brussels increased sanctions as part of the "critical" component of its critical engagement policy. In particular, it imposed its own autonomous sanctions and pressed third countries to impose the UN Security Council sanctions regime as well (Pacheco Pardo 2018). While this was part of the policy toolkit available under the "critical engagement" policy first launched in the mid-2000s, it was also a means of supporting a core interest of the EU: good transatlantic relations. Indeed, support for US policy under Obama was a way to show that, on this issue, there is no transatlantic divide. In the case of Trump, the EU wanted to avoid yet another problem with the unorthodox president (*ibid.*). Therefore, Brussels used the North Korean nuclear issue as a way to pursue its core interests, not only with regards to the non-proliferation regime but in also terms of relations management of the great powers.

From the onset of the second North Korea nuclear crisis until Trump's election, there has been a general agreement that the North Korea nuclear issue should be solved through multilateral mechanisms. The rationale is that North Korean denuclearisation has to be put in a broader context including inter-Korean reconciliation, normalisation of diplomatic relations between the US and North Korea, a peace regime for the Korean Peninsula and North Korea's economic development (Funabashi 2007). Thus, the 6PT were the main venue for addressing the North Korea nuclear issue throughout the 2000s, and there were regular calls to restore them during the 2010s.

The 6PT were set up in 2003 under Bush and Hu. A trilateral meeting involving China, North Korea and the US was quickly expanded to include initially South Korea, and then Japan and Russia by the time the first meeting was held in August (*ibid.*). The last round of talks was held in December 2008, shortly before Bush left office. Obama for the US, Xi for China, and Lee and Park for South Korea supported continuation of the 6PT. However, North Korea's opposition to their restoration led to their eventual collapse (Hur 2018). It should also be noted that Obama, Lee and Park made continuation of the 6PT contingent on Pyongyang's moves towards denuclearisation (Pacheco Pardo 2019).

The situation with Trump was different. He made it clear that he did not believe in multilateralism, which he thought impinges on American policy. Thus, Trump pulled out of the Paris Agreement on climate change, the Joint Comprehensive Plan of Action or JCPOA to stop Iran's development of its nuclear programme and the Trans-Pacific Partnership trade agreement involving, among others, 11 Asia-Pacific countries (Council of Foreign Relations 2020). Similarly, Trump took a bilateral approach to the North Korean nuclear issue. Faced with this situation, South Korea's Moon refrained from calling for a resumption of the 6PT (Pacheco Pardo 2019). Having said that, implementation of any denuclearisation agreement with North Korea is a different matter. The Trump administration let European countries know that their support would be welcome during its implementation. Europe would also be called upon to contribute to a multilateral economic package to prop up the North Korean economy (Pacheco Pardo 2018).

The multilateralisation of the North Korean nuclear issue poses a dilemma for the EU. Support for multilateralism is a cornerstone of its foreign policy, as explained in the previous section. However, the EU was conspicuously excluded from the 6PT. This exclusion came in spite of the EU being one of four executive board members of the Korean Peninsula Energy Development Organisation (KEDO). KEDO was the organisation set up to provide two light-water reactors to North Korea in exchange for its denuclearisation under the Agreed Framework signed by President Bill Clinton and North Korean leader Kim Jong-un (KEDO 2020). The EU did repeatedly support the 6PT in public (Kim and Choi 2020) but being excluded from this process without being asked was a diplomatic blow. Thus, the EU would support a multilateral process, especially when it comes to implementation of an agreement. Crucially, however, the EU would not be willing to "pay without a say". In other words, it would have to be consulted when implementation decisions are made (Pacheco Pardo 2018). This reinforces the point that self-interest is paramount to the EU. It is not willing to simply provide support to a multilateral initiative that it cannot shape to try to achieve its goals. Its participation in multilateralism comes at a price. This is the realist approach to multilateralism, which emphasises its use if it strengthens its user's power.

Furthermore, there is in relation to multilateralism the question of taking advantage of the multilateralisation of the North Korea nuclear issue to build a Northeast Asian security mechanism. The thinking is that a shared interest in the denuclearisation of North Korea could be translated into a permanent security institution to integrate Pyongyang into security threat management in the region. The US pressed to include a Northeast Asia Peace and Security Mechanism (NAPSM) in the 6PT Joint Statement of September 2005 (Funabashi 2007). However, this mechanism did not prosper. Park then sought to launch a Northeast Asia Peace and Cooperation Initiative (NAPCI) when she came to power in 2013 (Ministry of Foreign Affairs of the Republic of Korea 2013) but this initiative did not gain major traction. Moon then picked up and expanded on NAPCI by suggesting the creation of a NAPCR when he took office in 2017. Interestingly for the EU, it is explicitly included in NAPCR (Ministry of Foreign Affairs of the Republic of Korea 2017) in sharp contrast to NAPSM and NAPCI, from which it was excluded.

Multilateralism is a core interest of the EU, so logically it has been supportive of the potential creation of multilateral security institutions in Northeast Asia (Lee 2016). This is especially the case with NAPCR, of which the EU would be a part. This is an example of the EU siding with South Korea since the US has not seriously pressed for a regional security mechanism since the 2000s, and China has not made any serious suggestion in this respect. It is in the self-interest of the EU to support the establishment of a multilateral security institution in Northeast Asia. Brussels has its own experience of multilateral peace and cooperation to share; it can make pragmatic use of one of its normative components to enhance its soft power in the region. It is also, at best, a middle power in the Northeast Asian context. It thus makes sense to side with one of the middle powers in the region—South Korea—to press for an institution that would give voice to non-great powers. Furthermore, supporting a multilateral mechanism for Northeast Asia would give the EU a seat at the discussion table that it currently lacks, boosting its presence in the region.

Conclusions: The EU's permanent interests and Sino-American relations over North Korea

The EU has a set of permanent interests over North Korea. These include non-proliferation of nuclear weapons, the stability of the Korean Peninsula and improving the human rights situation of ordinary North Koreans. On the issue of non-proliferation, Brussels is concerned with the development of nuclear weapons programs across the Middle East, nuclear technology falling into the hands of terrorist groups, the example that North Korea may set for other would-be nuclear powers and the undermining of international law. This suggests an approach premised on the realist assumptions that actors prioritise self-preservation.

Brussels also has a set of well-defined tactics for addressing the North Korea nuclear issue: the use of partnerships, multilateralism, sanctions, direct bilateral dialogue and the forceful interdictions of North Korea's WMD. These tactics are also informed by a realist approach to international relations. They do include policies from the liberal toolkit but, from a realist perspective, these can be used to boost relative power. Furthermore, EU policies also involve the decidedly non-normative approach of the use of force and the controversial use of sanctions. In other words, the EU is open to use all tools at its disposal in order to strengthen its own security.

Taking a realist, self-interest first approach to dealing with North Korea leads to instances of both convergence and divergence with China and the US, as well as with South Korea. There is an agreement on the ultimate goal by American, Chinese and South Korean administrations dating back at least to the early 2000s: denuclearisation through engagement. This suits the EU since it links with its ultimate goal and preferred policy. The EU's self-interest thus aligns with the interests of the three key players—North Korea aside—on Korean Peninsula affairs.

Notwithstanding the above, the EU has had differences with China over the use of sanctions and with the US when it has refrained from supporting multilateralism under Trump. The latter is particularly interesting, for it shows that Washington might not always support common liberal foreign policy tactics. These cases matter insofar as they show that the EU's approach might not always align with those of the key actors on the Korean Peninsula.

What should the EU do when its approach is at odds with that of China and/or the US? Taking a cue from its realist turn—more clearly exemplified by its Global Strategy and von der Leyen's call to "learn the language of power" —Brussels should not budge. Neither the US nor China will look after Europe's interests when dealing with North Korea. Consequently, the EU should not necessarily follow American and Chinese policy when it goes against its preferred approach. In practical terms, this means following a policy that will mix both cooperation with China and the US, plus South Korea, as well as, in some cases, divergence.

The EU should therefore take a pragmatic approach to the North Korea nuclear issue, using all policies at its disposal. It cannot afford to make symbolic gestures if it wants to be taken seriously as a security actor in Asia-Pacific affairs. Even more importantly, its own security interests are at stake when it comes to the denuclearisation of North Korea. In this sense, norms and values should be part of the EU's thinking about the North Korea nuclear conundrum but should not determine it. Liberal tools may be used but so should all components of the EU's power projection capabilities. Following from this realist logic, the EU should not align with China or the US. Thankfully, its position is very similar to Beijing's and Washington's when it comes to North Korea's denuclearisation. But full alignment is counterproductive for there have been, and will be, cases when thinking about tactics will differ.

In summary, the main policy recommendation for the EU is to continue to pursue its main goals by using a mix of tactics. When it comes to goals, Brussels' prioritisation of non-proliferation aligns with the focus of Beijing, Seoul and Washington on denuclearisation. As for tactics, there is a high degree of convergence with China, South Korea and, especially, the US. Nevertheless, there are bound to be differences in approaches with Beijing and Washington, for their interests in the Korean Peninsula and approaches to world politics will not always match. In these instances, the EU should focus on its own self-interest and not deviate from its goals and tactics. This consistency will enhance its role in Korean Peninsula affairs.

Notes

1 The UN Security Council Committee established pursuant to Resolution 1718 (2006), or the North Korea sanctions committee, has confirmed Pyongyang's proliferation activities. Alleged recipients of North Korea's nuclear exports and/or expertise include Egypt, Iran, Libya and Syria (Berger 2016).

2 Certainly, China also considers stability on the Korean Peninsula to be central to its foreign policy. However, both Hu Jintao's and Xi Jinping's administrations consider North Korea's nuclear weapons programme a threat to stability; hence, their prioritisation of denuclearisation. Likewise, South Korean leaders dealing with a nuclear North Korea consider inter-Korean reconciliation and, potentially, reunification as important—especially the liberal Moon Jae-in. But both conservative and liberal South Korean leaders consider North Korea's denuclearisation a pre-condition for full reconciliation (see Funabashi 2007; Hur 2018; Pacheco Pardo 2019).

3 Not being a central actor in the Korean Peninsula nuclear issue should not lead to buck-passing from the EU. To begin with, the EU's security is directly affected by North Korea's nuclear program, as explained in this chapter. Furthermore, the EU's Asia Security Strategy explicitly posits that the EU should become more involved in the region's security affairs; among other things, this enhances the EU's prestige—and therefore power—at the global level and in the region. In addition, three of the EU's strategic partners, China, South Korea and the US, are the key players in solving the North Korea nuclear issue; supporting their position *vis-à-vis* Pyongyang can help Brussels receive their support on other security matters. Finally, and from a theoretical point of view, buck-passing is not possible in cases of bipolarity because there is no third power to catch the buck (Mearsheimer 2001). This applies to bipolar East Asia, where the EU has no third power to pass the buck to.

4 For a list of UN Security Council sanctions on North Korea, see United Nations Security Council. 2020. *Resolutions*. www.un.org/securitycouncil/sanctions/1718/resolutions.

5 The US Treasury Department imposed sanctions on Macau-based Banco Delta Asia in September 2005, accusing it of facilitating North Korea's money laundering. The Bush administration also led UN sanctions imposed on North Korea following its July 2006 missile tests and September 2006 nuclear test. However, enforcement was weak. Bush administration officials have confirmed that the main policy towards North Korea was engagement through the Six-Party Talks (Funabashi 2007; Hur 2018; Pacheco Pardo 2019).

References

Aggarwal, Vinod K., and Simon J. Evenett. 2017. "The Transatlantic Trade and Investment Partnership: Limits on Negotiating Behind the Border Barriers." *Business and Politics* 19 (4): 549–572.

Berger, Andrea. 2016. *Target Markets. North Korea's Military Customers*. London: Routledge.

Bolton, John. 2007. *Surrender Is Not an Option: Defending America at the United Nations and Abroad*. New York: Simon & Schuster.

Borrell, Josep. 2019. "HighRepresentativeoftheUnionforForeignPolicyandSecurityPolicy/ Vice-President-designate of the European Commission." Brussels, September 10. https:// mediawijs.be/dossiers/dossier-mediawijs-beleid/2019-the-eu's-next-digital-agenda.

Borrell, Josep. 2020. "Embracing Europe's Power." *Project Syndicate*, February 8. www.project-syndicate.org/commentary/embracing-europe-s-power-by-josep-borrell-2020-02?barrier=accesspaylog.

Center for Strategic and International Studies (CSIS). 2020. "Missiles of North Korea." Missile Defense Project. https://missilethreat.csis.org/country/dprk/.

Cha, Victor D., and Katrin Katz. 2011. "South Korea in 2010: Navigating New Heights in the Alliance." *Asian Survey* 51 (1): 54–63.

Council of the European Union. 2003. *European Security Strategy: A Secure Europe in a Better World*. Brussels: Council of the European Union, December 12. www.consilium. europa.eu/media/30823/qc7809568enc.pdf.

Council of the European Union. 2008. *Report on the Implementation of the European Security Strategy*. Brussels: Council of the European Union, December 11. www.consilium. europa.eu/ueDocs/cms_Data/docs/pressdata/EN/reports/104630.pdf.

Council of the European Union. 2018. "Enhanced EU Security Cooperation in and with Asia—Council Conclusions." Brussels, May 28. https://data.consilium.europa.eu/doc/document/ST-9265-2018-INIT/en/pdf.

Council on Foreign Relations. 2020. "Trump's Foreign Policy Moments." www.cfr.org/timeline/trumps-foreign-policy-moments.

European Commission. 2016. "Joint Communication to the European Parliament and the Council." *Elements for a New EU Asia Strategy*. Brussels, June 22. http://eeas.europa.eu/archives/docs/china/docs/joint_communication_to_the_european_parliament_and_the_council_-_elements_for_a_new_eu_strategy_on_china.pdf.

European External Action Service. 2015. "EU-DPRK Political Dialogue—14th Session." June 25. https://eeas.europa.eu/headquarters/headquarters-homepage/6336/node/6336_ko.

European External Action Service. 2016. "DPRK and the EU." June 26. https://eeas.europa.eu/diplomatic-network/north-korea/4186/dprk-and-eu_en.

European Union. 2016. *Shared Vision, Common Action: A Stronger Europe. A Global Strategy for the European Union's Foreign and Security Policy*. Brussels: European Union, June. https://eeas.europa.eu/archives/docs/top_stories/pdf/eugs_review_web.pdf.

Europol. 2019. *Terrorism Situation and Trend Report 2019*. The Hague: European Union Agency for Law Enforcement Cooperation, June 27. www.europol.europa.eu/activities-services/main-reports/terrorism-situation-and-trend-report-2019-te-sat.

Ferreira-Pereira, Laura C., and Alena Vysotskaya Guedes Vieira. 2016. "Introduction: The European Union's Strategic Partnerships: Conceptual Approaches, Debates and Experiences." *Cambridge Review of International Affairs* 29 (1): 3–17.

Funabashi, Yoichi. 2007. *The Peninsula Question: A Chronicle of the Second Korean Nuclear Crisis*. Washington, DC: Brookings Institution Press.

House of Commons Debates (Hansard). 1848. "Treaty of Adrianople—Charges Against Viscount Palmerston." *HC Deb* 97, cc. 66–123, March 1.

Hur, Mi-Yeon. 2018. *The Six-Party Talks on North Korea: Dynamic Interactions Among Principal States*. Singapore: Palgrave Macmillan.

KEDO. 2020. "About Us: Our History." http://kedo.org/au_history.asp.

Kim, Min-hyung, and Jinwoo Choi. 2020. "What Kind of Power Is the EU? The EU's Policies Toward North Korea's WMD Programs and the Debate About the EU's Role in the Security Arena." *Asia Europe Journal* 18 (1): 1–16.

Lee, Moosung. 2016. "The EU, Regional Cooperation, and the North Korean Nuclear Crisis." *Asia Europe Journal* 14 (4): 401–415.

Lee, Moosung. 2017. "The EU and the Six-Party Talks." IAI Working Papers 17. www.iai.it/sites/default/files/iaiwp1709.pdf.

Logan, Samuel E. 2005. "The Proliferation Security Initiative: Navigating the Legal Challenges." *Journal of Transnational Law & Policy* 14 (2): 253–274.

Manners, Ian. 2002. "Normative Power Europe: A Contradiction in Terms?" *Journal of Common Market Studies* 40 (2): 235–258.

Mearsheimer, John J. 2001. *The Tragedy of Great Power Politics*. New York: W. W. Norton & Company.

Ministry of Foreign Affairs of the Republic of Korea. 2013. *Northeast Asia Peace and Cooperation Initiative: Moving Beyond the Asian Paradox Towards Peace and Cooperation in Northeast Asia*. Seoul: Ministry of Foreign Affairs of the Republic of Korea.

Ministry of Foreign Affairs of the Republic of Korea. 2017. *Northeast Asia Platform for Peace and Cooperation*. Seoul: Ministry of Foreign Affairs of the Republic of Korea.

Morgenthau, Hans J. 2006. *Politics Among Nations: The Struggle for Power and Peace*, 7th ed. New York: McGraw-Hill.

Pacheco Pardo, Ramon. 2018. *North Korea in Focus: Towards a More Effective EU Policy*. Brussels: Wilfried Martens Centre for European Studies, September 2018. https://martenscentre.eu/sites/default/files/publication-files/infocus_north-korea-v2.pdf.

Pacheco Pardo, Ramon. 2019. *North Korea-US Relations from Kim Jong Il to Kim Jong Un*, 2nd ed. London: Routledge.

U.S. Department of State. 2020. "About the Proliferation Security Initiative." Bureau of International Security and Nonproliferation, March 19. www.state.gov/about-the-proliferation-security-initiative/.

Von der Leyen, Ursula. 2019. "Europe Address—Dr. Ursula von der Leyen President-Elect of the European Commission—Allianz Forum (Pariser Platz), Berlin." European Commission, Speech, November 10.

Part III

Geo-economic issues and Europe's welfare

8 Europe's economic and technological relationship with the United States and China

A difficult balancing act

Margot Schüller

Introduction

A European Union (EU)-wide survey conducted in September 2019 revealed that 75 percent of interviewees were either concerned or very concerned about the impact of the United States (US)-China trade conflict on Europe; in Germany, more people (81 percent) than in any other of the EU Member States felt such alarm.[1] With both the US and China being the most important trading partners for the EU (see Table 8.1), the US' protectionist trade policy vis-à-vis China represents a strong threat to European businesses. The fear of a trade war associated with a breakdown of supply chains looms on the horizon: more than two-thirds of world trade occurs through global value chains in which China plays a crucial role as the "factory of the world" (WTO 2019). Against this background, the next section in this contribution analyses how the EU has responded to the many challenges associated with the US-China trade conflict. This requires a careful look at the US administration's trade policy measures introduced since 2018, which aim at redirecting trade policies towards ones favouring the US economy. While China has been singled out by the US government as the number one target for punitive tariffs, the EU too has also been threatened with higher tariffs on a number of its own export products. Therefore, both the EU and China could have coordinated their responses to the current US trade policy in order to put more weight behind their respective policy reactions. The question of whether and how they have cooperated will be discussed in the next part of this contribution as well.

The third section then studies another major battlefield within US-China competition and how Europe is caught in the crossfire. China's transition towards being a new science, technology and innovation superpower and its strong ambitions to become technologically independent and a leading country worldwide in cutting-edge science and technology (S&T) practice are challenging the US' traditional roles in these fields. While the two countries have cooperated on higher education and S&T for more than four decades now, current US restrictions have nevertheless increased and cover a broad range of areas. They relate to joint research projects in China and the US, visa regulations for Chinese scientists and students and access to US technologies. Recently, the US administration also extended the dispute to third countries' cooperation with Chinese information technology (IT) companies (Gold 2020).[2] The final section raises the question of the likely nature of the EU's future relationship with the US and China amidst the discussion of partial disengagement or decoupling on the US' part. Related to this, it is asked whether the EU should choose sides in the US-China conflict and furthermore, which strategy it should pursue in order to best balance its own relationship with the two superpowers. The major argument put forth by the chapter is that even though the EU has recently adopted a more critical view on China with regards to its economic model and political assertiveness, Europe is not prepared to take sides in US-China geopolitical rivalry. To balance the US and China, the EU needs, however, to become less dependent on both economies.

The US-China trade conflict: responses from the EU

The US' trade imbalance with China has been a topic of discussion for policy-makers and scholars in both countries for a long time now (Lau 2019; Moosa et al. 2020). After China joined the multilateral regulatory framework of the World Trade Organization (WTO) at the end of 2001, trade disputes between both sides were supposed to be handled through that body's dispute settlement mechanism (Adekola 2019). The shift of bilateral trade controversies to a multi-lateral institution based on internationally agreed rules and norms of behaviour for fixing trade conflicts was one of the main reasons why China applied for membership of the WTO in the first place. That the US government unilaterally started to impose tariffs on China, which are inconsistent with WTO regulations, and tried to solve the trade conflict outside of the institution is now undermin-ing the reputation and legitimacy of the latter. It prevents the solution of the trade conflict on the basis of a rules-based system that reflects supposedly core US values, such as non-discrimination, transparency and the rule of law, and impedes the application of the WTO's global set of trade rules as a baseline for judging whether China reneges on its related commitments (Meltzer and Shenai 2019, 16–17).

While the EU shares some of the concerns that the US has about China's mixed record on adherence to WTO rules, especially with regards to reciprocity and transparency, it follows a different strategy vis-à-vis China. Although the EU has adopted a more critical stance towards China in recent years, it still sees, how-ever, the country not only as its competitor but also as an important cooperation partner—and the WTO still as the appropriate forum in which to resolve trade conflicts (European Commission 2019). When the US imposed punitive tariffs on the EU's exports of steel and aluminium to that country, claiming security rea-sons, in March 2018 and afterwards threatened to extend these tariffs to the export of cars from the EU as well, the political climate worsened between the two sides (González and Véron 2019, 4). The EU addressed its concerns immediately to the WTO and claimed that the US had adopted safeguard measures that took the form of a tariff increase on these products. The EU argued that: "Notwithstanding the United States' characterisation of these measures as security measures, they are safeguard measures. The United States failed to notify the WTO Committee on

Safeguards under Article 12.1(c) on taking a decision to apply safeguard measures" (WTO 2018).

That the EU regards China as a partner in preserving the WTO and modernising it is reflected in the joint statement given at the EU-China Summit of April 2019:

> The EU and China firmly support the rules-based multilateral trading system with the WTO at its core, fight against unilateralism and protectionism, and commit to complying with WTO rules. The two sides reaffirm their joint commitment to co-operate on WTO reform to ensure its continued relevance and allow it to address global trade challenges.
>
> (EU-China Joint Statement 2019)

Two particular topics have taken priority in the newly established Joint EU-China Working Group on WTO Reform: the international rules for industrial subsidies and the resolving of the crisis in the WTO Appellate Body. The US has continued to block the nomination of new Appellate Body members, with the aim of forcing changes to the dispute settlement system. Since the middle of December 2019, the forum has had only one member left, and is thus unable to form the quorum necessary to hear disputes. As a result, a country that loses its case at the panel level of the dispute will be able to block the decisions by filing an appeal, and the case will languish (Packard 2020).

As announced during his election campaign in 2016, China has become the focus of Trump's "America First" policy. The former was blamed for the loss of millions of jobs in the US and for the increase in social insecurity there. In fact, the impact of China's competitive pressure on US manufacturing industries has been revealed in various studies of local voting patterns. In the states of Michigan, Pennsylvania and Wisconsin, for example, the Democrats would have gained the majority of votes if the growth of import competition from China had been only half as large (Autor et al. 2020; Schüler-Zhou and Schüller 2017). The election of a protectionist presidential candidate cannot, however, be judged a purely economic phenomenon, having also a cultural dimension to it (Noland 2019, 9–10).

In order to redirect trade policies in favour of the US economy, the Trump administration has resorted to a number of measures—including the renegotiation of existing trade agreements with a preference for bilateral rather than multilateral ones. The withdrawal from the Trans-Pacific Partnership agreement was the first policy decision taken by Trump, followed by the renegotiation of the free trade agreement with Mexico and Canada (NAFTA) as well as the one with Korea (KORUS). Understanding foreign trade as a "zero-sum game", US trade policy associates a negative trade balance with a certain country as proof that the respective trade partner employs unfair policies. Besides China, therefore, the EU and Japan too became targets of US punitive tariffs. Unlike previous administrations, the current one also stresses the need for trade policies serving national security. Following this view, the decision to increase tariffs on EU steel and aluminum exports to the US is in line with Section 232 of the US Trade Law (Mildner 2020).

Most of the tariff increases on Chinese products are related to US Trade Law Section 301.[3] Following an investigation of China's policy on technology transfers, intellectual property rights (IPR) and innovation under Section 301 in March 2018, the US Trade Representative (USTR) came to the conclusion that tariff increases were justified. Four IPR-related policies were found: "forced technology transfer requirements; cyber-enabled theft of U.S. IP and trade secrets; discriminatory and non-market licensing practices; and state-funded strategic acquisitions of U.S. assets" (CRS Report 2019, 19). Starting in July 2018, the Trump administration imposed 25-percent tariff increase on imports from China, with a total volume of US$250 billion on three tranches of imports up until January 2019. China reacted with increased tariffs on US products of around US$110 billion. With bilateral negotiations not achieving the desired goals, the US government announced an additional 10-percent tariff increase on the remaining imports from China starting 1 September 2019 (CRS Report 2019, 19–21).

The Chinese position on the US government's trade policy is summarised in a White Paper published by the State Council in June 2019. Although the Chinese government stressed that it was willing to further work with the US to find solutions to contested issues, it pointed at bottom lines for future consultations. It argued, for example, that the US side had turned a blind eye to the improvement of IPR protection in China and to the development of the international industrial division of labour. Pointing to the integration of both economies and industrial chains, the Chinese side rejects the US' accusation that it pursues "unfair" and "non-reciprocal" trade policies that create deficits (The State Council Information Office of the People's Republic of China 2019, 6–8).

Bilateral negotiations continued in the second half of 2019 and resulted in an economic and trade agreement signed into being in January 2020 (USTR 2020a). The so-called Phase One Agreement is described in the USTR fact sheet of the president's trade agenda as a great success, requiring China to make structural changes that relate to IPR protection, technology transfers, agricultural standards, financial services and currency; it maintains leverage, meanwhile, with tariffs on US$370 billion worth of imports from China. Another achievement stressed by the USTR is China's commitment to increase purchases of US exports by around US$200 billion within the next two years; the focus herein is on manufactured goods, agriculture, energy and services (USTR 2020b).

Although the bilateral economic and trade agreement has been presented by the Trump administration as a great success, the global spread of the COVID-19 pandemic and the associated economic depression in many countries including China could leave the deal "dead on arrival" (Alam 2020). Both sides have stated their commitment to it, but China's economic slowdown might call the promised increase of purchases of US products into question. While forecasting how the US-China trade conflict will develop in the near future seems to be difficult, a look back at past years' trade performance shows that not many of the Trump administration's goals vis-à-vis the "America First" policy have been achieved.

When the trade balance turned in favour of China for the first time since 1983, the country's share in total US trade in goods was, however, negligible

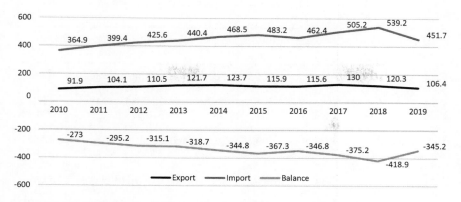

Figure 8.1 US trade in goods with China, 2000–2019 (in million US$)

Source: US Department of Commerce. Website: www.census.gov/foreign-trade/blance/c5700.html.

Notes: Figures are on a nominal base, not seasonally adjusted. Due to rounding, details may not equal totals.

(0.9 percent). With China's growing competitiveness—and especially after the country became a member of the WTO—the export surplus became a matter of great concern to the US government. By 2019, China's share in total US trade of goods had increased to 13.5 percent, and the US trade deficit therewith accounted for 40 percent (US$345 million) of the total US trade deficit.

US statistics reveal that despite the restrictive trade policies, the total deficit in trade of goods further went up to US$854 billion in 2019—an increase of 7.8 percent compared to 2017. While the deficit in trade with China declined by 8 percent, that with the EU grew by 18 percent (United States Census Bureau 2020a, 2020b, 2020c). With the Trump administration's focus on balanced trade, it can be expected that the EU will be the next target of USTR investigation. In the fact sheet about the president's 2020 Trade Agenda, the USTR already announced the extension of the "America First" trade agenda to the EU:

> For many years, U.S. businesses have been at a disadvantage in doing business in the EU. In a fair trade agreement with the European Union, the United States seeks to eliminate EU barriers to its markets and seeks a more balanced trade relationship.
>
> (2020b)

In the EU, there is strong concern about potential national security tariffs imposed on the automotive industry, a sector of great importance in many Member States. Similar to its response to the US' increased tariffs on aluminum and steel, the EU could again file a WTO case against the country and adopt "rebalancing measures" under the WTO safeguard process (González and Véron 2019, 17).

Table 8.1 Extra EU27 merchandise trade with largest trading partners in 2019 (excluding intra-EU trade)

Total trade with		EU imports from		EU exports to		EU trade balance with	
Country	million euro	Country	million euro	Country	million euro	Country	million euro
USA	616,386	China	361,855	USA	384,435	USA	152,484
China	560,146	USA	231,951	UK	318,099	UK	124,401
UK	511,798	UK	193,698	China	198,290	Switzerland	36,515
Switzerland	257,036	Russia	144,573	Switzerland	146,775	UAE	22,621
Russia	232,360	Switzerland	110,261	Russia	87,787	Australia	22,593
Turkey	138,065	Turkey	69,782	Turkey	68,283	Hong Kong	19,706
Japan	123,983	Japan	62,849	Japan	61,134	Canada	17,603
Norway	105,578	Norway	53,984	Norway	51,594	Mexico	13,327
S. Korea	90,685	S. Korea	47,352	S. Korea	43,334	Singapore	11,125
India	77,782	India	39,547	Canada	38,324	Egypt	19,756

Source: EU Commission. Directorate General for Trade. https://trade.ec.europa.eu/doclib/docs/2006/september/tradoc_122530.pdf.

Against this background, the EU has a keen interest in strengthening the multilateral trading system and in bringing together a broad coalition to implement WTO reforms. Conversely, the US-China economic and trade agreement does not seem to represent a challenge to the EU. On the contrary, the EU has a chance to freeride on topics of key interest to its companies, such as IPR protection and the avoidance of compulsory technology transfers.

The protectionist and aggressive US trade policy has, however, not only been criticised by its partner countries but also increasingly within the US itself. That this policy is working to the disadvantage of domestic companies is stressed by the US Chamber of Commerce (2020). On its website, the Chamber requests its members to send an appeal about the current trade policy to Congress. Under the heading "Trade works. Tariffs don't", it points to the implications of the global trade war that the government has started:

> Trade actions by the Trump administration threaten as many as 2.6 million American jobs and will stymie our economic progress. Tariffs on imported goods are hitting American consumers and businesses—including manufacturers, farmers, ranchers, and technology companies—with higher costs on commonly used products and materials.
>
> (US Chamber of Commerce 2020)

The EU's position amid US-China competition for global technological leadership

China has clearly benefited from globalisation. The relocation of labour-intensive production there from EU Member States and the US since the 1990s is associated with a transfer of both implicit and explicit knowledge. While foreign companies accepted the transfer of technology in exchange for having access to the huge Chinese market in the beginning, the rapid improvement of Chinese companies' competitiveness would change their stance with regards to the compulsory request for technology transfers—especially after China's accession to the WTO. Although membership thereof committed the Chinese government to restricting this practice, foreign companies have frequently continued to complain about its occurrence even in recent years.

The rise of Chinese companies in the global value chains of manufactured goods was strongly supported by ambitious industrial and science policies, which usually overlap. While the country would gradually emerge as a leading player in S&T (Suttmeier 2020), the development of high-tech products and processes still lagged behind the level found in the US—on whom China remained dependent for key technical components, such as semiconductors. Against this background, the Chinese political leadership started to steer the country's economic model in a new direction, with the aim of achieving innovation-driven growth and a technological upgrade of its industry. Although the industrial modernisation programme presented by the government in 2015, the "Made in China 2025" (MIC) plan, was basically an extension of already-existing industrial policies (Schüller 2015), it still startled governments and companies worldwide—especially in the US.

In 2017 the US Chamber of Commerce published a report on the MIC plan, analysing its basic goals and instruments—as well as implications for the US. The Chamber interpreted the plan as an industrial policy that aims at transforming China into a global manufacturing leader. With its focus on ten strategic industries, including next-generation IT, aviation, rail, new energy vehicles and agricultural machinery, the Chamber saw the plan as being very ambitious but not compatible with US policies because of its state-led approach, the central role of state planning and guidance and heavy state subsidies for the support of strategic industries: "Plans like MIC and their implementation are putting the two economies on a path of separation rather than integration in critical commercial areas" (US Chamber of Commerce 2017).

Following Segal (2018), China's intention via MIC is not so much to join the ranks of high-tech economies but rather to replace them altogether, as the plan strives to achieve self-sufficiency through technology substitution and to support the rise of China as a manufacturing superpower that dominates global markets. When the Trump administration imposed increased tariffs of US$60 billion based on the Section 301 investigation of 2018, the MIC plan was cited as a proof that China pursues unfair trade practices and that tariffs were thus justified. That the plan represents a great challenge to the US economy and requires an appropriate policy response is the message of the report titled "Made in China 2025 and the Future of American Industry". Presented in September 2019 by the chairman of the Senate Committee on Small Business and Entrepreneurship, Senator Marco Rubio, it invites the Senate to understand the MIC plan as a wake-up call for American political economy and demands the increase of high-value, high-labour production in the US (Rubio 2019).

In sum, such competition over technological leadership seems to be even more important than the US-China trade conflict. In order to contain China's technological rise, perceived as a threat to its national economy and security, the US government employs four different approaches (Segal 2019a). First, a 25 percent tariff increase is imposed on those Chinese products supported by the MIC policy; the focus is on 1,300 industrial technological, transport and medical ones. Second, Chinese investment in US technology sectors is restricted by revised export control laws. The new Export Control Reform Act (ECRA) was introduced in 2018 to prevent China from obtaining technologies suspected of being later used for military purposes (Lazarou and Lokker 2019). From the list of 14 emerging technologies, the initial focus will be on artificial intelligence (AI), quantum computing and 3D printing (Barkin 2020). Another control mechanism is the Entity List, an export blacklist. Moreover, reviews of the investment application procedure conducted by the Committee on Foreign Investment in the US (CFIUS) have become stricter; such investment now has to follow additional security criteria, too. Third, the US government is imposing restrictions on Chinese information technology (IT) companies, especially Huawei, ZTE and China Mobile, regarding doing business in the US; these companies are excluded from selling network equipment or telecommunication services to federal agencies, for example. US government officials have also put pressure on countries outside the US not to use Huawei for 5G infrastructure, including ones in the EU. Fourth, tightening the prosecution of Chinese companies for intellectual property theft. Taking these restrictions on access to US technology together, from the Chinese perspective, even more emphasis now has to be put on indigenous innovation in key technologies in order to become technologically independent from the US (Sun 2019, 201–204).

During the year 2019, the "tech Cold War" between the US and China further unfolded—with the Trump administration placing Huawei and 68 of its affiliates on a blacklist of companies to which US firms are not allowed to sell technologies without official approval, especially advanced semiconductors and software. Some large US companies such as Google and Micron have reacted to these restrictions and consequently suspended their business dealings with Huawei. In October 2019, an additional 28 Chinese companies—this time from the AI sector—were added to the blacklist, among them SenseTime, Megvii, Yitu and iFlytek. China's response to the latest restrictions keeping its IT companies out of government networks in the US is very similar to the latter's policy: namely, all government offices and public institutions in China being required to remove foreign computer equipment and software within three years (Segal 2019b).

Although policies that restrict China's access to US technology might demonstrate some success in the short term, there are doubts about whether they can hold back the country's technological progress in the long run. Suttmeier, for example, expects that "pressures from the United States could stimulate renewed efforts in China to build more independent systems for research and innovation" (2020, 59). With regards to the rapid development of S&T over the last few decades, he is, however, quite optimistic that China will be able to manage should a prolonged technology war ensue: "US policies can impose costs on China in the short run, but the trajectory of Chinese development over the past several decades strongly suggests that China has the financial, human, and institutional resources to manage the costs over the longer run" (ibid., 63).

Europe's strong S&T ties with both the US and China see its companies and scholars caught in the crossfire of this tech Cold War. The overall policy climate with regards to S&T cooperation with China has not, however, changed in the EU to the same extent as it has in the US. In view of China's increased weight in the international economy and the associated impact on the system of global governance, the European Commission (EC) has nevertheless adapted its policy towards China in recent years. The communication of the EC to the Council in March 2019, "EU-China—A Strategic Outlook", reflects this change, stressing that "there is a growing appreciation in Europe that the balance of challenges and opportunities presented by China has shifted" (EC 2019). It continued by remarking that the EU needs to take a fair, balanced and mutually beneficial course moving forwards.

In its new approach on China, the EU not only views the country as an important cooperation partner but at the same time also as "an economic competitor in the pursuit of technological leadership, and a systemic rival promoting alternative models of governance" (EC 2019). Three objectives regarding the relationship with China were proposed: first, closer engagement in order to foster common interests at the international level (including support for multilateralism, sustainable development and climate change mitigation); second, more balanced and reciprocal conditions within the two sides' economic relationship; and, third, changes within the EU itself so as to make the Union more globally competitive (Schüller 2020). On the level of individual European countries, reactions to the US-China trade conflict have varied markedly (Esteban et al. 2020)—as has their reactions regarding S&T cooperation with China. The largest countries, though—especially France, Germany and the United Kingdom (UK)—closely cooperate with China both on higher education and S&T (Kroll et al. 2020).

The situation for European companies doing business with China is becoming increasingly difficult with the unfolding of the US-China trade conflict and tech war. European business associations such as the European Chamber of Commerce have already closely studied the negative impact of this trade conflict on European companies. They are also very concerned about the collateral damage caused by a potential tech war. In October of last year, the Chamber (2019) conducted a survey among its member companies working in China. It showed that about one in four respondents who import goods from the US were affected by the tariffs and associated changes in prices. Out of this group, 44 percent changed suppliers and others redirected their global production away from the US-China "border". Among the companies exporting goods to the US, meanwhile, about 25 percent were hit by the punitive tariffs. With a US-China tech war looming on the horizon, the president of the European Chamber of Commerce, Jörg Wuttke, has stressed the impending challenges for European companies doing business with China. Taking the new controls imposed on Huawei as an example, Wuttke believes that all global chipmakers that supply the company are under threat, as they all depend on US tools equipment.

The future of the EU's Relations with the US and China

China's emergence as a global power is challenging US supremacy in many ways, especially because of its different political system and the central role of the state in the economy. While their bilateral trade and investment relationship has seen its ups and downs over the years, it is under the Trump administration that the US' relations with China have shifted from engagement to confrontation (European Parliament 2020). Other countries are increasingly being drawn into this competition, with the US government putting pressure on allies to choose sides. Some recently published contributions by the "Taskforce on Transforming the Economic Dimension of the U.S. China Strategy" reflect the ongoing discussion about partial disengagement from China as a new approach for increasing economic competitiveness with that country.

The final report for this taskforce from Boustany and Friedberg (2019) reveals the extent to which economic nationalism and political goals overlap. The authors reiterate their suggestion to cooperate more closely with like-minded nations "to develop a common negotiating position towards China". Under the heading of "Self-strengthening", they suggest intensifying "defensive measures to protect against Chinese penetration and exploitation of the U.S. economy and the economies of other advanced industrial democracies". Four scenarios for the development of bilateral relations between the US and China are discussed by the authors. There are two extreme ones, namely the "free trade" and the "Cold War/Containment" scenarios: 1) China liberalises its economy, resulting in a convergence of interests between the US and China. Although the "free trade" scenario is the preferred outcome, the authors doubt whether it can be achieved with the Chinese Communist Party in power. Alternatively: 2) disengagement, with trade and investment flows restricted. The other two more moderate scenarios are: 3) "status quo", characterised by the openness of the US economy and China being partially closed, and 4) "partial disengagement"—with both countries' economy partially closed.

The idea of disengagement or decoupling from China has so far not received much support in Europe. In contrast, EC High Representative/Vice-President Josep Borrell underlined the importance of China and cooperation with this country at the press conference following the EU-China High Level Strategic Dialogue: "China is without doubt one of the key global players. This is a fact, and China will increase its global role. We have to engage with China to achieve our global objectives, based on our interests and values" (Borrell 2020). That Europe needs an independent strategy towards China is one of the key messages in the research report "EU-China Trade and Investment Relations in Challenging Times", a study requested by the European Parliament (2020). With reference to the EC communication of March 2019 in which the Commission defined China as a systemic rival, the study emphasises that "the EU needs to reassess its longer-term strategy of engagement with China. Systemic rivalry is, of course, one option but cannot be the only one. China is too big a partner for the EU, and systemic rivalry as a starting point can easily lead to deteriorating relations and even outright confrontation. As China's importance is likely to grow, the EU will need to define a nuanced approach to China, setting out conditions for a fruitful co-existence with China while also strengthening instruments to defend EU interests and EU values" (European Parliament 2020, 69).

In their own study on strategic rivalry between the US and China, Lippert and Perthes (2020) note that rivalry has become a dominant paradigm in international relations again over the past two years. This new outlook determines not only strategic debates but also real-world political, military and economic dynamics. The authors also see Sino-American global competition over power and status as being shaped by growing threat perceptions and an increasingly important political/ideological component on both sides. Lippert and Perthes strongly recommend that "Europe needs to escape the bipolar logic that demands it choose between the American and Chinese economic/technological spheres" (2020, 2). For the EU, it will be important to design its own China policy.

That European policymakers and companies do not fully share the US approach to China is also highlighted in the discussion about export controls and the inclusion of Chinese 5G technologies. In his study on export controls and the US-China tech war, Barkin notices what he calls a "healthy scepticism in European capitals about Washington's use of offensive economic tools, such as export controls, to counter China" (2020, 5). Critics of the US approach see export controls as an inadequate policy in a world of global supply chains and assume that the US' motivation in employing such measures is predominantly based on the idea of containing China's technology development.

To summarise, many European policymakers and business associations understand that the US-China trade conflict is first of all a political one over power and spheres of influence, including the field of technology. The EU has become more critical towards China's economic model, including with regards to the lack of reciprocity for European investors and its "divide-and-rule approach" in the Belt and Road Initiative vis-à-vis the Central and Eastern European countries. In contrast to the current US administration, however, China is not only seen as a competitor but as a cooperation partner. With the EU being dependent on global rules-based institutions, and especially on the WTO, the inclusion of China in the process of reforming it is of the utmost importance.

What are the policy implications for Europe amidst the US-China conflict? Starting from a position of strength as one of the world's largest markets, the EU should rely more on its counterbalancing power within multilateral organisations—especially the WTO. The overall goal should be reform of the WTO together with like-minded countries, focusing for example on the dispute settlement system, the role of state-owned enterprises, industrial subsidies and digital trade. Due to its dependence on trade with both the US and China, the EU cannot and should not choose sides, but rather intensify collaboration on reform issues with other important trading nations such as Japan.

Being one of the most important locations for research and innovation, and due to the inclusion of many countries in its huge research programmes such as Horizon 2020, the EU should use its role as a "rule-maker" to influence global governance regarding S&T. In this context, the most important goal for the EU should be preserving the openness of the international research and innovation system. Without China, global challenges such as climate change, health or the depletion of natural resources cannot be tackled.

While the digital transformation of industry and society in European countries is ongoing and will be supported by the EU's long-term budget 2021–2027, short-term answers to the positioning of Europe amidst the US-China tech war still need to be found. Depending on global information and communications technology (ICT) supply chains, the EU needs to design an overall regulatory framework of how to assess that suppliers do indeed guarantee data privacy and overall network security (Rühlig et al. 2019).

In sum, Europe should not take sides in the US-China geopolitical rivalry. By overcoming its own economic, technological and political weaknesses, the EU should start to act as a global power in its own right.

Notes

1　Conducted by the Bertelsmann Stiftung (2020), this survey included 12,263 people from 28 EU Member States.
2　See the decision of the United Kingdom (UK) government to ban Huawei from involvement in the country's 5G networks (Gold 2020).
3　Schneider-Petsinger et al. (2019, 6) point to four primary concerns laid down in the USTR's Section 301 report: foreign ownership restrictions; regime of technology regulations; cyber theft; and outbound investments.

References

Adekola, Tolulope Anthony. 2019. "US—China Trade War and the WTO Dispute Settlement Mechanism." *Journal of International Trade Law and Policy* 18 (3): 125–135.

Alam, Mayaz. 2020. "Where the US-China Trade War Should Go from Here: More Tariffs Cannot Be the Answer Amid the Pandemic." *The Diplomat*, July 6. https://thediplomat.com/2020/07/where-the-us-china-trade-war-should-go-from-here/.

Autor, David H., David Dorny, Gordon H. Hanson, and Kaveh Majlesi. 2020. "Importing Political Polarization? The Electoral Consequences of Rising Trade Exposure." May 2020. www.ddorn.net/papers/ADHM-PoliticalPolarization.pdf.

Barkin, Noah. 2020. "Export Controls and the US-China Tech War: Policy Challenges for Europe." *Merics China Monitor*, March 18. https://merics.org/de/studie/exportkontrollen-und-der-us-chinesische-technologiekrieg.

Bertelsmann Stiftung. 2020. "Survey: Europe's View of China and the US-China Conflict." January 2020. www.bertelsmann-stiftung.de/fileadmin/files/BSt/Publikationen/GrauePublikationen/eupinions_China_DA_EN.pdf.

Borrell, Josep. 2020. "EU-China Strategic Dialogue: Remarks by High Representative/Vice-President Josep Borrell at the Press Conference." *European External Action*, June 9. https://eeas.europa.eu/headquarters/headquarters-homepage/80639/eu-china-strategic-dialogue-remarks-high-representativevice-president-josep-borrell-press_en.

Boustany, Charles W., and Aaron L. Friedberg. 2019. "Partial Disengagement. A New U.S. Strategy for Economic Competition with China." The National Bureau of Asian Research, BNR Special Report 82, November 4. www.nbr.org/publication/partial-disengagement-a-new-u-s-strategy-for-economic-competition-with-china/.

CRS (Congressional Research Service). 2019. "U.S.—China Relations." CRS Report, September 3. https://crsreports.congress.gov/product/pdf/R/R45898.

Esteban, Mario, Miguel Otero-Iglesias, Una Aleksandra Bērziņa-Čerenkova, Alice Ekman, Lucrezia Poggetti, Björn Jerdén, John Seaman, Tim Summers, and Justyna Szczudlik, eds. 2020. "Europe in the Face of US-China Rivalry." European Think-Tank Network on China Report, January. www.ifri.org/en/publications/publications-ifri/europe-face-us-china-rivalry.

EU-China Summit Joint Statement. 2019. Brussels, April 9. www.consilium.europa.eu/media/39020/euchina-joint-statement-9april2019.pdf.

European Chamber of Commerce. 2019. "European Chamber Survey on the US-China Trade War Finds More Companies Making Difficult Strategic Changes to Adapt to the Indefinite Nature of the Tensions." https://static.europeanchamber.com.cn/upload/medianews/attachments/September_Trade_War_Survey_Results_and_Findings_Final_1.1[24].pdf.

European Commission. 2019. "EU-China—A Strategic Outlook." European Commission and HR/VP Contribution to the European Council, March 12. https://ec.europa.eu/commission/sites/beta-political/files/communication-eu-china-a-strategic-outlook.pdf.

European Commission Directorate General for Trade. 2020. "Client and Supplier Countries of the EU 27 in Merchandise Trade (Value %), 2019, Excluding Intra-EU Trade."https://trade.ec.europa.eu/doclib/docs/2006/september/tradoc_122530.pdf.

European Parliament. 2020. "EU-China Trade and Investment Relations in Challenging Times." Policy Department for External Relations Directorate General for External Policies of the Union, Study requested by the INTA Committee, May. www.europarl.europa.eu/RegData/etudes/STUD/2020/603492/EXPO_STU(2020)603492_EN.pdf.

Gold, Hadas. 2020. "UK Bans Huawei from Its 5G Network in Rapid About-face." *CNN Business*, July 14. https://edition.cnn.com/2020/07/14/tech/huawei-uk-ban/index.html.

González, Anabel, and Nicolas Véron. 2019. "EU Trade Policy Amid the China-US Clash: Caught in the Cross-Fire?" Bruegel Working Paper 7, September 16. www.bruegel.org/wp-content/uploads/2019/09/WP-2019-07.pdf.

Kroll, Henning, Markus Conlé, Julia Hillmann, Peter Neuhäusler, Margot Schüller, and Iris Wieczorek. 2020. "Monitoring des Asiatisch-Pazifischen Forschungsraums (APRA)." *Kooperation International*. https://www.kooperation-international.de/fileadmin/user_upload/apra_2020.pdf.

Lau, Lawrence J. 2019. *The China-U.S. Trade War and Future Economic Relations.* Hong Kong: Chinese University Press.

Lazarou, Elena, and Nicholas Lokker. 2019. "United States: Export Control Reform Act (ECRA): European Parliamentary Research Service." www.europarl.europa.eu/RegData/etudes/BRIE/2019/644187/EPRS_BRI(2019)644187_EN.pdf.

Lippert, Barbara, and Volker Perthes, eds. 2020. "Strategic Rivalry Between United States and China: Causes, Trajectories, and Implications for Europe." SWP Research Paper, April. https://doi.org/10.18449/2020RP04.

Meltzer, Joshua P., and Neena Shenai. 2019. "The US-China Economic Relationship: A Comprehensive Approach." Global Economy and Development at Brookings/ American Enterprise Institute, February. www.brookings.edu/wp-content/uploads/2019/02/us_china_economic_relationship.pdf.

Mildner, Stormy-Annika. 2020. "'America First'—U.S. Trade Policy Under President Donald Trump." *BDI: The Voice of German Industry*, March 11. https://english.bdi.eu/article/news/america-first-u-s-trade-policy-under-president-donald-trump/.

Moosa, Nisreen, Vikash Ramiah, Huy Pham, and Alastair Watson. 2020. "The Origin of the US-China Trade War." *Applied Economics* 52 (35): 3842–3857.

Noland, Marcus. 2019. *Protectionism under Trump: The China Shock, Intolerance, and the 'First White President'.* Washington, DC: Peterson Institute for International Economics, Working Paper, June. www.piie.com/publications/working-papers/protectionism-under-trump-china-shock-intolerance-and-first-white.

Packard, Clark. 2020. "Trump's Real Trade War Is Being Waged on the WTO." *Foreign Policy*, January 9. https://foreignpolicy.com/2020/ 01/09/trumps-real-trade-war-is-b.

Rubio, Marco. 2019. "Made in China 2025 and the Future of American Industry." *Medium*, September 17. https://medium.com/@SenatorMarcoRubio/made-in-china-2025-and-the-future-of-american-industry-c7532c35168c.

Rühlig, Tim, John Seaman, and Daniel Voelsen. 2019. "5G and the US-China Tech Rivalry—A Test for Europe's Future in the Digital Age: How Can Europe Shift from Back Foot to Front Foot? SWP Comment." June 29. www.swp-berlin.org/fileadmin/contents/products/comments/2019C29_job_EtAl.pdf.

Schneider-Petsinger, Marianne, Jue Wang, Yu Jie, and James Crabtree. 2019. "US-China Strategic Competition: The Quest for Global Technological Leadership." Chathamhouse Research Paper, November. www.chathamhouse.org/sites/default/files/publications/research/CHHJ7480-US-China-Competition-RP-WEB.pdf.

Schüler-Zhou, Yun, and Margot Schüller. 2017. "Trumps Shadow Over US-China Economic Relations." *GIGA Focus Asia* 4, June. www.giga-hamburg.de/en/publication/trumps-shadow-over-us-china-economic-relations.

Schüller, Margot. 2015. "Chinas Industriepolitik: auf dem Weg zu einem neuen Erfolgsmodell?" *WSI-Mitteilungen* 7: 542–549. www.wsi.de/data/wsimit_2015_07_schueller.pdf.

Schüller, Margot. 2020. "The Belt and Road Initiative's (BRI) Impact on the Economic Policy of the European Union: A Preliminary Assessment." Forthcoming. https://www.tandfonline.com/doi/full/10.1080/16081625.2020.1686841.

Segal, Adam. 2018. "Made in China 2025: Why Does Everyone Hate It?" *Global Trade*, August 6. www.globaltrademag.com/made-in-china-2025-why-does-everyone-hate-it/.

Segal, Adam. 2019a. "Seizing Core Technologies: China Responds to U.S. Technology Competition." *China Leadership Monitor.* https://3c8314d6-0996-4a21-9f8a-a63a59b09269.filesusr.com/ugd/10535f_4b07cc3458014c47a03b3f23cae5fde1.pdf.

Segal, Adam. 2019b. *Year in Review 2019: The U.S.-China Tech Cold War Deepens and Expands*. Londres: European Council on Foreign Relations, Blog Post, December 18. www.cfr.org/blog/year-review-2019-us-china-tech-cold-war-deepens-and-expands.

The State Council Information Office of the People's Republic of China. 2019. "China's Position on the China-US Economic and Trade Consultation." http://images.mofcom.gov.cn/fj2/201906/20190606114029957.pdf.

Sun, Haiyong. 2019. "U.S.-China Tech War. Impacts and Prospects." *China Quarterly of International Strategic Studies* 5 (2): 197–212. www.worldscientific.com/doi/pdf/10.1142/S237774001950012X.

Suttmeier, Richard P. 2020. "Chinese Science Policy at a Crossroads." *Issues in Science and Technology* 2: 58–62, Winter.

United States Census Bureau. 2020a. "Trade in Goods with the European Union." www.census.gov/foreign-trade/balance/c0003.html.

United States Census Bureau. 2020b. "Trade in Goods with China." www.census.gov/foreign-trade/balance/c5700.html.

United States Census Bureau. 2020c. "Trade in Goods with World, Seasonally Adjusted." www.census.gov/foreign-trade/balance/c0004.html.

United States Trade Representative (USTR). 2020a. "Economic and Trade Agreement Between the Government of the United States of America and the Government of the People's Republic of China." https://ustr.gov/sites/default/files/files/agreements/phase%20one%20agreement/Economic_And_Trade_Agreement_Between_The_United_States_And_China_Text.pdf.

United States Trade Representative (USTR). 2020b. "Fact Sheet: The President's 2020 Trade Agenda and Annual Report." https://ustr.gov/about-us/policy-offices/press-office/fact-sheets/2020/february/fact-sheet-presidents-2020-trade-agenda-and-annual-report.

US Chamber of Commerce. 2017. "Made in China 2025: Global Ambitions Built on Local Protections." www.uschamber.com/report/made-china-2025-global-ambitions-built-local-protections-0.

US Chamber of Commerce. 2020. "Trade Works. Tariffs Don't." https://www.uschamber.com/tariffs.

World Trade Organization (WTO). 2019. "Technological Innovation, Supply Chain Trade, and Workers in a Globalized World." *Global Value Chain Development Report 2019.* www.wto.org/english/res_e/booksp_e/gvc_dev_report_2019_e.pdf.

WTO Council for Trade in Goods. Committee on Safeguards. 2018. "Immediate Notification Under Article 12.5 of the Agreement on Safeguards. . . ." https://docs.wto.org/dol2fe/Pages/FE_Search/FE_S_S006.aspx?DataSource=Cat&query=@Symbol=%22G/L/1240%22%20OR%20@Symbol=%22G/L/1240/*%22&Language=English&Context=ScriptedSearches&languageUIChanged=true.

9 European and American approaches towards Chinese foreign direct investment in post-COVID times

Opportunities, challenges and policy responses

Philippe Le Corre

Introduction

Over the past decade, China has affirmed its position as one of the world's largest economic powerhouses and, more significantly, as a key global investor. Since 2005, by some accounts (American Enterprise Institute and The Heritage Foundation 2005–2020), it has invested nearly €2trillion abroad. Three decades ago, the Chinese government began encouraging an investment drive focused on national resources, justifying the deployment of capital in Africa and Latin America. Most recently, Beijing has encouraged a more active presence for its companies in Western countries. While America has always been attractive to Chinese investors, the European continent began to shine in the eyes of the Chinese leadership during the 2008 Global Financial Crisis (GFC), with many opportunities arising in large and smaller countries. Foreign direct investment (FDI) is now viewed by Beijing as both a means of securing international influence geopolitically and advancing China's own economic development. Europe[1] and the United States (US) have been key destinations of Chinese capital, receiving respectively €43 billion and €41 billion in the peak year of 2016. Due to factors explained below, numbers have since decreased dramatically (Baker McKenzie 2020).

Beijing seems to be reconsidering how it should conduct its business abroad, contrasting with the unbounded spending that had catapulted China to its leading investor status in the years 2015–2017. There are various reasons for such a shift in the environment. A combination of increased scrutiny from FDI recipient countries and domestic concerns about the high levels of capital outflows are causing a new moderation in Chinese overseas investment since 2018. While it is too early to predict the long-term macroeconomic consequences of the damaging COVID-19 pandemic, continuing tensions with the US and the economic repercussions of the US-China trade war have already cast Beijing's international FDI strategy in doubt.

The case of an emerging market which invests considerably in advanced economies is in itself rare and is especially remarkable in the context of the economic and geopolitical challenges that China poses to both Europe and the US. This chapter describes the phenomenon of Chinese FDI on both sides of the Atlantic, looking at specific concerns that the European Union (EU) and the US may particularly have when dealing with the "China challenge". Chinese overseas investment raises important questions for Europe and the US, particularly with regards to balancing their traditional openness and the economic benefits of foreign capital with the security risks of welcoming Chinese money. The longstanding belief that China would liberalise as it integrates into the existing rules-based global economic order is wearing off, so Europe and the US are left to reconsider how to manage the inflow of investments from their "strategic competitor".

The chapter is organised thus. Part 1 is an overview of the challenges presented by Chinese FDI in the US and Europe. Part 2 examines the responses from both sides. Part 3 identifies some common ground between European countries, looks at commonalities and discrepancies between the US and Europe and analyses areas where they could engage in dialogue and possibly deeper cooperation. Finally, in light of China's aspiring global role, it will conclude with the long-term possibilities in a post-COVID-19 world and recommend that Europeans regroup under a joint legal framework and common values.

Dealing with Chinese outbound FDI: challenges for the US and Europe

Beijing's "going global" strategy, originally designed by the government of Prime Minister Zhu Rongji in the 1990s, has had one primary goal: to encourage the international expansion of Chinese companies and increase technology transfer from Western countries to China (Le Corre and Sepulchre 2016). Until 2009, Chinese enterprises believed that European markets were too complex and over-regulated. Many of them could not adjust their business practices to meet European standards and habits. In the US, the growth of the Chinese diaspora in the early part of the 21st century led to more Chinese businessmen, scientists and students settling there. Chinese private companies began investing in New York and California but also in several industrial states such as Washington, Texas and Iowa. Projects multiplied around 2012,[2] with several high-profile acquisitions by Chinese firms of Canadian energy (CNOOC-Nexen) and US food producing (Shuanghui-Smithfield) firms (Dollar 2015). These transactions have gone through the Committee on Foreign Investment in the US (CFIUS) process[3] and been approved. In 2015, as Beijing launched its Made in China 2025 (MIC 2025) policy, China's presence in the American high-tech industry increased. Many of China's relatively small-sized investments did not register on the CFIUS radar. They involved early-seed funding of tech firms in Silicon Valley and low-profile purchases, such as in the Delaware bankruptcy court. They included joint ventures with microchip manufacturers and research and development centres created with international partners (Bennet and Bender 2018).

China has tailored its policies to the different political and economic contexts prevailing in the two regions. In the case of Europe, its approach towards "large countries" such as Germany, France and the UK (all of which have had special ties to the People's Republic of China since the 1970s) differs greatly from that of smaller Southern and Eastern European states. Deals with the latter are increasingly geared towards consolidating China's status as an economic superpower and earning foreign validation for its global projects. The group formerly known as 16 + 1, and which now includes Greece, is seen by local experts as a tool of Chinese influence and support for the Belt and Road Initiative (BRI, or "One Belt, One Road" in Chinese (Turcsányi 2020). The BRI was originally launched by President Xi Jinping in the fall of 2013 with the aim of creating new links between China and Europe, well-served in Beijing's eyes by its 500-million strong consumer market. The original concept was to build a network of regional infrastructure projects, encompassing road and rail routes as well as oil and gas pipelines and facilities. The scope of the BRI has continued to expand over the past few years, and the initiative has become part of the Chinese "going abroad" narrative. Although the geographical coverage of the BRI has repeatedly expanded, the outreach to Europe has been a long-lasting trend. In fact, several projects that were originally not BRI-related have become prime examples of "success stories" which China wants to project to European public opinion. These include the Piraeus harbor of Athens and plans around Italian ports such as Genova and Trieste following the signing of an Italy-China memorandum of understanding (MOU) during Xi's state visit there in April 2019.[4]

A surge of Chinese FDI into Europe and the US in the mid-2010s has sparked security and economic competition concerns on both sides of the Atlantic. The US saw a higher volume of primarily private Chinese investments beginning a decade ago, but Europe received an almost equal amount of investment: in 2016, Europe attracted €41 billion of Chinese investment while the US attracted €43 billion (Baker McKenzie 2017). This investment included mergers and acquisitions (M&A), greenfield investments and construction projects across the board. Although the past couple of years have seen a significant decline in both the US and Europe, due to fewer large transactions by state-owned enterprises and a refocus on BRI-related projects, China's rise as a financial power will continue.

In the US, Chinese investment has been driven more by private commercial incentives and, crucially, by the acquisition of advanced technologies firms and their intellectual property. Meanwhile, according to the American Enterprise Institute (AEI), the stock of Chinese FDI in the US (excluding bonds) has amounted to US$180 billion since 2005 and is spread across the country and sectors (Hanemann et al. 2019a). It includes almost every single US state in the fields of technology, chemicals, telecommunications, textile, health, entertainment, transport and real estate.

The two blocs have reacted in different ways. The US responded much earlier to China's surge in FDI on its soil, perceiving China as a geopolitical challenger from early on. For years, Washington politicians have confronted China, either for its effect on the US economy and job losses (Democrats) or regarding strategic competition in the Asia-Pacific (Republicans). This attitude limited, in part, the scope for Beijing to deploy an economic "charm offensive". Nevertheless, a number of US states, such as Texas, California, Washington, Virginia and Iowa, have attracted a fair amount of Chinese capital (Rhodium Group n.d.), pushing state governors and city mayors into the hands of opportunistic Chinese investors, while American multinationals increased their presence in China from the 1990s onwards. Thus, from 2017, China has experienced difficulties with its image in America. Since the election of Donald Trump as US President, both sides of the political spectrum have been highly critical of China, leading to a generally negative public perception (O'Keeffe and Hughes 2018), both of China and Chinese FDI (Zeng and Li 2019).

European countries have had significantly different experiences dealing with Chinese FDI. Besides individual cases, ranging from the Piraeus Port Authority (Cosco) in Greece to PSA Peugeot-Citroën in France (Dongfeng), Italian tire manufacturer Pirelli (ChinaChem) or Sweden's Volvo (Geely), the real transformation came right after the 2008 GFC, when Beijing started buying Eurobonds and investing massively in state assets to bail out several European countries such as Portugal, Italy and Greece. This led three large European countries (France, Germany and Italy) to suggest a new investment screening mechanism to the European Commission in early 2017. In 2019, the new process was first adopted by the European Parliament, then—unanimously—by the European Council and came into law in 2020. In fact, the EU now has a coherent policy, supplementing national policies. The EU as a collective body has been late in consolidating its stance on conducting business with China but is now increasingly standing up to Beijing.

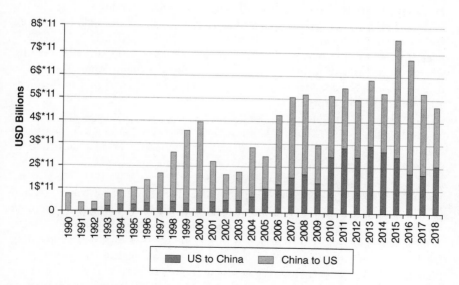

Figure 9.1 Annual value of FDI transactions between the US and China, 1990–2018
Source: Rhodium Group, Report on China-US Investment Trends.

U.S. and European responses

The American and European responses to the growth of Chinese FDI have diverged significantly, based on different perceptions of the challenge but also in reaction to a diversified Chinese approach to investing in each region. For the US, the primary challenge is to maintain its superiority in the context of advanced technologies, especially artificial intelligence, biotechnology, semiconductors and robotics, which have dual implications for America's economic competitiveness and military superiority. The same technologies form a substantial part of the MIC 2025 strategy which, in previous years, motivated many of the China-led deals in the US and Europe as means of acquiring visible brands and existing R&D (European Union Chamber of Commerce in China 2017).

Already under the Obama administration and more forcefully so under Trump, the US has responded by taking a tough stance, primarily by bolstering its FDI screening body, the CFIUS, to effectively ban any deals in sensitive technologies—sometimes even those not directly involving Chinese parties. Among the deals deemed sensitive to US national security interest, five investments have been blocked, although proposed transactions may have been withdrawn by the firms involved in lieu of being blocked. According to public records, President Barack Obama used the Foreign Investment and National Security Act of 2007 (FINSA) authority in 2012 to block an American firm, Ralls Corporation, owned by Chinese nationals, from acquiring a US wind farm energy firm located near a Department of Defense facility (Younglai 2012). He also blocked a Chinese investment firm in 2016 from acquiring Aixtron, a Germany-based firm with assets in the US (Financial Times 2016). In 2017, President Trump blocked the acquisition of Lattice Semiconductor Corp. by the Chinese investment firm Canyon Bridge Capital Partners; in 2018, he blocked the acquisition of Qualcomm by Broadcom; in 2019, CFIUS raised concerns over Beijing Kunlun Company's investment in Grindr LLC, an online dating site, over concerns of foreign access to the personally identifiable information of US citizens. Subsequently, the Chinese firm divested itself of Grindr (Congressional Research Service 2020).

The US has an established track record of screening investments from China, and the peak inflow of FDI in the mid-2010s has caused a backlash motivated chiefly by strategic and security considerations in industries deemed of strategic importance, primarily relating to advanced technologies. This has translated into emboldening CFIUS through the Foreign Investment Risk Modernization Act (FIRRMA), passed by Congress in 2018. The purpose was to tighten CFIUS against the risk to US national security posed by certain types of foreign investments. FIRRMA, which was incorporated into the 2019 National Defense Authorization Act, created four categories of "covered transactions", expanding the definition of "critical technology" to include "emerging and foundational technologies". It also imposed a deadline on the CFIUS response to written notices, created the option for a written declaration, imposed a CFIUS filing fee and established a process to identify non-notified transactions (Sanchez and Daya 2018).

From 2015 to 2017, CFIUS reviewed 473 cases with those from China ranking number one (143 cases), followed by Canada (66) and Japan (46).

However, tougher investment screening measures under the Trump administration also went hand in hand with trade tariffs aimed directly against China's grand development strategy MIC 2025. These tariffs, introduced under Section 301 on US$50 billion of Chinese imports of mainly high-tech products, are a direct retaliation for China's forced technology transfer and intellectual property infringements that contribute to an advantage by Chinese firms in strategic sectors. Huawei's ban can be similarly considered to form part of this general policy of protecting the US lead in strategic advanced technologies.

The Trump administration acted through punitive tariffs against Chinese competitors in the same sectors in which it is trying to maintain its edge, which are also justified by Washington as responses to Chinese forced technology transfers and intellectual property (IP) theft practices. In July 2018, President Trump imposed sweeping tariffs on China for its alleged unfair trade practices. Over the following 18 months, the two countries were embroiled in countless back-and-forth negotiations and a tit-for-tat tariff war; they introduced foreign technology restrictions and fought several WTO cases which consequently led U.S.-China trade tensions to the brink of full-blown trade war (Lee 2020). So far, the US has imposed tariffs on US$550 billion worth of Chinese products; China, in turn, has set tariffs on US$185 billion worth of US goods. In January 2020, the two sides agreed on a "Phase One deal", which was revealed to be more limited in scope than the comprehensive deal that both sides had been seeking (Politi 2020). The agreement addresses in unspecific terms the issues of intellectual property, technology transfers, food and agriculture, financial services and currency management.

The Trump administration had equally tried to export its approach to its European allies with mixed—albeit, not meagre—results. Through CFIUS, it weighed in on a number of technology deals, and through diplomatic channels it has urged the banning of Chinese telecommunication giant Huawei Technologies from 5G procurement. At the February 2020 annual Munich Security Conference, former Secretary of State Mike Pompeo urged Europeans to rally behind Washington on China, given that there was "more to unite than divide" across the Atlantic, and considering China's attempt to set up an "empire" (Barkin 2020). However, the Trump administration lacked the same pull with Brussels and European capitals that its predecessors enjoyed, and its erratic policy approach towards China had arguably given further reason to Europeans not to dismiss the Chinese as a potential partner just yet.

On their part, Europeans have different concerns about China which focus partly on critical infrastructure. This term refers to the vast investment projects in ports, railways, energy, and utilities that have been financed largely by state-linked financial vehicles and sometimes under the banner of the BRI, President Xi's signature project. Examples of European utilities that were entirely or partly taken over by Chinese state entities include the *Piraeus* harbour of Athens (China Ocean Shipping Company, 67 percent); *Energias de Portugal* (China Three Gorges, 28 percent); *Redes Electricicas Nacionais*, Portugal's public power transmission company (China State Grid, 25 percent) (Le Corre 2018), as well as acquisitions of *Noatum* Ports Holdings in Spain (Ports Europe 2017) and *CSP Zeebrugge Terminal* in Belgium (both controlled by Cosco). In Germany, China Logistics (a subsidiary of China Chengtong Holding Group) invested €100 million in JadeWeserPort (Wilhelmshafen) (Österreichische Verkehrszeitung 2019).

However, recent statements by the EU and Member States suggest that the definition of critical infrastructure seems to be expanding to encompass key technologies as well. Physical infrastructure remains the primary target of European screening. Nevertheless, more EU members, including Italy, Greece, Croatia and Hungary, have signed BRI-related MOUs and are welcoming its presence in their infrastructure markets. In the UK, China has helped finance a major nuclear plant, Hinkley Point C, with possible extensions (Vaughan and Kuo 2018). Croatia agreed to commission Chinese companies to build the Pelješac Bridge (85 percent financed by EU structural funds), while other companies are bidding to construct the Rijeka-Zagreb highway or the Hålogaland Bridge in Norway (built in cooperation with Serbian firm VNG) (Bastian 2018). In Serbia itself, China Railways Corporation, a vast state-owned company, is meant to start building the new Budapest-Belgrade railway, although multiple obstacles have slowed the project—mainly on the Hungarian side (Ferchen 2018). In April 2020, the Hungarian government classified details of the Budapest-Belgrade railway plan, ostensibly to protect "national interests". This followed a controversial "coronavirus law" granting populist Prime Minister Viktor Orbán the right to rule by decree, raising serious questions about transparency and accountability (Inotai 2020).

Overall, the above suggests that certain European countries (especially outside the EU) have enhanced their dependence on China during the pandemic and are even less prepared to compromise their access to Chinese capital. This is especially so in countries bordering the EU, such as the West Balkan states (Conley et al. 2020).

Diverging US and European approaches towards Chinese FDI

Although a united European posture on China has only been superficial at best (Le Corre 2019), EU members are mending their divisions on the subject. In February 2017, the economy ministers of Germany and France, as well as the industry minister of Italy, wrote a joint letter (Reuters 2017) to the former European Commissioner for Trade Cecilia Malmström, voicing concern that a growing number of non-EU investors were "buying up European technologies for the strategic objectives of their home country". At the same time, "EU investors often face barriers when they try to invest in other countries", the ministers wrote. "As a consequence, we are worried about the lack of reciprocity and about a possible sell-out of European expertise, which we are currently unable to combat with effective instruments". The lack of reciprocity was clearly a major factor in the three countries' letter, reflecting toughening market conditions in China itself. Their request for the Commission to review the possibility of EU Member States being able to outright block a foreign investment or make it subject to conditions led to an EU-process and the adoption of a new EU screening mechanism in 2019, coming into effect in the autumn of 2020.

According to the European Commission paper (European Commission 2019), the EU framework will:

- Create a cooperation mechanism where Member States and the Commission will be able to exchange information and raise concerns related to specific investments.
- Allow the Commission to issue opinions when an investment poses a threat to the security or public order of more than one Member State, or when an investment could undermine a project or programme of interest to the whole EU, such as Horizon 2020 or Galileo.
- Encourage international cooperation on investment screening, including sharing experience, best practice and information on issues of common concern.
- Set certain requirements for Member States who wish to maintain or adopt a screening mechanism at a national level. Member States also retain the last word on whether a specific investment operation should be allowed in their territory.
- Take into account the need to operate under short business-friendly deadlines and strong confidentiality requirements.

The introduction of this new official process shows the concerns of large Member States for a more balanced situation between the EU and China. In particular, the regulation encourages Member States to specifically review state-supported investments in sensitive technologies and critical infrastructure. Some experts estimate that 82 percent of Chinese M&A transactions in Europe during the year 2018 would fall under at least one of those criteria. In other words, a broader scrutiny of the Chinese commercial presence in Europe will impact Chinese investors (Hanemann et al. 2019b). This will need to be complemented by national schemes, which are also taking shape. Several countries (such as Sweden or Estonia) have, since 2019, launched their own process, but others (such as Belgium, Ireland and most Eastern European states) do not have such a scheme. Only 15 Members out of 27 have national screening mechanisms. The COVID-19 pandemic has pushed the European Commission president, Ursula von der Leyen, to issue even stronger guidelines to ensure "a strong EU-wide approach to foreign investment screening in a time of public health crisis and related economic vulnerability". The aim, said the Commission, was "to preserve EU companies and critical assets, notably in areas such as health, medical research, biotechnology and infrastructures that are essential for our security and public order, without undermining the EU's general openness to foreign investment" (European Commission 2020).

The recent critical steps taken by the EU represent a rather fresh policy trend, but China's popularity has continued in many European capitals. The decline of overall FDI to EU countries disguises net and significant increases in a number of smaller states, where even comparatively small sums carry some weight. These budding investment relations play into China's general approach to "divide and conquer" and can potentially earn it new friends.

Among sub-regions that have nurtured a close relationship with China, the Western Balkans is perhaps the most obvious. Three decades after the fall of the Berlin Wall, the region significantly lags behind the EU in terms of economic clout and badly lacks foreign investment. In particular, it has massive infrastructure deficits combined with a lack of capital, loose regulatory practices, lax public procurement rules and poor labour regulations. As non-members of the EU, those markets that have still not recovered from the former Yugoslavia's civil war in the 1990s have appealed to Chinese investors looking to easily establish bases at the EU's gate.

In addition, Chinese companies are willing to build at low costs without the stringent and costly requirements of meeting environmental and social standards. According to AEI figures (see Figure 9.2) (American Enterprise Institute and The

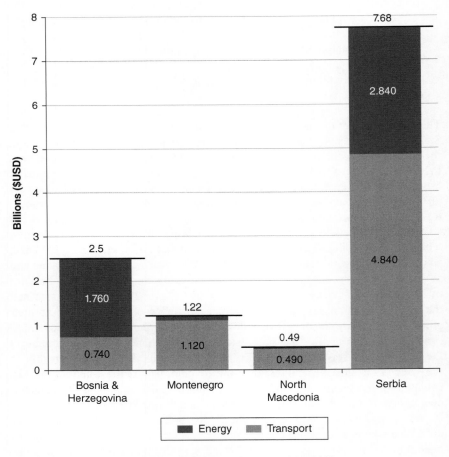

Figure 9.2 Chinese investment in the Western Balkans, 2005–2019

Source: American Enterprise Institute Global China Investment Tracker.

Heritage Foundation 2005–2020), Chinese investment in the four Western Balkan countries (Serbia, Bosnia-Herzegovina, Montenegro and North Macedonia) over 2005–2019, mainly through loans in the key sectors of energy and transport, have reached US$14.6 billion—Serbia leading with US$10.3 billion. About half of Chinese investment in the Western Balkans is for transport and infrastructure public contracts financed by Chinese banks—precisely US$7.2 billion—the rest going to the energy sector. In total, more than 80 percent of total investment in the region is financed by loans.

Can the EU and US engage in a dialogue on China's FDI?

The US and EU share concerns that their economies are threatened from the often asymmetrical and illegitimate commercial practices promoted by the Chinese state. These concerns have been fed by annual reports published by various organisations, from the EU Chamber of Commerce in China to the American Chamber, Germany's Bundesverband der Deutschen Industrie (BDI, Confederation of German Industries) and, more recently, Brussels-based Business Europe,[5] in addition to numerous think-tanks (Brattberg and Le Corre 2020). In addition, the COVID-19 crisis has underlined the fact that both the US and EU economies are over-reliant on Chinese supply chains (The Economist 2020).

As for the US, it has not limited its actions in this competition to domestic markets but has actively used its powers and a good dose of political pressure to bring its European allies into line. The US has taken positions on Chinese deals with EU companies such as France's Lumileds (Meunier 2019), Germany's Aixtron and Kuka (Hooijmaaijers 2019), and other major German technology brands on national security grounds. In some cases, it has succeeded in stopping the deals, in others its warnings resulted in either reviewing the terms of the deal or had no effect. The US has also actively tried to shape the approach of EU countries to Huawei (and its smaller Chinese competitor ZTE) and encouraged them to follow US policy that bans the Chinese from 5G procurement. This has the dual goal of protecting sensitive data from China's cyber espionage but also, significantly, to curb the advance of Huawei and its Chinese peers from "winning" the 5G race, thereby preserving the US lead. Multiple delegations travelled to Europe, trying to persuade governments to use alternatives to Chinese technology, including companies such as Ericsson, Nokia and Samsung. This has not prevented the British government from originally allowing Huawei into its 5G network, despite heavy pressure from the White House (Benner 2020).

The EU, on the other hand, is only starting to respond to this challenge; for the most part, it has not found the answer to weighing the economic interests of engaging with China and the security risks it poses with an approach from its main transatlantic ally that remains largely hostile and unconstructive. The union is divided on Huawei and on the BRI. Despite the new investment screening measures, current domestic applications signal mixed results, and it will likely take several years for most Member States to conform to Brussels' line. Having recognised China as a "systemic rival" (European Commission and High Representative of the Union for Foreign Affairs and Security 2019), the EU has taken a firmer approach in 2019 on reciprocity and fairness. This is a meaningful departure from its usual caution but does not reveal what tangible steps the EU is prepared to take to act on its concerns. Besides its own relations with Beijing, Brussels needs to keep a close eye on developments in the US-China trade dispute negotiations for the repercussions it could have on its own economy and strategic position.

These developments occur against the backdrop of a stark decline in Chinese FDI in both the US and the EU, although the latter is less pronounced and more diversified on a country-by-country basis. Beijing has curbed capital outflows and is finding increasing resistance to its plan for "going global" on its own terms. Fearing the rapid depletion of its foreign reserves and the loss of capital to foreign enterprises, China's State Administration of Foreign Exchange set the threshold for the state review of capital outflows from US$1 billion down to just US$5 million in November 2016 (U.S.-China Economic and Security Review Commission 2018). This change comes at the end of a peak year for outbound FDI and accounts for the ensuing decline in the aggregate volume of investments, especially by those large conglomerates such as Anbang Insurance Group, HNA Group (CNBC 2020) and Dalian Wanda that had driven much of the previous growth (these companies had been put under closer scrutiny from mid-2017). Additional policies aimed at controlling and limiting outbound FDI include a 2017 investigation by the China Banking Regulatory Commission into the use of financial tools and foreign loans for financing of deals abroad and the State Council's announcement of new policies to curb "irrational" investment which did not align with Beijing's state economic objectives (U.S.-China Economic and Security Review Commission 2018, 37).

China is now less amenable to its capital flowing abroad; this domestic crackdown will likely make it easier for European and American policymakers to point to deals that are overtly motivated by the MIC 2025 agenda (European Union Chamber of Commerce in China 2017). On the other hand, the current context also sees China grappling to adjust its strategy to address heightened concern from every corner of the world over its BRI and MIC 2025 plans, not to mention the aftermath of the COVID-19 pandemic. Whether China will become more accommodating or more astute in pursuit of its goals will be the main question for the coming years.

Finally, the domestic political context in Europe and linkages to the much-debated rift in the transatlantic relationship should not be overlooked. Populist and anti-establishment parties in various European countries have used China as a pawn in their pursuit of popular support. Hungary's conservative prime minister Viktor Orban has been welcoming Chinese investment from the mid-2000s, and Budapest has tried to leverage its "special relationship" with Beijing *vis-à-vis* Brussels (Reuters 2019). Portugal and Greece both warmed to Chinese investment during the privatisation wave that followed the 2008 GFC. In Italy, the populist coalition that came to power in May 2018 displayed the various facets of the European populist stance on China. In a bid to clash with Brussels, the coalition seemed initially united in pursuing a closer relationship with Beijing, including signing a BRI MOU in March 2019. This position remained prevalent with the left-leaning Five Star Movement (M5S), which sees such a pro-Beijing policy as a break with established Europe- and NATO-oriented foreign policies, and, indeed, something of a golden goose. The far-right Northern League leader Matteo Salvini ultimately came out firmly against vast Chinese FDI, lashing out on camera that Italy would not sell out as Greece did (Rossi 2019)—a stark reassertion of his "sovereigntist" line. From September 2019 under the new coalition (without the Northern league), Rome seems much more cautious when dealing with China.

Conclusion

According to the Organization for Economic Cooperation and Development (OECD) FDI regulatory restrictiveness index, China has remained one of the most restrictive economies with respect to inward investment. Despite some improvement over the past 20 years, the FDI restrictiveness index for China (0.32) is still much higher than the OECD average (0.07) (Dollar 2015). In contrast, almost all EU nations have consistently been among those countries with the lowest levels of FDI restrictiveness, which is about to change.

In 2019, the EU-China strategic outlook proposed ten action points, including the promotion of reciprocity and opening up procurement opportunities for European companies in China (Action 6). It also specified that, in the EU itself, high levels of labour and environmental standards are taken into account in the participation of foreign bidders and goods in the EU procurement market (Action 7).

One year and many months following this statement, little progress had been made in the negotiations for an EU-China comprehensive investment agreement. Market access for European companies in China has remained highly restricted. Meanwhile, the severity of the COVID-19 crisis made negotiations difficult and the probability of a signed agreement by the end of 2020 unlikely.

At least in rhetoric, Washington and Brussels are becoming increasingly aligned, but they have pursued separate policies, with Brussels and key EU states reacting somewhat forcefully (Financial Times 2018) to the escalating US-China clash during the Trump presidency (Noack 2020). Still, the years 2017–2020 have shown a remarkable similarity in the analysis of Washington and Brussels *vis-à-vis* Chinese investments. Although US policy toward Chinese investment has become very defensive, to say the least, the 2019 EU-level new screening framework is also more ambitious than anticipated and creates incentives for Member States to establish robust FDI monitoring mechanisms (Hanemann et al. 2019b). While proposing guidelines for information exchange, coordination and empowerment for national screening, it could impact Chinese investors and should eventually lead to a reassessment of inbound investments if not a review of Europe's policy toward trade and investment with China. It should also fill the long-awaited bilateral treaties between the EU and China and between the US and China (the latter being a more remote possibility until the next US administration takes office in 2021).

Can the US and Europe collaborate on a multilateral approach to get China to play by international rules? Or will they simply go on to develop fragmented responses to the challenge? Will they see each other's approaches through a competitive lens?

While transatlantic divisions remain on many economic issues, the US and the EU have started an informal dialogue through the Geneva-based World Trade Organisation or the Paris-based OECD. In early 2020, for the first time, a formal meeting on the topic of investment screening took place between American, EU and Japanese government officials. The EU and US share a substantial interest in jointly developing a common approach to Chinese investment, one focused on the rule of law and reciprocity. For its part, the US system can share its best practice when it comes to national security issues. The North Atlantic Treaty Organization could also provide assistance to its members on strategic thinking on global affairs.

Another aspect that is often overlooked is the role of the business community. On both sides of the Atlantic, companies have faced restrictions on the China market and, at the same time, seen the emergence of Chinese state-owned enterprises as competitors in their own domestic markets. The two main chambers of commerce in China (of the EU and US) have already worked collaboratively for quite some time.

The OECD has been following the issue of "Chinese innovation mercantilism" for over a decade (OECD 2008) and was instrumental in 2016 in helping the G20 pass a set of non-binding guiding principles for global investment policymaking. It is likely that the next few years will see more effective, coordinated action on foreign investment screening between like-minded countries.

The US and Europe together represent roughly 850 million people with a total GDP of nearly US$40 trillion. They should try to coordinate their policies towards China, in conjunction with like-minded countries such as Japan, South Korea, Canada, New Zealand and Australia. This should especially be the case concerning technology, where China has been promoting its own model. In this context, the outcome of the 5G debate across the developed world will be critical.

In addition, it is recommended that the EU should:

- Stand for European norms and values.
- Promote unity in the defence of European infrastructures.
- Use OECD norms of transparency.
- Invest in regional connectivity.
- Invest in regional multilateralism.
- Encourage European industrial champions.
- Build a European consensus on China.

Overall, following the election of Joe Biden as US President in November 2020, much will also depend on future domestic economic outlooks as well as who is in power in the key capitals of Berlin, Paris, London and Rome. The latter, which had appeared to have broken ranks with other G7 countries by signing on to the

BRI in 2019, had a major political shift six months later under a new coalition government. Following a public debate and the COVID-19 crisis (where Italy banned all inbound flights from China), it is no longer perceived as a close Beijing ally in Europe. When it comes to dealing with the world's second most powerful economy, China, it is time for cooperation rather than for unilateral approaches. The EU's High Representative for Foreign Affairs and Security Policy, Josep Borrell, wrote:

> When it comes to Europe itself, there are also lessons to be learnt from the crisis—some of which will play into our relations with our international partners including China. We should avoid excessive dependence in strategic sectors by building stockpiles of critical materials. We also need to shorten and diversify our supply chains. Since diplomacy is best grounded in clear principles, the watchwords for EU-China should be trust, transparency and reciprocity. We should move forward together, based on a realistic assessment of China's strategic intent and the EU's common interests.
>
> (EEAS 2020)

Exchange among allies, cherishing a shared decades-long history of struggle to defend and expand freedom and democracy, should be the main priority.

Notes

1 This chapter will alternately refer to "Europe" (including the EU, Norway, the United Kingdom (UK), Switzerland and the Western Balkans) or to "the European Union" (its 28 members until January 2020, now 27 without the UK).
2 For a good overview of Chinese FDI in the United States, see Dollar (2015).
3 CFIUS: Committee of Foreign Investment of the United States.
4 As of May 2020, Chinese investment in the ports of Trieste and Genova had failed to materialise.
5 See BDI (2019), European Union Chamber of Commerce in China (2019), Business-Europe (2020), AmCham China (2020).

References

AmCham China. 2020. "2020 American Business in China." AmCham China White Paper. www.amchamchina.org/policy-advocacy/white-paper/.

American Enterprise Institute, and The Heritage Foundation. 2005–2020. "China Global Investment Tracker." www.aei.org/china-global-investment-tracker/.

Baker McKenzie. 2017. "Rising Influence: Assessing China's Record FDI Surge in North America and Europe." www.bakermckenzie.com/-/media/files/insight/publications/2017/03/chinafdi/chinafdi_2017.pdf?la=en.

Baker McKenzie. 2020. "Chinese Investment in Europe and North America Hits 9-Year Low; Signs of Recovery for 2020." January 8. www.bakermckenzie.com/en/newsroom/2020/01/chinese-investment-in-europe-na.

Barkin, Noah. 2020. "The U.S. and Europe Are Speaking a Different Language on China." *Foreign Policy*, February 16. https://foreignpolicy.com/2020/02/16/the-u-s-and-europe-are-speaking-a-different-language-on-china/.

Bastian, Jens. 2018. "China's Expanding Presence in Southeast Europe." Center for Strategic & International Studies (CSIS), December 19. https://reconnectingasia.csis.org/analysis/entries/chinas-expanding-presence-southeast-europe/.

BDI (Bundesverband der Deutschen Industrie). 2019. "Strengthen the European Union to Better Compete with China." October 1. https://english.bdi.eu/article/news/strengthen-the-european-union-to-better-compete-with-china/.

Benner, Thorsten. 2020. "Britain Knows It's Selling Out Its National Security to Huawei." *Foreign Policy*, January 31. https://foreignpolicy.com/2020/01/31/boris-johnson-britain-knows-its-selling-out-its-national-security-to-huawei/.

Bennet, Cory, and Bryan Bender. 2018. "How China Acquires 'the Crown Jewels' of U.S. Technology." *Politico*, May 22. www.politico.com/story/2018/05/22/china-us-tech-companies-cfius-572413.

Brattberg, Erik, and Philippe Le Corre. 2020. *The EU and China in 2020: More Competition Ahead*. Beijing: Carnegie Endowment for International Peace, February 19. https://carnegieendowment.org/2020/02/19/eu-and-china-in-2020-more-competition-ahead-pub-81096.

BusinessEurope. 2020. "EU Should Fundamentally Rebalance Its Relationship with China." Press Release, January 16. www.businesseurope.eu/publications/eu-should-fundamentally-rebalance-its-relationship-china.

CNBC. 2020. "China Plans to Take Over HNA Group and Sell Its Airline Assets as Coronavirus Hits Business, Report Says." February 19. www.cnbc.com/2020/02/19/china-to-take-over-hna-group-and-sell-its-airline-assets-report-says.html.

Congressional Research Service. 2020. "The Committee on Foreign Investment in the United States (CFIUS)." *CRS Report*. https://fas.org/sgp/crs/natsec/RL33388.pdf.

Conley, Heather A., Jonathan E. Hillman, Donatienne Ruy, and Maesea McCalpin. 2020. "China's 'Hub-and-Spoke' Strategy in the Balkans." Center for Strategic & International Studies, Report, April. https://csis-website-prod.s3.amazonaws.com/s3fs-public/publication/200427_ChinaStrategy.pdf.

Dollar, David. 2015. *United States-China Two-Way Direct Investment: Opportunities and Challenges*. Washington, DC: Brookings Institution Press, January. www.brookings.edu/wp-content/uploads/2016/06/us-china-two-way-direct-investment-dollar.pdf.

The Economist. 2020. "Covid-19 Is Teaching Hard Lessons About China-Only Supply Chains." *The Economist*, February 29. www.economist.com/china/2020/02/29/covid-19-is-teaching-hard-lessons-about-china-only-supply-chains.

EEAS (European External Action Service). 2020. "Several Outlets—Trust and Reciprocity: The Necessary Ingredients for EU-China Cooperation." May 15. https://eeas.europa.eu/headquarters/headquarters-homepage_en/79355/Trust%20and%20reciprocity:%20the%20necessary%20ingredients%20for%20EU-China%20cooperation.

European Commission. 2019. "EU Foreign Investment Screening Regulation Enters into Force." Press Release, April 10. https://ec.europa.eu/commission/presscorner/detail/en/IP_19_2088.

European Commission. 2020. "Coronavirus: Commission Issues Guidelines to Protect Critical European Assets and Technology in Current Crisis." Press Release, March 25. https://ec.europa.eu/commission/presscorner/detail/en/ip_20_528.

European Commission, and High Representative of the Union for Foreign Affairs and Security. 2019. "Joint Communication to the European Parliament, the European Council and the Council: EU-China—A Strategic Outlook, JOIN(2019) 5 Final." March 12. https://ec.europa.eu/commission/sites/beta-political/files/communication-eu-china-a-strategic-outlook.pdf.

European Union Chamber of Commerce in China. 2017. "China Manufacturing 2025: Putting Industrial Policy Ahead of Market Forces." www.europeanchamber.com.cn/en/china-manufacturing-2025.

European Union Chamber of Commerce in China. 2019. "Annual Report 2020." www.europeanchamber.com.cn/en/publications-annual-report.

Ferchen, Matt. 2018. *China's Troubled Hungary-Serbia Railway Project: A Case Study*. Leiden: Leiden Asia Center, December 12. https://carnegietsinghua.org/2018/12/12/china-s-troubled-hungary-serbia-railway-project-case-study-pub-78100.

Financial Times. 2016. "Obama Blocks Chinese Takeover of Tech Group Aixtron." *Financial Times*, December 2. www.ft.com/content/0c940900-b8e2-11e6-ba85-95d1533d9a62.

Financial Times. 2018. "German Manufacturers Fear Fallout from US-China Trade War." *Financial Times*, April 5. www.ft.com/content/5a9a71d0-38c9-11e8-8b98-2f31af407cc8.

Hanemann, Thilo, Mikko Huotari, and Agatha Kratz. 2019b. *Chinese FDI in Europe: 2018 Trends and Impact of New Screening Policies*. Rhodium Group and Mercator Institute for China Studies, Report, March 6. https://merics.org/de/studie/chinese-fdi-europe-2018-trends-and-impact-new-screening-policies.

Hanemann, Thilo, Daniel H. Rosen, Cassie Gao, and Adam Lysenko. 2019a. *Two-Way Street: 2019 Update US-China Direct Investment Trends*. Rhodium Group, Report, May 8. https://rhg.com/research/two-way-street-2019-update-us-china-direct-investment-trends/.

Hooijmaaijers, Bas. 2019. "Blackening Skies for Chinese Investment in the EU?" *Journal of Chinese Political Science* 24 (3): 451–470.

Inotai, Edit. 2020. "Budapest to Belgrade: All Aboard the Secret Express." *Balkan Insight*, April 22. https://balkaninsight.com/2020/04/22/budapest-to-belgrade-all-aboard-the-secret-express/.

Le Corre, Philippe. 2018. *China's Rise as a Geoeconomic Influencer: Four European Case Studies*. Washington, DC: Carnegie Endowment for International Peace, October 15. https://carnegieendowment.org/2018/10/15/china-s-rise-as-geoeconomic-influencer-four-european-case-studies-pub-77462.

Le Corre, Philippe. 2019. "A Divided Europe's China Challenge." *East Asia Forum*, November 11. www.eastasiaforum.org/2019/11/26/a-divided-europes-china-challenge/.

Le Corre, Philippe, and Alain Sepulchre. 2016. *China's Offensive in Europe*. Washington, DC: Brookings Institution Press.

Lee, Amanda. 2020. "China to Refund US Trade War Tariffs on Some Medical Devices amid Coronavirus Outbreak." *South China Morning Post*, February 21. www.scmp.com/economy/china-economy/article/3051824/china-refund-us-trade-war-tariffs-some-medical-devices-amid.

Meunier, Sophie. 2019. "Beware of Chinese Bearing Gifts: Why China's Direct Investment Poses Political Challenges in Europe and the United States." In *China's International Investment Strategy: Bilateral, Regional, and Global Law and Policy*, edited by Julien Chaisse. London: Oxford University Press.

Noack, Rick. 2020. "Now that Trump Has a Trade Deal with China, Some Europeans Fear He Will Focus His Trade Threats on Them." *The Washington Post*, January 17. www.washingtonpost.com/world/2020/01/17/now-that-trump-has-a-trade-deal-with-china-some-europeans-fear-he-will-focus-his-trade-threats-them/.

OECD (Organisation for Economic Co-Operation and Development). 2008. *OECD Benchmark Definition of Foreign Direct Investment*, 4th ed. Paris: OECD. www.oecd.org/daf/inv/investmentstatisticsandanalysis/40193734.pdf.

O'Keeffe, Kate, and Siobhan Hughes. 2018. "Congress Passes Defense Bill That's Tough on China." *The Wall Street Journal*, August 1. www.wsj.com/articles/u-s-defense-bill-seeks-to-counter-china-1533127150.

Österreichische Verkehrszeitung. 2019. "Chinese Logistics Centre to Be Built at the JadeWeserPort Freight Village." June 12. https://oevz.com/en/chinese-logistics-centre-to-be-built-at-the-jadeweserport-freight-village/.

Politi, James. 2020. "What's in the US-China 'Phase One' Trade Deal? A Chapter-by-Chapter Guide to the Deal Aimed at Pausing the Conflict Between Washington and Beijing." *Financial Times*, January 15. www.ft.com/content/a01564ba-37d5-11ea-a6d3-9a26f8c3cba4.

Ports Europe. 2017. "Noatum Port's Purchase by Cosco to Reshape Spanish Ports Industry." June 15. www.portseurope.com/noatum-ports-purchase-by-cosco-to-reshape-spanish-ports-industry/.

Reuters. 2017. "France, Germany, Italy Urge Rethink of Foreign Investment in EU." *Reuters*, February 14. www.reuters.com/article/uk-eu-trade-france/france-germany-italy-urge-rethink-of-foreign-investment-in-eu-idUKKBN15T1ND.

Reuters. 2019. "Hungary PM Orban's Ally to Co-Build Chinese Railway for $2.1 Billion." June 12. www.reuters.com/article/us-hungary-china-railways-opus-global-idUSKCN1TD1JG.

Rhodium Group. n.d. "The US-China Investment Hub." www.us-china-investment.org/us-china-foreign-direct-investments/.

Rossi, Sara. 2019. "China Must Not 'Colonize' Italian Business: Ruling League." March 11. www.reuters.com/article/us-china-italy-belt-and-road-govt/china-must-not-colonize-italian-business-ruling-league-idUSKBN1QS2A7.

Sanchez, Ignacio E., and Christine Daya. 2018. *Congress Finalizes CFIUS Reform Bill to Broaden National Security Reviews of Foreign Investments*. London: DLA Piper Publications.

Turcsányi, Richard Q. 2020. "China and the Frustrated Region: Central and Eastern Europe's Repeating Troubles with Great Powers." *China Report* 56 (1): 60–77.

U.S.-China Economic and Security Review Commission. 2018. *2018 Report to Congress of the U.S.-China Economic and Security Review Commission*. Washington, DC: U.S. Government Publishing Office. www.uscc.gov/sites/default/files/annual_reports/2018%20Annual%20Report%20to%20Congress.pdf.

Vaughan, Adam, and Lily Kuo. 2018. "China's Long Game to Dominate Nuclear Power Relies on the UK." *The Guardian*, July 26. www.theguardian.com/environment/2018/jul/26/chinas-long-game-to-dominate-nuclear-power-relies-on-the-uk.

Younglai, Rachelle. 2012. "Obama Blocks Chinese Wind Farms in Oregon Over Security." *Reuters*, September 29. www.reuters.com/article/us-usa-china-turbines/obama-blocks-chinese-wind-farms-in-oregon-over-security-idUSBRE88R19220120929.

Zeng, Ka, and Xiaojun Li. 2019. "Geopolitics, Nationalism, and Foreign Direct Investment: Perceptions of the China Threat and American Public Attitudes Toward Chinese FDI." *Chinese Journal of International Affairs* 12 (4): 495–518.

10 Europe and the Belt & Road Initiative (BRI)

Infrastructure and connectivity

Claude Zanardi

Introduction

This chapter examines the Belt and Road Initiative (BRI) as a leading Chinese strategy that is reshaping Eurasia through the building of infrastructure and connectivity. It considers Europe as a region in Eurasia (Zanardi 2019) that includes the European Union (EU) and its neighbouring countries. Regions are increasingly studied in world politics (Andrew 1995): departing from a geographically-based view of regions as "self-evident blocks of space" (Agnew 2013, 12), functional approaches focus on how regions are changed through international flows of goods, investment and information. For instance, Katzenstein has studied how globalisation and internationalisation increase the openness of regions and blur their boundaries (Katzenstein 2015).

China has a functional idea of regions, which strengthens its international connections and widens the economic benefits of globalisation (Kaczmarski 2017). Not only does the BRI reshape China's periphery, but it also impacts Europe and the EU by enhancing Eurasian connectivity and, thus, changing its geo-economics. Hence, the BRI can be seen as an ambitious transnational "space planning strategy" that highlights the gap between existing borders and the functions exercised by territorial entities (Feng and Huang 2016).

This chapter focuses on the Central and Eastern European Countries (CEECs), particularly Poland and Serbia, as well as on the digital dimension of the BRI, to show that the BRI poses several challenges to the EU. The author argues that while Asia is increasingly important to the EU, the footprint of the EU has shrunk (Wolf et al. 2016), and the EU currently has neither the resources nor the political willingness to play a significant role in Asia. Brussels should rather refocus on strengthening the EU and its relations with its neighbouring countries, define its own interests and develop a more comprehensive foreign policy towards China. This would allow it to cope with the long-term consequences of the BRI without being drawn into Sino-American competition. This certainly entails a review of its normative foreign policy.

Foreign policy based on norms and values underpins the nature of the normative power attributed to the EU (Manners 2002; Mattlin 2012). Some have examined whether the EU acts as a normative power (Tocci 2009) or whether it only aspires towards an ideal type of normative power (Forsberg 2011). Others have highlighted the political "value gap" between the EU's liberal approach and China's authoritarian regime (Gottwald et al. 2010, 29). As a "norm exporter" (Michalski 2017, 71), the EU diverges from China with regard to both internal norms (e.g., democracy, the rule of law) and external norms (multipolarity vs multilateralism) (*ibid.*).

The chapter argues that, as a normative power, the EU still needs to work with the United States (US) to defend its norms and values while overcoming the exclusive focus of a normative foreign policy. Therefore, a more geopolitical approach is welcomed but requires further institutional changes that are difficult to make. In view of deteriorating transatlantic relations and of growing Sino-American competition, the EU should take a more pragmatic approach guided by its own interests. Since the BRI is much more a challenge for Europe than for the US, and since the EU lacks the resources to also get deeply involved in a region as distant as the Asia-Pacific, it should cooperate with Asia-Pacific powers where possible to defend international norms and standards.

The BRI's footprint on the CEECs

The BRI may spread the authoritarian Chinese model (Fukuyama 2016; Thompson 2019; Ortmann and Thompson 2018), thus undermining democratic governments. The case of the CEECs suggests that such a possibility exists. Due to their geographic position, they are an important logistic subregion for the BRI; they have relatively cheap labour costs and high expectations as to the potential benefits of participating in the BRI. Through the "17 + 1" framework,[1] China has built its influence on the CEECs as a hub for the development of both land and sea routes to Europe; its trade and investment with the CEECs reached US$58.7 billion in 2016, up from US$43.9 billion in 2010 (Kuo 2017), and Chinese companies are increasingly targeting strategic assets (Szunomar 2018).

Since Chinese loans represent an alternative financial source, they offer the CEECs more economic independence from international actors (e.g., International Monetary Fund (IMF), EU, Russia). China's growing economic footprint likely increases its political leverage and can induce an attitude of self-censorship, which can work against EU positions on issues as diverse as democracy or the arms embargo on China. The belief that China lacks both capacity and intention "to alter the strategic and policy choices of the Balkan states" (Pavlićević 2019, 270) is contradicted by several instances of CEECs that have modified their stance in favour of Beijing. For example, Hungary, Greece and Slovenia blocked or adulterated resolutions on human rights and on international arbitration over the South China Sea (Leonard et al. 2019). This is in line with China's divide and rule approach (Vasselier and Godement 2018), which increases competition for funding between European countries (Heilman and Schmidt 2014) and is facilitated by the absence of an overall European strategy.

China's geographic reconfiguration of Eurasia through the BRI implies the reorganisation of space in sub-regions that serve Chinese needs while straddling existing frontiers. For instance, Beijing has entrusted Shandong province with dealing with the French regions of Britany and the Loire even before Paris redesigned its regional administrative map (Interview with Philippe LeCorre 2018). The 17+1 includes Member States, candidate countries (Serbia, Montenegro, Albania and North Macedonia), a potential candidate (Bosnia and Herzegovina) and the Baltic states (Interview with Una Aleksandra Bērziņa-Čerenkova 2018), while leaving out Ukraine and Byelorussia so as not to upset Moscow. Hence, this geographical reorganisation does not always respect the EU as a unified actor: it initially excluded Brussels, which sought to attend the 16+1 annual summits. Despite appearing as multilateral, the BRI functions in bilateral frameworks (Kratz 2018).

Following the idea of regions as linking-hubs, China focused on Poland to set up a European intermodal transportation multi-logistic hub. In 2009, it launched the "Riga-based 'silk roads' project [and] proposed a 'new silk [rail-]road'" (Palonka 2010, 370), the Łódz-Chengdu, which is the only railroad to provide regular connections—other Sino-European railways only leave when fully loaded (Szczudlik 2016). However, the first Polish cargo from the Łódz-Chengdu railway to reach China did not leave until 2015 (*ibid.*) as rail trade is extremely unbalanced due to Chinese overcapacity (Goh and Goettig 2018).

Poland is along the New Eurasian Land Bridge; during President Xi's visit in 2016, its Strategic Partnership with China from 2011 was upgraded to a comprehensive level. Warsaw welcomed Beijing as an alternative source of funding, despite receiving the highest level of funding from the EU Cohesion Policy (Musiałkowska 2018). Furthermore, Poland became a founder of the Asian Infrastructure Investment Bank (AIIB) and signed a memorandum of understanding (MOU) on the BRI in 2015; however, it quickly faced unintended implications, particularly with Washington. For instance, the Polish Minister of Defence cited national security reasons for preventing a Chinese company from buying land belonging to the Polish army to create a logistic hub in Łódz (Góralczyk 2017). China, however, circumvented the problem by signing an agreement with the mayor of Kutno, just 15 kilometres from Lodz (*ibid.*). Thus, the BRI is a multidimensional initiative which can also develop at the subnational level (Kamiński 2019).

Despite being directed against Russia, a 2015 Polish law against hostile takeovers that lists key sectors for national security (energy, oil, telecommunications, explosives, weapons and ammunition)[2] also limited Chinese investment in sensitive sectors. For example, the purchase agreement of the China Security and Fire Company with V4C Eastern Europe for Konsalnet Holdings S.A. was blocked (Reuters 2017) because Konsalnet's activities were too sensitive (Bloomberg n.d.). Nevertheless, the same law did not prevent the signing of a cooperation agreement between the Polish Space Agency (POLSA) and China's National Space Administration (CNSA) on joint research, monitoring and developing new telecoms solutions with "transfers of technology from the Chinese space sector" (Berger 2016). Poland's first space strategy (Adamowski 2016) provided China with the opportunity to further expand its Beidou Navigation Satellite system along the BRI by making Poland a digital hub. Eventually, with Poland being a member of North Atlantic Treaty Organization (NATO), deeper cooperation became problematic. Furthermore, China's promise of massive funding for infrastructure has yet to materialise, causing frustration in the Polish government and business community (Interview with Polish Expert 2018).

One of China's priorities is to ink the communications hubs horizontally (east to west) and vertically (south to north): the Balkan countries make it possible to link the Piraeus Port controlled by the state-owned enterprise, China Ocean Shipping Company (COSCO) (van der Putten 2016), to northern Europe through the China-Europe Land-Sea Express Corridor (Pavlićević 2019). Hence, Serbia is another key-country for the BRI: not being part of the EU or NATO, Belgrade welcomes Chinese financial support as an alternative to international institutions. For example, two years after the IMF suspended credit to Belgrade in 2014 (Ramani 2016), China and Serbia signed several agreements on "energy, infrastructure, military industry, science and technology, culture and media" (Jian 2018, 253). China also backs Serbia's position on Kosovo, which makes Beijing and Belgrade "normative partners in sovereignty disputes" (Ramani 2016).

During Xi's visit in 2016, the Sino-Serbian strategic partnership was updated to a comprehensive strategic partnership (Jian 2018) and, in 2019, China became Serbia's main source of investment, with its foreign direct investment up to 20 percent of Serbia's total (Shehadi and Hopkins 2020). Beijing is not alone in investing to create a transport hub in the Balkans centred on Serbia: Moscow also aims at building a Balkan energy line centred in Serbia and BRI's projects often overlap with previous European projects. In fact, Brussels committed to provide Western Balkan countries with "financial assistance, political dialogue, trade relations and regional cooperation" by building infrastructure to connect them to the EU by railway, and the second Pan European Transport Conference of 1994 identified several Pan European corridors (Jian 2018, 248–249).

Since Piraeus is at the core of the BRI in Europe, Greece joined the 16 + 1 framework in 2019. The Chinese Ambassador to Greece explained that Sino-Greek collaboration is rooted in the creation of a fast-track to link the Maritime Silk Road (MSR) and the Silk Road Economic Belt (Sellier 2016). This land route includes the Belgrade-Budapest railway (Rogers 2019) but was frozen by an EU investigation (Hu 2017). The corresponding maritime route links Piraeus to Chinese ports (Li 2019). While helping Greece to recover economically, the growing importance of Piraeus as a Southern European logistic hub has diminished the relevance of other European ports (Ekman 2018).

China's approach *vis-à-vis* Southern European countries is linked more to the MSR: in 2013, Beijing organised a conference to strengthen cooperation in agriculture, another on maritime cooperation in 2015, and established a global maritime cooperation partnership with six southern Member States (Cyprus, Greece, Italy, Malta, Portugal and Spain) (Ekman 2016). All except Spain signed an MOU on the BRI.[3]

Through group-cooperation diplomacy (*ibid.*), China creates sub-regional fora that cut across the EU territory. This approach does not consider the EU as a sum of sub-regions according to the geographic divisions of the Chinese administration (*ibid.*). This has made the EU more aware of the importance of unity when dealing with China: "all [Member States], individually and within sub-regional cooperation frameworks . . . have a responsibility to ensure consistency with EU law, rules and policies" (European Commission and High Representative of the Union for Foreign Affairs and Security 2019, 2).

The BRI: connecting Eurasia through infrastructure

China's re-emergence spans from the economic to the normative dimensions; its size means that, whatever stance it takes, it has a global impact. Its integration into the international system increased its economic activities worldwide (Taylor 2010) and changed its attitude towards the international community. The People's Republic of China joined the World Trade Organisation in 2001 (Cass et al. 2003), becoming increasingly involved in multilateral organisations (Medeiros and Fravel 2003) and creating new institutions, such as the Shanghai Cooperation Organisation in 2001.

Built on vast foreign exchange reserves of more than US\$3 trillion in 2017 (Babones 2018), the BRI was launched by Xi Jinping in 2013 under the name "New Silk Roads", then "One Belt One Road" in 2014 and, finally in 2015, the Belt and Road Initiative. Incorporated into the charter of the Chinese Communist Party (CCP) (Xinhua 2017), a 2018 amendment to the constitution included the mantra of a "community with a shared future for humanity" (Manuel 2019). By focusing on connectivity and infrastructures from railways to pipelines, fibre optic and submarine cables, but also on the diffusion of standards and norms (Kratz 2018), the BRI aims at improving Eurasian connectivity along two integrated dimensions: a land route called the Silk Road Economic Belt (SREB) and a maritime route called the 21st Century Maritime Silk Road (MSR).

Although it is Xi's flagship policy tool (Rolland 2019), the BRI is a unifying brand of pre-existing projects which rationalise dispersed infrastructure, such as the New Eurasian Land Bridge of 1990[4] that connects Lianyungang to Rotterdam by rail (Xu 1997). By the mid-2000s, scholars had traced the development of China's land transport links with several peripheral sub-regions, namely Central, Southwest and South Asia (Garver 2006).

The term "connectivity" highlights the need for infrastructure building in Eurasia, as happened in China's western provinces; thanks to the BRI, China's economic development spills over into its periphery and across Eurasia. Xi stated that "Connectivity is vital to advancing Belt and Road cooperation . . . Infrastructure is the bedrock of connectivity" (Xi 2019, 8). Connectivity also has a more political dimension: "China's political room for manoeuvre stems . . . from the consistent enforcement of proactive connectivity power" (Kohlenberg and Godehardt 2018, 1), defined as setting standards and rules, multidimensionality, discourse power and the implicit internationalisation of the CCP's rule (*ibid.*). Hence, the BRI indirectly facilitates the dissemination of Chinese standards through investment and bilateral cooperation (Seaman 2020).

Whilst it is called a "strategy" in China (Xue 2015), this term is carefully avoided among foreign audiences. Some consider the BRI as a grand strategy "to re-constitute the Eurasian regional order with new governance ideas, norms, and rules" (Callahan 2016, 1). With its organisations, such as the AIIB and the Silk Road Fund, it establishes a Chinese-led financing framework promoting Chinese norms and values, often in contrast with European norms and values, and contributing to the internationalisation of the Yuan renminbi.

As a normative power, the EU should stress its commitment to the normative objectives of multilateralism, transparency, accountability and the rule of law in an open, rules-based global order (Callahan 2016). For instance, at the BRI International Forum of 2017, the EU Member States refused to sign a statement on the BRI due to a lack of guarantees regarding transparency, sustainability and tendering processes. In fact, complaints about restrictions on European companies entering the Chinese market increasingly include projects within the BRI (Keegan 2018): in 2018, 28 EU ambassadors in Beijing, excepting Hungary, signed a report condemning the BRI for hampering free trade, giving Chinese companies an unfair advantage and attempting to remake globalisation in China's national interests (Rolland 2019).

The limits to the EU's belief that integrating China into the international trading system would socialise it are evident (Ferenczy 2019). Although it does not seem to impose conditions,[5] China indirectly promotes an alternative model of development such as establishing new institutions and norms (Jones 2018). This may have indirect consequences, such as facilitating anti-liberal/democratic norms and practices that contrast with European ones (Pavlićević 2019).

The challenge of the digital silk road

Some see the BRI as a Chinese tool for backdoors intelligence gathering through hardware and software (Palma 2018). This is especially the case regarding the digital dimension of the BRI, referred to as the Digital Silk Road (DSR). While it has the potential to enhance digital connectivity in Eurasia, it simultaneously has the capacity to spread authoritarianism and curtail democracy and fundamental human rights (Cheney 2019). By promoting in-depth cooperation with other countries, the DSR provides China with a platform for disseminating its "telecom standards and technology in new generation information" (National Development and Reform Commission, Ministry of Foreign Affairs and Ministry of Commerce of the PRC 2015, 7). By establishing a China-centric digital infrastructure, exporting industrial overcapacity, facilitating the expansion of Chinese technology corporations and accessing large pools of data, it indirectly helps authoritarian countries develop a domestic system of surveillance, censorship and propaganda (Lucas and Feng 2018). Communications infrastructure built along with the BRI could become sources of vast amounts of real-time data but could also enhance China's influence through the spreading of its governance, surveillance and financial systems (Hemmings 2020). Countries along the DSR could shift towards a more Chinese "political, digital and economic order" (Hemmings and Chan 2020), as the cases of Serbia or Hungary seem to demonstrate. In exchange, authoritarian countries will back China's attempts to shape cyber norms; in particular, they will make use of China's experience in applying information technology in its surveillance system in Xinjiang.

The DSR concentrates new technologies "in smart cities, smart ports, and satellite-networked communications, using 5G as a baseline for other technologies like artificial intelligence, data analytics, and the Internet of Things" (Hemmings 2020). For instance, in Greece, the centralisation of data in smart port systems could be used to "create a deniable, surgical sanctions system by interdicting or slowing the container traffic of states or their leaders" (*ibid.*).

The centralisation of data also exposes host countries to the danger of authoritarian influence since access to data could become a liability in the diplomatic issues or divergences with Beijing (Hemmings and Chan 2020) and could also expose the EU if the host country is a Member State. Therefore, the DSR may indirectly export Chinese digital authoritarianism and become a challenge to the EU's regulations and norms (Eder et al. 2019). Brussels and Beijing have committed to strengthen cooperation between China's Internet Plus strategy (The State Council of the PRC n.d.) and the EU Digital Agenda (European Commission 2010). The Internet Plus strategy is linked to the "Made in China 2025" plan and aims at restructuring the Chinese economy through the integration of "network connectivity and networked applications" (Hong 2017). Launched in 2015 by the Internet Plus Action Plan, it relies on the Internet to integrate the technological, industrial and service sectors.

Although both China's Internet Plus Strategy and the European Digital Agenda have similar goals, limitations on cooperation remain important because of the opposing approach of China and the EU on the Internet; the EU notably adopts an open multi-stakeholders' approach while China backs a heavily state-controlled online system. Furthermore, the People's Liberation Army is traditionally a key player in Chinese telecommunications (Mulvenon and Bickford 1999); unsurprisingly, Huawei Technology Corporation was created by a former general, Ren Yunfei (Barré 2016). As the second largest company selling network equipment worldwide, Huawei is well established in European countries. Since its 5G technology is cheap and advanced, it is one of the recipients of the EU's push to deploy 5G (Cerulus 2017). As an EU representative explained, Huawei "present themselves as a private company but the links with the CPC are well-known" (Interview with EU Representative 2014); thus, its activity in sensitive sectors raises security questions. Furthermore, Chinese companies are heavily subsidised by the government and the EU's approach to Huawei is creating friction with Washington, which has excluded Chinese providers for its 5G wireless network due to national security concerns (Rogers and Ruppersberger 2012).

Within the CEECs, Huawei in 2008 replaced "Ericsson in the production of equipment for wireless internet in Serbia" (Shehadi and Hopkins 2020). In 2014, Serbia's Ministry of the Interior signed a MOU with Huawei which inaugurated an Innovation Centre for Digital Transformation in Belgrade in 2020. Serbia is expected to become a sub-regional digital hub in the Balkans; its government also signed a MOU with Huawei for its Smart City project (Shehadi and Hopkins 2020). In Poland, Huawei entered the market in 2004 to become the leading smartphone provider in 2018 (Xinhua 2018). A member of NATO that permanently hosts 4,000 American soldiers, Poland signed an arms deal with the US to deploy a missile defence system on its soil (Kelly 2018) and host an American military base (Shotter and Manson 2018). Therefore, when the Pentagon declared its intention to stop the sale of mobile phones produced by Huawei and ZTE within its military bases because of "potential security threats" (Woo and Lubold 2018), Huawei became a hot topic of bilateral negotiations. In 2019, following pressure from Washington, Warsaw arrested a Huawei employee and a former Polish security officer on spying allegations (Plucinska et al. 2019) before finally banning Huawei from the 5G national plan (Sink and Sebenius 2019).

Hence, because it will likely shape the future of digital connectivity, 5G is a key-normative issue for the EU. Its presence in European countries has become a political issue because network equipment companies that manage the infrastructure have direct access to data flows and could thus access European critical information and communications technology infrastructure. Washington has stepped up bipartisan pressure on European countries to boycott Huawei, destabilising the implementation of 5G by 2020 that was promised by the EU 5G Action Plan. Nancy Pelosi has publicly linked the danger posed by Huawei to China's authoritarian system, saying that European countries will have to "choose autocracy over democracy" (Peel and Warrell 2020).

The EU toolbox for 5G security is a welcome tool for coordinating the European approach to secure 5G networks, and European countries have a less suspicious attitude towards Chinese companies and no military competition with China. The Serbian and Polish cases illustrate some of the challenges faced by the EU on the DSR and how different the outcome may be depending on the country and its links both to the EU and also Washington.

Conclusion

The BRI is a powerful foreign policy tool for realising the Chinese dream of rejuvenation by 2049 and poses institutional challenges to the EU. Although Chinese investment helps provide the necessary infrastructure at a time when Brexit has reduced the EU budget, growing relations between China and Member States may further divide the EU. Despite a more positive approach towards the BRI, European concerns exist over the lower standards of Chinese companies, links to the CCP, lack of transparency and accountability, economic inefficiency and corruption. Furthermore, the authoritarian tendencies of certain CEECs, such as Hungary (Rácz 2011), suit China's regime (Bergsten et al. 2008); participating in BRI projects may increase China's influence on receiving countries and decrease their allegiance to the EU and its standards of good governance while exposing host countries to excessive public debt.

Therefore, the EU should work to strengthen the democratic institutions in CEECs and make greater effort to provide infrastructure, particularly for 5G where the role of Chinese companies should remain weak for security reasons. Brussels should also accelerate the accession of western Balkan countries to enhance their resilience in the face of growing authoritarian influence. Opening these countries to EU membership would end an impasse while strengthening their adherence to European rules. However, this would inevitably increase diversity within the EU and further complicate the already difficult decision-making process. Therefore, the EU should review its governance before enlargement to the Western Balkans.

China is redrawing its periphery according to its interests and has the potential to reshape the whole of Eurasia in the long-term (Zanardi 2019). This may bring to a shift in Katzenstein's analysis of how Asia and Europe change according to how the US changes (Katzenstein 2015): in fact, in the 21st century, the focus may increasingly be on how the US and Europe change according to how Asia changes. As Eurasia is expected to become more interconnected, the analysis should thus shift towards how Asia and Europe will change according to China rather than the US.

Through the 17 + 1 and the BRI, China promotes "sub-regional economic integration that transcend [*sic.*] national borders" (Vangeli 2017, 60) as well as those of the EU. The 17 + 1 could also signal the very inception of a regional institution. Therefore, it is crucial for the EU to speak with one voice to China and prevent any erosion of its identity. As the German foreign minister called on China to respect "one Europe" and on Europeans to develop "a single strategy towards China" to prevent it from "dividing Europe" (Kynge and Peel 2017), so the EU as a whole should openly make the same request to Beijing.

The EU is as dependent on China as China is on the EU and should therefore not be afraid of defending its own positions *vis-à-vis* China—the latter certainly does not respect weakness and kowtowing. The BRI is not a thing that should be opposed, and cooperation is preferred to antagonism. However, it is necessary for the EU to clearly define its own interests and the best way of achieving them. For instance, despite the EU-China summit incorporating the BRI into its 2015 agenda, the 2015 EU-China Connectivity Platform looking for connectivity cooperation, the European Commission's Joint Communication "Elements for a new EU strategy on China", the 2016 European Global Strategy, and the 2018 EU-Asia Connectivity Strategy, the EU's approach towards China remains reactive and underdeveloped.

Since it is up to China to demonstrate that the BRI is open, respects market rules and international norms, and is beneficial for all, the EU needs to closely cooperate with Washington to maintain these norms. Despite the election of Donald Trump in 2017 increased tensions between the US and the EU, there remains room for cooperation with the US on countering Chinese influence in Eurasia, especially on avoiding the degradation of international norms and standards in favour of China's lower norms and standards. Although working with Washington would help defend the EU's increasingly challenged normative power (Sjursen 2017), the EU and its Member States risk being trapped "in the great power game between China and the US" (Okano-Heijmans and Montesano 2016, 4).

Therefore, since the BRI is a much more important challenge for Europe—which lacks the resources to also develop a significant role in the Asia-Pacific region—the EU should rather focus on strengthening its relations with its immediate neighbourhood. This does not mean that it should completely neglect the Asia-Pacific but simply that it should recognise the impossibility of it promoting order in that region. While a Geopolitical European Commission is a first step forward because the EU cannot either just rely on its normative power or on the erratic foreign policy of the current US administration, the Commission should be given the tools to be a geopolitical actor. Since this requires changes in the current institutional settings of the EU, it should, in the meantime, take a pragmatic approach guided by its own interests and cooperate with Asia-Pacific powers wherever possible in order to defend international norms and standards. Finally, the EU should avoid siding with Washington in the latter's confrontational relations with Beijing and instead choose its partners on a case-by-case basis according to its own interests. The issue remains of how to define and defend these interests amidst the current internal and external crises facing the EU.

Notes

1 "16+1" before Greece joined: Albania, Bosnia-Herzegovina, Bulgaria, Croatia, Czech Republic, Estonia, Hungary, Latvia, Lithuania, North Macedonia, Montenegro, Poland, Romania, Serbia, Slovakia and Slovenia.
2 Law of July 24, 2015, Journal of Laws of 2015, item 1272.
3 Cyprus, Greece, Malta and Portugal in 2018; Italy in 2019.
4 "New" or Second Eurasian Land Bridge, the first being the Eurasian Land Bridge of the Trans-Siberian Railway of 1916.
5 It implies at least the adherence to the One China Policy and China's core interests.

References

Adamowski, Jaroslaw. 2016. "Poland Unveils New Space Strategy, Eyes Space Spending Hike." *Spacenews*, October 12.
Agnew, John A. 2013. "Arguing with Regions." *Regional Studies* 47 (1): 6–17.
Andrew, Hurrell. 1995. "Explaining the Resurgence of Regionalism in World Politics." *Review of International Studies* 21 (4): 331–358.
Babones, Salvatore. 2018. "China Is Sitting on $3 Trillion in Currency Reserves, But Is That Enough?" *Forbes*, May 24.
Barré, Geneviève. 2016. *Quand les entreprises chinoises se mondialisent: Haier, Huawei et TCL*. Paris: CNRS Editions.
Berger, Brian. 2016. "Poland Signs Space Partnership Deal with China, Eyes Increased Industry Cooperation." *Spacenews*, July 4.
Bergsten, C. Fred, Charles Freeman, Nicholas R. Lardy, and Derek J. Mitchell. 2008. *China's Rise. Challenges and Opportunities*. Washington, DC: Peterson Institute for International Economics.
Bloomberg. n.d. "Company Overview of Konsalnet Holding S.A. Bloomberg Commercial Services and Supplies." www.bloomberg.com/research/stocks/private/snapshot. asp?privcapId=49280320.

Callahan, William A. 2016. *China's Belt and Road Initiative and the New Eurasian Order*. Oslo: Norwegian Institute of International Affairs Policy Brief 22.

Cass, Deborah Z., Brett G. Williams, and George Barker. 2003. *China and the World Trading System: Entering the New Millennium*. Cambridge: Cambridge University Press.

Cerulus, Laurens. 2017. "China's Ghost in Europe's Telecom Machine." *Politico*, December 11.

Cheney, Clayton. 2019. *China's Digital Silk Road: Strategic Technological Competition and Exporting Political Illiberalism*. Londres: European Council on Foreign Relations, September 26. s. https://www.cfr.org/blog/chinas-digital-silk-road-strategic-technological-competition-andexporting-political.

Eder, Thomas S., Rebecca Arcesati, and Jacob Mardell. 2019. "Networking the 'Belt and Road'—the Future Is Digital." *Merics*, August 28. www.merics.org/en/bri-tracker/networking-the-belt-and-road.

Ekman, Alice. 2016. "La Chine en Méditerranée: un nouvel activisme." *Politique Etrangère* 81 (4): 73–84.

Ekman, Alice. 2018. "China in the Mediterranean: An Emerging Presence." *Notes de l'Ifri*, February.

European Commission. 2010. "A Digital Agenda for Europe." May 19. https://eur-lex.europa.eu/legal-content/EN/TXT/HTML/?uri=CELEX:52010DC0245&from=en.

European Commission, and High Representative of the Union for Foreign Affairs and Security. 2019. "Joint Communication to the European Parliament, the European Council and the Council: EU-China—A Strategic Outlook, JOIN(2019) 5 Final." March 12. https://ec.europa.eu/commission/sites/beta-political/files/communication-eu-china-a-strategic-outlook.pdf.

Feng, Zhongping, and Jing Huang. 2016. "Sino-European Cooperation on the Belt and Road Initiative: Drive, Dynamics and Prospect." *Contemporary International Relations* 26 (2): 11–24.

Ferenczy, Zsuzsa Anna. 2019. *Europe, China, and the Limits of Normative Power*. Cheltenham: Edward Elgar Publishing.

Forsberg, Tuomas. 2011. "Normative Power Europe, Once Again: A Conceptual Analysis of an Ideal Type." *Journal of Common Market Studies* 49 (6): 1183–1204.

Fukuyama, Francis. 2016. "Exporting the Chinese Model." *Project Syndicate*, January 12. www.project-syndicate.org/onpoint/china-one-belt-one-road-strategy-by-francis-fukuyama-2016-01.

Garver, John W. 2006. "Development of China's Overland Transportation Links with Central, South-West and South Asia." *The China Quarterly* 185: 1–22.

Goh, Brenda, and Marcin Goettig. 2018. "In Europe's East, a Border Town Strains Under China's Silk Road Train Boom." *Reuters*, June 27. www.reuters.com/article/us-china-europe-silkroad-insight/in-europes-east-a-border-town-strains-under-chinas-silk-road-train-boom-idUSKBN1JM34M.

Góralczyk, Bogdan. 2017. "China's Interests in Central and Eastern Europe: Enter the Dragon." *European View* 16 (1): 153–162.

Gottwald, Jörn-Carsten, Andrew Cottey, and Natasha Underhill. 2010. "The European Union and China: Status, Issues, Prospects." In *Civil Society in European-Chinese Relations, Challenges of Cooperation*, edited by Nora Sausmikat and Klaus Fritsche, 7–32. Essen: Asienstiftung.

Heilman, Sebastian, and Dirk Schmidt. 2014. *China's Foreign Political and Economic Relations: An Unconventional Global Power*. Lanham: Rowman and Littlefield.

Hemmings, John. 2020. "Reconstructing Order: The Geopolitical Risks in China's Digital Silk Road." *Asia Policy* 27 (1): 5–21.

Hemmings, John, and Patrick Chan. 2020. "Exploring China's Orwellian Digital Silk Road." *The National Interest*, January 7. https://nationalinterest.org/feature/exploring-china%E2%80%99s-orwellian-digital-silk-road-111731.

Hong, Yu. 2017. "Pivot to Internet Plus: Molding China's Digital Economy for Economic Restructuring?" *International Journal of Communication* 11: 1486–1506.

Hu, Yongqi. 2017. "Li Calls to Accelerate China-Europe Land-Sea Express Line." *China Daily*, November 29.

Interview with EU Representative. 2014. Brussels, May 22.

Interview with Philippe LeCorre. 2018. Frankfurt, November 2.

Interview with Polish Expert. 2018. Warsaw, October 30.

Interview with Una Aleksandra Bērziņa-Čerenkova. 2018. Turku, October 11.

Jian, Junbo. 2018. "China in Central Asia and the Balkans: Challenges from a Geopolitical Perspective." In *The Belt & Road Initiative in the Global Arena: Chinese and European Perspectives*, edited by Yu Cheng, Lilei Song, and Lihe Huang, 241–261. Singapore: Palgrave Macmillan.

Jones, Catherine. 2018. *China's Challenge to Liberal Norms: The Durability of International Order*. Basingstoke: Palgrave Macmillan.

Kaczmarski, Marcin. 2017. "Non-Western Visions of Regionalism: China's New Silk Road and Russia's Eurasian Economic Union." *International Affairs* 93 (6): 1357–1376.

Kamiński, Tomasz. 2019. "What Are the Factors Behind the Successful EU-China Cooperation on the Subnational Level? Case Study of the Lodzkie Region in Poland." *Asia European Journal* 17 (2): 227–242.

Katzenstein, Peter J. 2015. *A World of Regions: Asia and Europe in the American Imperium*. Ithaca: Cornell University Press.

Keegan, Elmer. 2018. "EU Presents (Nearly) United Front Against China's 'Unfair' Belt and Road Initiative." *South China Morning Post*, April 20.

Kelly, Lydia. 2018. "Poland Signs $4.75 Billion Deal for U.S. Patriot Missile System Facing Russia." *Reuters*, March 28. http://reuters.com/article/us-raytheon-poland-patriot/poland-signs-4–75-billion-deal-for-u-s-patriot-missile-system-facing-russia-idUSKBN1H417S.

Kohlenberg, Paul J., and Nadine Godehardt. 2018. "China's Global Connectivity Power: SWP Comment." April 17. www.swp-berlin.org/fileadmin/contents/products/comments/2018C17_khb_gdh.pdf.

Kratz, Agatha. 2018. *Implication de la Chine dans le secteur des transports en Europe Centrale et Orientale: Formes, réalisations et limites. Étude de l'IRSEM* 55. Paris: Irsem.

Kuo, Mercy A. 2017. "China in Eastern Europe: Poland's Perspective." *The Diplomat*, December 19. https://thediplomat.com/2017/12/china-in-eastern-europe-polands-perspective/.

Kynge, James, and Michael Peel. 2017. "Brussels Rattled as China Reaches Out to Eastern Europe." *Financial Times*, November 27. www.ft.com/content/16abbf2a-cf9b-11e7-9dbb-291a884dd8c6.

Leonard, Mark, Jean Pisani-Ferry, Elina Ribakova, Jeremy Shapiro, and Guntram Wolff. 2019. "Securing Europe's Economic Sovereignty." *Survival* 61 (5): 75–98.

Li, Xue. 2019. "China-Europe Land-Sea Express Route with the Belt and Road Initiative." In *Routledge Handbook of the Belt and Road*, edited by Fang Cai and Peter Nolan, 453–456. Abingdon: Routledge.

Lucas, Louise, and Emily Feng. 2018. "Inside China's Surveillance State." *Financial Times*, July 20. www.ft.com/content/2182eebe-8a17-11e8-bf9e-8771d5404543.

Manners, Ian. 2002. "Normative Power Europe: A Contradiction in Terms." *Journal of Common Market Studies* 40 (2): 235–258.

Manuel, Ryan. 2019. "Twists in the Belt and Road." *China Leadership Monitor*, September 1. www.prcleader.org/manuel-belt-road.

Mattlin, Mikael. 2012. "Dead on Arrival: Normative EU Policy Towards China." *Asia-Europe Journal* 10 (2–3): 181–198.

Medeiros, Evan S., and Taylor M. Fravel. 2003. "China's New Diplomacy." *Foreign Affairs* 82 (6): 22–35.

Michalski, Anna. 2017. "Europe, China, and the Diffusion of Norms." In *Unlikely Partners? China, the European Union and the Forging of a Strategic Partnership*, edited by Anna Michalski and Zhongqi Pan. Basingstoke: Palgrave Macmillan.

Mulvenon, James, and Thomas J. Bickford. 1999. "The PLA and the Telecommunications Industry in China." In *The People's Liberation Army in the Information Age*, edited by James C. Mulvenon and Richard H. Yang, 245–257. Santa Monica, CA: RAND Corporation.

Musiałkowska, Ida. 2018. "Subnational Development Policy as the Area of Common Interest Under the One Belt One Road Initiative? The Case of Regional Policy-Making in Poland." In *The Belt & Road Initiative in the Global Arena: Chinese and European Perspectives*, edited by Yu Cheng, Lilei Song, and Lihe Huang, 141–161. Singapore: Palgrave Macmillan.

National Development and Reform Commission, Ministry of Foreign Affairs and Ministry of Commerce of the PRC. 2015. "Vision and Actions on Jointly Building Silk Road Economic Belt and 21st Century Maritime Silk Road." March 28. https://reconasia-production.s3.amazonaws.com/media/filer_public/e0/22/e0228017-7463-46fc-9094-0465a6f1ca23/vision_and_actions_on_jointly_building_silk_road_economic_belt_and_21st-century_maritime_silk_road.pdf

Okano-Heijmans, Maaike, and Francesco Saverio Montesano. 2016. *Who Is Afraid of European Economic Diplomacy?* Clingendael Policy Brief. The Hague: Netherlands Institute of International Relations 'Clingendael', April 5.

Ortmann, Stephan, and Mark R. Thompson. 2018. "Introduction to the Special Section: The 'Singapore Model' and China's Neo-Authoritarian Dream." *The China Quarterly* 236: 930–945.

Palma, Stefania. 2018. "China Accused of Using Belt and Road Initiative for Spying." *Financial Times*, August 15.

Palonka, Krystyna. 2010. "Economic and Trade Relations Between Poland and China Since 2004." *Asia Europe Journal* 8 (3): 369–378.

Pavlićević, Dragan. 2019. "A Powershift Underway in Europe? China's Relationship with Central and Eastern Europe under the Belt and Road Initiative." In *Mapping China's 'One Belt One Road' Initiative*, edited by Li Xing. Cham: Palgrave Macmillan.

Peel, Michael, and Helen Warrell. 2020. "Nancy Pelosi Warns Europe Over Huawei 5G Dangers." *Financial Times*, February 14. www.ft.com/content/c2fbacf2-4f43-11ea-95a0-43d18ec715f5.

Plucinska, Joanna, Karol Witenberg, and Jack Stubbs. 2019. "Poland Arrests Huawei Employee, Polish Man on Spying Allegations." *Reuters*, January 11. www.reuters.com/article/us-poland-security/poland-arrests-huawei-employee-polish-man-on-spying-allegations-idUSKCN1P50RN.

Rácz, András. 2011. "A Limited Priority: Hungary and the Eastern Neighbourhood." *Perspectives: Review of Central European Affairs* 19 (2): 143–163.

Ramani, Samuel. 2016. "China's Growing Ties With Serbia." *The Diplomat*, February 29. https://thediplomat.com/2016/02/chinas-growing-ties-with-serbia/.

Reuters. 2017. "BRIEF-China Security & Fire Scraps Plan to Buy Poland's Konsalnet." *Reuters*, June 30.

Rogers, Mike, and Charles A. Ruppersberger. 2012. *Investigative Report on the U.S. National Security Issues Posed by Chinese Telecommunications Companies Huawei and ZTE*. Washington, DC: U.S. House of Representatives, 12th Congress, October 8.

Rogers, Samuel. 2019. "China, Hungary, and the Belgrade-Budapest Railway Upgrade: New Politically-Induced Dimensions of FDI and the Trajectory of Hungarian Economic Development." *Journal of East-West Business* 25 (1): 84–106.

Rolland, Geneviève. 2019. "Beijing's Response to the Belt and Road Initiative's 'Pushback': A Story of Assessment and Adaptation." *Asian Affairs* 50 (2): 216–235.

Seaman, John. 2020. "China and the New Geopolitics of Standardisation." *Notes de l'Ifri*, January 27. www.ifri.org/sites/default/files/atoms/files/seaman_china_standardization_2020.pdf.

Sellier, Elodie. 2016. "China's Mediterranean Odyssey." *The Diplomat*, April 19.

Shehadi, Sebastian, and Valerie Hopkins. 2020. "Serbia's Embrace of Chinese FDI Raises Questions of Transparency." *Financial Times*, February 7.

Shotter, James, and Katrina Manson. 2018. "Poland Woos White House with 'Fort Trump' Pitch." *Financial Times*, September 24.

Sink, Justin, and Alyza Sebenius. 2019. "U.S. and Poland Ink 5G Security Agreement Amid Anti-Huawei Campaign." *Bloomberg*, September 2.

Sjursen, Helene. 2017. "Principles in European Union Foreign Policy, 3rd." In *International Relations and the European Union*, edited by Christopher Hill, Michael Smith, and Sophie Vanhoonacker, 3rd ed., 445–462. Oxford: Oxford University Press.

The State Council of the PRC. n.d. "Internet Plus." http://english.www.gov.cn/2016special/internetplus/.

Szczudlik, Justyna. 2016. "Poland on the Silk Road in Central Europe: To Become a Hub of Hubs?" In *Europe and China's New Silk Roads. ETNC Report December 2016*, edited by Frans-Paul van der Putten, John Seaman, Mikko Huotari, Alice Ekman, and Miguel Otero-Iglesias, 45–48. www.iai.it/sites/default/files/2016_etnc_report.pdf.

Szunomar, Agnes. 2018. "One Belt One Road: Connecting China with Central and Eastern Europe?" In *The Belt & Road Initiative in the Global Arena: Chinese and European Perspectives*, edited by Yu Cheng, Lilei Song, and Lihe Huang, 71–85. Singapore: Palgrave Macmillan.

Taylor, Ian. 2010. *The Forum on China-Africa Cooperation (FOCAC)*. London: Routledge.

Thompson, Mark R. 2019. *Authoritarian Modernism in East Asia*. New York: Palgrave Macmillan.

Tocci, Nathalie. 2009. *Who Is A Normative Power? The European Union and Its Global Partners*. Brussels: CEPS.

van der Putten, Frans-Paul. 2016. "Infrastructure and Geopolitics: China's Emerging Presence in the Eastern Mediterranean." *Journal of Balkan and Near Eastern Studies* 18 (4): 337–351.

Vangeli, Anastas. 2017. "The Impact of China." In *Resilience in the Western Balkans: EUISS Report* 36, edited by Sabina Lange, Zoran Nechev, and Florian Trauner, 57–62. Paris: EUISS.

Vasselier, Abigaël, and François Godement. 2018. *China at the Gates: A New Power Audit of EU-China Relations*. London: ECFR.

Wolf, Reinhard, Markus Liegl, and Sebastian Biba. 2016. "Introduction: Perils of US-China Confrontation—Implications for Europe." *European Foreign Affairs Review* 21 (3/1): 1–10.

Woo, Stu, and Gordon Lubold. 2018. "Pentagon Orders Stores on Military Bases to Remove Huawei, ZTE Phones." *Wall Street Journal*, May 2. www.wsj.com/articles/pentagon-asking-military-bases-to-remove-huawei-zte-phones-1525262076.

Xi, Jinping. 2019. *Working Together to Deliver a Brighter Future for Belt and Road Cooperation*. Keynote Speech by Xi Jinping at the Opening Ceremony of the Second Belt and Road Forum for International Cooperation, Beijing: National People's Congress, 6–11.

Xinhua. 2017. "Belt and Road' Incorporated into CPC Constitution." *Xinhua*, October 24. www.xinhuanet.com//english/2017-10/24/c_136702025.htm.

Xinhua. 2018. "China's Huawei Becomes Largest Smart Phone Seller in Poland: Report." May 27. www.xinhuanet.com/english/2018-05/27/c_137210290.htm.

Xu, Shu. 1997. "The New Asia-Europe Land Bridge-Current Situation and Future Prospects." *Japan Railways and Transport Review* 14: 30–33.

Xue, Li. 2015. "Zhongguo 'Yidai Yilu' zhanlüe miandui de waijiao fengxian' [Diplomatic Risks Facing the Belt and Road Strategy]." *Guoji Jingji Pinglun [International Economic Review]* 2: 68–79.

Zanardi, Claude. 2019. "The Rise of China and Connecting Eurasia and Asia Pacific." In *Beyond Europe. Reconnecting Eurasia*, edited by Tadeusz Wallas, Andrzej Stelmach, and Rafal Wiesniewski, 13–32. Berlin: Logos Verlag.

11 EU-China cooperation amidst fragmented climate leadership[1]

Mario Esteban and Lara Lázaro Touza

Introduction

Navigating the current geopolitical rivalry between the United States (US) and China is one of the key foreign policy issues for the European Union (EU). This big power rivalry might be seen as entailing difficult *a priori* choices for the EU, one of which is related to concerted climate action. Should the EU follow a normative approach or pursue its own interests in building international climate cooperation? Should it continue cooperating with the US, a long-term strategic and economic partner which is expected to rejoin the Paris Agreement under the Biden administration? Or should the EU reinforce existing cooperation with China, the EU's second most important market, arguably the next economic superpower and the self-proclaimed bedrock of the Paris Agreement?

Unlike other issues on the global agenda, the choice of normative versus interest-based interaction on climate change may be deemed irrelevant as there is arguably no significant normative conflict at present between European and Chinese stakeholders. Additionally, while development goals have historically limited Chinese climate ambition, China's embrace of a "New Normal" development model, its energy dependence, renewable energy leadership and quest for international recognition provide enough interest-based reasons for engaging in joint climate action with willing partners such as the EU.

On the other hand, the US withdrew from the Paris Agreement on 4 November 2020, after being one of its key architects alongside China and the EU. Until the US regains a seat at the global climate partnership table the question remains who could help fill America's climate void internationally and what type of alliances could historic (EU) and new (China) climate heavyweights build. China, accounting for 25 percent of global greenhouse gas (GHG) emissions, and the EU, whose emissions amount to 9 percent of global GHG emissions, have been singled out as the two obvious choices. They are also two of the three leading actors in the international climate change regime. As such, they seem to be in a privileged position to jointly fill America's leadership gap.[2]

In this context, the EU is seeking to strengthen a rules-based multilateral order to avoid the bipolarisation that could result in it being forced to forsake relations with one of the two global powers, most likely China (Casarini 2019; Esteban et al. 2020; Garcia-Herrero 2019; Niblett 2018). China, meanwhile, strives to boost its international status, projecting itself as a structural leader[3] that can meet its climate commitments and safeguard the Paris Agreement.

Considering the current fragmentation of the climate leadership space (Falkner 2018), this chapter explores three interconnected issues. The first is how America's withdrawal from the Paris Agreement could affect its role in the international climate change regime. The second is China's evolving cooperation on climate change with both the US and the EU. The third is the prospects for EU-China climate leadership, based on their enhanced climate change cooperation and domestic developments in China under the leadership of Xi Jinping. The chapter concludes by highlighting climate change as an issue on which Europe's preference for a rules-based multilateral order—aligned with both the EU's values and interests—signals its willingness to continue cooperating with both the US and China in order to ensure a stable climate.

The US in the international climate regime post Trump

America's withdrawal from the Paris Agreement and its failure to honour its nationally determined contribution (NDC) will increase the current emissions gap (Dai et al. 2017), reduce the overall carbon budget available to meet the agreed temperature goals (Sussams 2018) and increase mitigation costs for the agreement's other parties (Dai et al. 2018), including China and the EU.

With the US withdrawal from the Paris Agreement, its leadership role, exercised very effectively since the inception of the international climate regime in the 1990s, could logically be expected to come to an end. In fact, there are authors that contend that the US withdrawal from the Paris Agreement will lead to a three-pronged leadership gap: the mitigation gap, the climate finance gap and the governance gap (Chai et al. 2017). However, given the timing of its withdrawal as per Article 28 of the Paris Agreement and the "tsunami" of non-state climate action, the US could retain some mitigation and governance leadership, reducing the space for other potential leaders while maintaining its pull as a climate companion to the EU.

The partial retention of climate leadership by the US is explained by the substantive role it has played in the development, adoption and entry into force of the Paris Agreement, as well as during the development of the Katowice rulebook at COP 24 that (almost) completed the implementation guidelines of the Paris Agreement. Even if leaving the Paris Agreement means that the US no longer has a say in international climate negotiations under that framework for the duration of the withdrawal, it is still a party to the United Nations Framework Convention on Climate Change (UNFCCC) and retains its observer status within the Paris Agreement negotiations, as it did with the Kyoto Protocol (Chestnoy and Gershinkova 2017). This could present opportunities for cooperation between the EU and US on climate change.

Moreover, the US withdrawal from the Paris Agreement does not preclude climate leadership by non-state actors, essential (both globally and in the US) for achieving the goal of avoiding dangerous human interference with the climate system. Regarding non-state actions, the US can pride itself in having reacted decisively in the aftermath of Trump's Rose Garden withdrawal speech (Averchenkova 2019). The most salient initiatives at the time this withdrawal was announced were America's Pledge (Bloomberg Philanthropies 2018) and We Are Still In (We Are Still in 2017).

According to an America's Pledge report, non-state action in the US analysed by this initiative will deliver two-thirds of America's climate commitment under its NDC (Bloomberg Philanthropies 2018). Therefore, although insufficient to fulfil its international commitments, non-state actions could afford the US some international mitigation leadership for the duration of the withdrawal.

However, regarding climate finance, it seems clear that, under former President Trump, the US has partially relinquished its leadership role to other parties to the Paris Agreement. A US$2 billion funding gap remains, for instance, in the US contribution to the Green Climate Fund (Taraska et al. 2017; GCF 2018). The long-term international climate finance goal under the Paris Agreement is to provide US$100 billion annually from 2020 onwards to foster developing countries' mitigation and adaptation actions, and other parties would have to increase their contributions to fill America's financial gap. More recently, the fact that the Democrats won a majority in the House of Representatives has led to a partial reversal of former President Trump's pledge of radically scaling down US international climate finance (Thwaites 2020), arguably mitigating US leadership loss on climate finance.

It is also interesting to note that, to a certain extent, EU-US climate cooperation was still ongoing under the Trump administration. According to the US Environmental Protection Agency (EPA), cooperation included air quality and vehicle emission testing, the control of Montreal Protocol regulated substances, the Global Methane Initiative (GMI) and joint efforts in the area of energy efficiency (EPA 2019). There was no mention of the Paris Agreement in cooperation arrangements, even though US negotiators still attended international climate conferences and interacted in a relatively constructive manner with EU negotiators (Roberts 2018). There was hence both an openly acknowledged cooperation agenda on climate-related issues and unpublicised ongoing cooperation on the international climate regime. This cooperation was geared towards allowing the US to re-enter the Paris Agreement.

In the (temporary) absence of the US in the international climate regime, the leadership binomial of EU-China has been touted by scholars as needed after Trump's withdrawal (Kopra 2019; Lázaro Touza 2017) and even after the US may rejoin the Paris Agreement under the new Biden administration.

A realignment in Chinese climate change cooperation

Cooperation on climate change between the US and China boomed during Barak Obama's second term. Joint Sino-American climate leadership was key for the international community, with a bilateral US-China agreement being used to shape the international climate change regime. In November 2014, the two countries decided to jointly present their emission reduction targets for 2025 and 2030 respectively (The White House 2014a). These targets would then be included in their intended NDCs, setting the stage for other countries to announce their own contributions (The White House 2014b).

The bilateral US-China climate change cooperation was reinforced in 2015 with the US-China Joint Presidential Statement on Climate Change issued during Xi's visit to the US (The White House 2015). China assumed in that document—at least on paper—some key issues that would enable China to play a leadership role on climate change, such as providing more transparent information regarding greenhouse gas emissions and actions to fight climate change. China also committed to financing climate change actions in developing countries. Furthermore, joint US-China climate leadership was clearly shown in their simultaneous ratification of the Paris Agreement in 2016 which, along with the EU ratification, was key to the Agreement's entry into force.

The Trump administration, on the other hand, marginalised climate change in its policy agenda and followed a more confrontational approach towards China than Obama's administration (Pence 2019). That took a severe toll on US-China climate change cooperation (as illustrated by the ending of the US-China Climate Change Working Group) and has paved the way towards deeper EU-China cooperation in this field as Chinese leaders look for a new privileged partner on climate action, however, progress has been patchy.[4] The EU and China were supposed to issue a joint *communiqué* on climate change during their 19th summit on 2 June 2017, but the Chinese side decided not to move forward to protest the EU not granting them market economy status (Godement and Vasselier 2017).

Despite this setback, the EU and China finally decided to enhance their climate change cooperation during their 20th bilateral summit in 2018, when both sides underlined the privileged role that climate change and clean energy will play in their bilateral relations, expecting it to become "a main pillar of their bilateral partnership, including in their economic relations" (European Council 2018).[5] This was reflected in the Leaders' Statement on Climate Change and Clean Energy and in the Memorandum of Understanding to Enhance Cooperation on Emissions Trading between the European Commission and the Ministry of Ecology and Environment of the People's Republic of China (European Council 2018).

The two main innovations in the enhanced EU-China cooperation on climate change *vis-à-vis* the US-China partnership are related to emissions trading and triangular cooperation in developing countries. On the former, the EU and China are likely to have the two largest carbon markets in the world. They agree that emissions trading is potentially a cost-effective climate policy tool. Hence, the EU and China have agreed to expand their cooperation on emissions trading. China is trying to consolidate a national carbon emission market out of seven pilot projects, although it faces significant difficulties in attracting foreign investors (Goulder et al. 2017). The EU is therefore providing technical cooperation on how to develop, run and review emissions trading systems. Regarding the other innovation, triangular climate change cooperation in developing countries, it is significant that the EU has made explicit recognition of Chinese leadership in this field, particularly in the development of the G20 recommendations on green finance (European Council 2018).

Moreover, EU-China climate change cooperation also contains explicit calls for bilateral cooperation on climate change and related multilateral fora, including but not limited to the United Nations Framework Convention on Climate Change. This demand for deepening EU-China cooperation could potentially serve as a platform for jointly shaping the climate change regime, as the US and China did during Obama's second term.

Drivers of joint EU-China leadership on climate change

The EU has been one of the most committed actors in fighting climate change since its 1992 adoption of the United Nations Framework Convention on Climate Change (UNFCCC), despite different priorities across its Member States. The EU has consistently followed a strategy of "leading by example" (Gupta and Grubb 2000; Lázaro Touza 2018). Domestically, it has a broad climate *acquis*, a robust institutional set-up and a stable corpus of civil servants dedicated to climate action. It has established significant domestic targets, including that of becoming the first climate neutral region in the world. This was enshrined in the European Green Deal after the declaration of a climate emergency. It has pledged €1 trillion through the Sustainable Europe Investment Plan (European Commission 2020) for a low-carbon transition, although this is insufficient for meeting the goals of the Paris Agreement (Climate Action Tracker 2019; also see Table 11.1). The EU has also greened its multiannual financial framework (2021–2027) as well as the post COVID-19 recovery mechanism (NextGenerationEU) which together amount to €1.8 trillion, with 30 percent of these funds allocated to climate action (European Council, 2020).

The fact that EU emissions have dropped 22 percent between 1990 and 2017 while its GDP has grown 58 percent attests to its past success in curbing GHG within its borders (Eurostat 2019). In fact, meeting its 2020 climate commitments is not expected to weigh heavily on potential GDP growth, although energy intensive sectors that trade their goods internationally (e.g., steel and aluminium) are expected to lose from increasingly stringent climate policies (Carraro and Davide 2016).

Table 11.1 EU's climate and energy targets

Area	Target 2020 (base year/ reference)	Target 2030 (base year/ reference)	Target 2050 (base year/ reference)
GHG emission reduction	20% (1990)	55% (1990)	Climate neutrality. Net Zero emissions (1990)
Renewable energy	20%	32%	N/A
Energy efficiency	20% (BAU)	32.5% (BAU)	N/A

Sources: European Commission (2019, 2017); Arias Cañete (2018); European Council (2020).

The EU's significant energy dependence and the fact that several EU countries rank among the world's top-ten renewable energy powerhouses (IEA 2019) provides the energy security rationale for supporting the EU's concerted climate action.

As is the case in other areas, climate policies require at least a passive acceptance by citizens to be effectively implemented (Roberts 2011). According to recent surveys, Europeans (EU-28) perceive climate change as the second most serious problem facing the world, only behind poverty, hunger and lack of drinking water (European Commission 2019). Climate change also ranks as the top foreign policy concern for citizens in France, Germany and Spain (Elcano Royal Institute 2018a, 2018b, 2018c).

Internationally, the EU committed to an 8 percent reduction of its GHG emissions from 2008 to 2012 under the first commitment period of the Kyoto Protocol, a goal that the EU overachieved. Under the Paris Agreement, the EU's first NDC establishes the goal of reducing GHG emissions by 40 percent by 2030 from 1990 levels. This target will be revised upwards (55 percent) in the next round of NDC submissions.

In addition to its internal and international climate commitments, and acting as a self-proclaimed leader by example, the EU has actively and constructively cooperated in the development of the international climate change regime. It has sought to persuade other international actors of the relevance of ambitious and globally concerted climate action. It has also advocated robust rules, a strong transparency framework, and increasingly stringent targets and timelines to meet them. Europe is hence seen as a "leadiator" (leader-cum-mediator) in global climate action (Bäckstrand and Elgström 2013). Values, interests, policies and citizen support for climate action are arguably aligned, hence rendering the choice of interests versus values moot to a certain extent. The EU's quest for climate leadership is expected to continue. This remains so even if delivering on the carbon neutrality goal is fraught with difficulties that derive from the upfront and asymmetrically distributed costs of a low-carbon transition, despite recalcitrant EU states (e.g., Poland), despite the complex geopolitics of climate action (e.g., US, Brazil, Saudi Arabia) and in the face of shrinking emissions by the EU-27 *vis-à-vis* countries like China.

China has also adopted and ratified the UNFCCC, the Kyoto Protocol and the Paris Agreement, demonstrating its continued engagement with the international climate regime (Lázaro Touza and Esteban 2016), although it has been less proactive historically than the EU regarding climate action. On national climate action, China started including climate commitments in its five-year plans from 2006, when it became the largest GHG emitter. The Third Plenary Session of the 18th Congress of the Chinese Communist Party in November 2013 signalled a remarkable shift in economic policy that has been later presented by the Chinese authorities as the "new normal" that strives to achieve slower but more stable economic growth. This "new normal" is characterised by a transition from energy-intensive growth based on heavy industry, exports and investment to a more balanced economy characterised by slower growth, an increasing role for services and domestic consumption and a focus on innovation and low-carbon technologies (Hilton and

Kerr 2017). That structural economic change is considered inevitable in China as the economic, social and environmental costs of the highly-polluting economic model became more visible and its benefits shrank. The cost of China's pollution damage rose fourfold from 2004 to 2013, accounting for up to 3 percent of annual GDP; suspended particulate matter causes between 350,000 and 500,000 premature deaths per annum in urban China (Wang 2016). At the same time, excessive investment had started to generate over-capacity and mounting debt instead of development (Ding et al. 2016).

The 13th Five Year Plan (2016–2020) includes several quantified targets related to climate change that tend to be more ambitious than the ones set in the two preceding five-year plans (Grantham Research Institute on Climate Change and the Environment and Sabin Center for Climate Change Law, n.d.). It aimed to reduce CO_2 emissions per unit of GDP by 18 percent from 2015 levels by 2020, reduce energy consumption by unit of GDP by 15 percent from 2015 levels by 2020, cap total energy consumption at 5 billion metric tons of standard coal equivalent by 2020, increase non-fossil energy from 12 percent to 15 percent of primary energy consumption by 2020, raise forest cover from 21.66 percent to 23.04 percent, stabilise arable land at 124.3 million hectares by 2020, increase grassland vegetation cover to 56 percent by 2020 and reduce the area of land used for construction per unit of GDP by 20 percent by 2020—taking 2015 as a baseline—and ensure that natural shoreline does not fall below 35 percent by 2020 (2015 baseline).

China's interests and values also showed signs of aligning with a lower-carbon development model. Firstly, a profound change in China's economic structure which has led to lower GDP growth, improvements in the energy intensity per unit of GDP (since the Chinese economy became more efficient), a shift to services and a decline in carbon intensity in its energy mix, with fossil fuels losing ground to renewable energies (Peters et al. 2017, 118). Based on these trends, Chinese CO_2 emissions could peak before 2025 (Green and Stern 2016).

Secondly, China's concerns about energy security are also conducive for fostering climate change action. Since China became a net importer of crude oil in 1993, energy security (access to energy at affordable prices) (IEA 2020) has been a growing concern for Chinese policymakers (Wu et al. 2012). This concern about energy security has also translated into more vocal advocacy for a significant deployment of renewable energy and emissions controls (Yao and Chang 2014).

A third sign of China's alignment with a lower carbon development model is that problems such as poor air and water quality, desertification, health and the economic impacts of environmental deterioration have led to an increase in citizen concern about the environment and climate change (Albert and Xu 2016, also see Figure 11.1). Increasing awareness in China of the negative effects of air pollution makes it a politically salient issue because it erodes citizen support for the Chinese authorities and increases political pressure to improve air quality (Alkon and Wang 2018).

In addition to domestic factors, China began to suffer heavy criticism for its lack of climate action since the Conference of the Parties (COP) 15. Part of the international community, including both developed and some developing countries,

Views of pollution and climate change in China (%)
How big of a problem is ...?

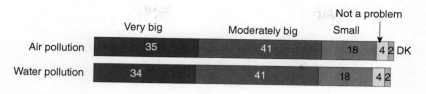

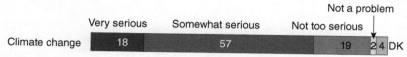

Figure 11.1 Views of pollution and climate change in China
Source: Gao (2015).[6]

no longer saw China as a typical developing country. Hence, there were growing expectations for China to assume greater responsibility for climate action. In this context, not shouldering such responsibility had a significant reputational cost for China (Kopra 2019).

Internationally, China has historically sided with the G77 and the Like-Minded Group of Developing Countries, consistently advocating for asymmetric requirements for developed and developing countries and being at times less than constructive regarding mitigation and transparency. China's stern defence of the principle of common but differentiated responsibilities, and its blocking of mitigation advancements in the run up to COP 24, are indicative of past dependencies in the international climate regime, despite welcome high-level political declarations (Xi 2017a).

On the positive side, China has stepped up its climate action in the international arena since COP 15. For the first time, it pledged to reduce its emission intensity (emissions per unit of GDP) by 40 percent to 45 percent by 2020 (compared with its 2005 levels), committed to increase its share of non-fossil fuels in its primary energy consumption to 15 percent and to significantly increase its forest cover and forest stock (Finamore 2010). In 2014, China pledged to reach its carbon emissions peak by 2030 and to reduce its emissions intensity (emissions per unit of GDP) by somewhere between 60 percent to 65 percent by 2030 (compared with 2005 levels). The share of non-fossil fuels—including nuclear—in primary energy consumption would increase to approximately 20 percent, with significant increases in forest stock.

In addition, Chinese leadership in renewable energy is one of the most significant contributions to global climate action. China has been the largest investor in renewable energy sources (RES) over the past decade, with US$785 billion from 2010 to the first half of 2019 followed by the US with US$356 billion. Furthermore, Chinese investment in RES amounted to under one-third of global renewable investment in 2018 (Frankfurt School-UNEP Centre 2019). It also leads the world in the production and net installed capacity of hydro, solar photovoltaic (PV) and wind. China also ranks among the top-ten producers and importers of oil, coal and gas. This energy portfolio and significant fossil fuel dependence is recognised as a driver of China's low-carbon transition (IEA 2017a, 2017b, 2019; Frankfurt School-UNEP Centre 2019).

China's international engagement and domestic actions to curb GHG emissions have been acknowledged by international climate negotiators. As a result, recognition by COP delegates of China's leadership increased to 54 percent, the highest ever recorded (COP 21), overtaking the EU for the first time.[7] Furthermore, China's more active engagement in the international climate change regime has paved the way for enhanced EU-China cooperation in this field. Structural changes in China's development model, energy security concerns, its prominent role in renewable energy markets and its citizens' demands for cleaner air (a co-benefit of climate action) are supporting growing long-term Chinese cooperation with the international climate change regime.

China's leadership on climate change would be aligned with the pro-active foreign policy pursued by Xi Jinping, partly oriented to increasing the international prestige of China and its leaders (Esteban 2017). Not all the international issues offer this opportunity to China, since its domestic conditions forestall Chinese leadership in other areas, such as civil liberties and political rights. Hence, climate change negotiations and cooperation with self-proclaimed climate leaders such as the EU (or the US during Obama's second term) offer China an excellent opportunity to present itself as a responsible power in the eyes of the international community and to enhance its soft power. This is even more so when the Chinese commitment to multilateralism for addressing climate change contrasts with the neo-Jacksoninan approach of the Trump administration. This commitment to multilateralism is shared by the EU and underpins bilateral EU-China cooperation on climate change (European Council 2018).

Both internal demands and international pressure have fostered greater cooperation by China both within the international climate change regime and with the EU. Additionally, the Chinese authorities have publicly announced their aspiration for China to play a leading role in international fora on climate change (Xi 2017b) and in the process of implementing the Paris Agreement (Zhu and Jun 2018). This latter point is also stressed in joint EU-China declarations: "The EU and China are determined to forge ahead with further policies and measures for the effective implementation of their respective nationally determined contributions and lead the clean energy transition" (European Council 2018, 10).

Barriers to joint EU-China climate leadership

Despite the window of opportunity for joint EU-China climate leadership created by the US withdrawal from the Paris Agreement, it is far from clear whether this leadership will materialise in the short term. China's self-proclaimed leadership in international climate change fora is not leading to more ambitious domestic action on climate change, nor is it fruitfully fostering diplomatic initiatives conducive to meeting the goals of the Paris Agreement. At the domestic level, China is on track to fulfil its 2030 NDC, but this is "highly insufficient" for keeping global warming below 2°C (Climate Action Tracker 2019). China therefore committed to update its NDC and present its long-term strategy (UNSG 2019) in 2020. The updated commitments now include a peaking in emissions before 2030 and reaching carbon neutrality by 2060—two significant improvements as compared to its previous commitments.

Moreover, there have been some setbacks in China's climate action since 2017. After decreasing coal consumption from 2013 to 2016, it flattened in 2017 and increased by 0.8 percent in 2018 (CEIC Data 2018). The Chinese government downscaled subsidies for solar power in 2018 and started the construction of new coal-fired power plants after a two-year freeze, adding 28GW of coal capacity. In April 2019, the National Energy Administration allowed 11 provinces and regions to resume building coal power plants to serve large industrial users (Bloomberg 2019). In addition, one of the most anticipated climate change policies of the 13th Five Year Plan, the implementation of a national emission trading system, has been postponed from 2017 to 2020 (Xu et al. 2019).

The loss of momentum for China's climate change action is mainly driven by domestic factors. Even if the salience of climate change in the agenda of the China's Communist Party has increased dramatically over the last decade, advances in this area are still contingent on social stability derived from economic growth (Heberer and Schubert 2017) and the legitimacy which such growth affords the government (Kopra 2019).

The trade war with the US and the slowdown of the Chinese economy have resulted in Chinese authorities prioritising pro-growth policies at the expense of sustainability, according to Chinese experts interviewed in 2019. This policy shift, which will probably be aggravated by the negative effects of the coronavirus crisis on economic growth, reflects a deep divide among different stakeholders in the Chinese regime and is expected to impact the extent to which these stakeholders integrate climate change into their decision-making processes. Pushback against climate action is being led by corporate interests and the less developed provinces, which are more reliant on the industrial sector. The dependence of China's regions and local governments on high-polluting industries for their development can limit climate action (Engels 2018; Hilton and Kerr 2017) and hence limit low-carbon cooperation between the EU and China.

A further obstacle limiting joint EU-China climate leadership is the asymmetric concern about climate change and demand for climate action by civil society. In the EU, 79 percent of citizens see climate change as a very serious problem (European Commission 2019) compared with 18 percent of China's citizens (Gao 2015; Liu et al. 2019). Differences in concern about climate change as a foreign policy priority are also significant. Citizens in large EU emitters such as France, Germany and Spain rank climate change as their first foreign policy priority. Citizens

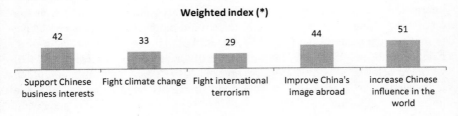

Weighted index (*)

| 42 | 33 | 29 | 44 | 51 |

Support Chinese business interests · Fight climate change · Fight international terrorism · Improve China's image abroad · increase Chinese influence in the world

(*) Index = (First *1) + (Second * 0,66) + (Third * 0,33)

Figure 11.2 Foreign policy priorities for Chinese citizens

Source: Elcano Royal Institute 2018b, 111.[8]

in China rank climate change fourth out of five possible foreign policy priorities (Elcano Royal Institute 2018a; also see Figure 11.2). There are also stark differences between China and the EU concerning civil society organisations. Whereas Europe has a wealth of environmental NGOs working on climate change, there are few NGOs that work on this in China (Engels 2018). The pressure that Chinese citizens and civil society exert on the Chinese government to lead international climate negotiations can be expected to be lower than the EU.

Finally, American officials resent how EU-China climate change cooperation may boost the international status of China by sanctioning its image as a responsible power. This may eventually exert pressure to limit joint EU-China climate leadership as US-China strategic rivalry becomes increasingly aggravated.

Policy recommendations

Climate governance space is currently riddled with radical uncertainty, leadership fragmentation, national retrenchment and a global health crisis derived from the coronavirus pandemic that will have lasting economic impacts. Political capital for non-COVID-19 issues is in short supply. In this context, joint EU-China climate co-leadership could focus on issues that are known cooperation levers and which will arguably have lasting impacts. These include:

- *Ideational cooperation.* Jointly analysing the current climate governance context to better understand the drivers and barriers to enhanced climate cooperation in the current context. This could include creating a high-level task force on climate action. Such a taskforce could analyse the climate impacts of the coronavirus and the impacts of the stimulus packages that will be adopted to respond to the health crisis, contain its economic impacts and help the economy recover while fostering transformative low-carbon transitions that are Paris-compatible. The response to the coronavirus will not be climate-neutral; if the EU and China wish to retain some form of joint climate leadership, they should help "green" the COVID-19 exit strategy. The EU can do this by implementing the European Green Deal; China can include a Paris-compatible stimulus in its 14th Five-Year Plan and in the Belt and Road Initiative.

- *Exploiting the climate finance lever.* Jointly supporting the work of the Coalition of Finance Ministers for Climate Action, encouraging China to join this coalition and supporting the work of the Network for Greening the Financial System. This support could include gathering and diffusing knowledge about the impacts of green recovery stimulus plans compared to those adopted in the aftermath of the 2008 financial crisis.
- *Broadening the climate scope.* The EU and China suppporting an enhanced framework on biodiversity protection while clearly linking it to climate. According to Chinese government officials, China's interest in biodiversity and European diplomatic support in COP 15 of the Convention on Biological Diversity (CBD) could help motivate greater Chinese climate ambition for its upcoming NDC to be submitted ahead of COP 26.

Conclusion

Climate change cooperation between the EU and the US has historically been easier than the EU's cooperation with China, due to normative and institutional similarities. Current climate policies enacted by the Trump administration, however, have stalled EU-US climate cooperation to a certain extent. The current US administration has additionally halted climate change cooperation with China; its announcement of withdrawal from the Paris Agreement has left a leadership void in the international climate change regime. In this context, the EU and China have reinforced their climate change cooperation since 2018.

Even if growing Sino-American confrontation is shaping the international order to one based less on rules and more on *realpolitik*, this chapter illustrates how the EU's staunch commitment to a rules-based multilateral order remains unscathed regarding climate change, despite the coronavirus pandemic having dampened the diplomatic thrust ahead of COP 26. Hence, the EU is expected to welcome cooperation from the willing, be they like-minded democracies such as the US or any concerned international actors, such as China. Concerted climate leadership is especially urgent in raising ambitions in the next round of NDCs, finalising the Katowice rulebook and enacting domestic policies, which are the *de facto* enforcement mechanisms of the Paris Agreement.

Joint EU-China cooperation on climate change is enabled due to the lack of a significant normative clash between the EU and China on this issue,[9] a shared awareness of the impacts of climate change, the quest for leadership in the low carbon transition and agreement about the need to provide a multilateral solution to climate change. Therefore, climate cooperation between the EU and China does not presently entail a significant values-interests dilemma.

In addition, since addressing climate change is a key priority for both European leaders and for their populations, effective cooperation is being sought by the EU over the preservation of international power balances. This means that European authorities will try to resist American pressure to reduce EU-China cooperation on climate change that could enhance China's international status.

Current headwinds for enhanced climate cooperation include the need to focus political capital and action to respond to the health crisis and economic fallout of the coronavirus pandemic, domestic factors in the US (e.g. the limited capacity by the Biden administration to enact federal climate action) and domestic factors in China (i.e., the severe slowdown of the Chinese economy even before the pandemic). Additionally, Chinese negotiators have not pursued a leadership role in the last COPs. More specifically, Chinese negotiators have been criticised as having sought to reopen differentiation debates that had been closed with the adoption of the Paris Agreement in 2015. They have also blocked progress on mitigation and transparency, and they have aligned themselves with less ambitious positions defended, among others, by the group of Like-Minded Countries. This is consistent with the response of the Chinese government to tackle the current slowdown of the Chinese economy, prioritising pro-growth policies at the expense of sustainability.

Therefore, regardless of growing confrontation between the US and China and the complex climate action context across the two largest GHG emitters, the EU will consider both countries as potential climate partners in order to promote ambitious international climate action. The EU's cooperative climate leadership efforts are more likely to be limited by domestic factors in the US and in China than by geostrategic considerations.

Notes

1 The authors would like to gratefully acknowledge the support of the Spanish Ministry of Economy, Industry and Competitiveness (grant number I+D project CSO2017–82921-P) and the comments of Antxon Olabe, Special Advisor to the Minister for Ecological Transition and Demographic Challenge in Spain.
2 Larger coalitions or "climate clubs" have, however, been suggested. One such proposal includes China, the EU, Brazil, India and South Africa (Zhang et al. 2017). However, Brazil's current stance on climate change would probably rule it out of any ambitious climate coalition.
3 Structural leadership requires the leader to follow through on its threats and comply with its commitments. It also requires the leader to pursue the common good as well as its own interests (Skovdin and Andresen 2006; Andresen and Agrawala 2002).
4 EU-China cooperation on climate change started in 2005, when they established a Climate Change Partnership, which was originally conceived as a platform for hierarchical cooperation, with the EU helping China with both mitigation and adaptation to climate change. Bilateral collaboration in this area has evolved to the point that the EU-China 2020 Strategic Agenda for Cooperation, which is the highest-level joint document in EU-China relations, in November 2013 listed climate change as one of the ten main common responsibilities shared by the EU and China for advancing global development (EEAS 2013).
5 Nevertheless, the relevance conferred by the Chinese side to climate change cooperation in the general framework of its bilateral relation with the EU should not be overstated.

The 19th EU-China summit (2017) provided an enlightening example of how the Chinese authorities may make further climate change cooperation conditional on other issues.

6 Pew Research Center bears no responsibility for the analyses or interpretations of the data presented here. The opinions expressed herein, including any implications for policy, are those of the author and not of Pew Research Center.

7 The information is based on questionnaires distributed among conference delegates at eight consecutive COP meetings, 2008–2015 (Parker et al. 2017).

8 Note that the survey was coordinated by Qíndice and was conducted via the internet with a panel of respondents. The fieldwork took place between 21 February and 14 May 2017. The sample amounted to 4,468 respondents (between 400 and 443 respondents per country). Quota sampling was used for age, gender and geographical location. The error margins vary from +/-5 percent for countries with 400 interviews to +/- 4.8 percent for the country (Turkey) where 443 surveys were completed, for a 95 percent confidence level and the most unfavourable case ($p = q = 0.5$). The age of respondents ranged from 18 to 70. For further details on the survey, see Elcano Royal Institute (2018b).

9 Their most significant normative disagreement is on the role of supranational institutions in the governance of climate change action: the EU is much more favourable to them than China.

References

Albert, Eleanor, and Beina Xu. 2016. *China's Environmental Crisis*. Londres: European Council on Foreign Relations. www.cfr.org/backgrounder/chinas-environmental-crisis.

Alkon, Meir, and Erik H. Wang. 2018. "Pollution Lowers Support for China's Regime: Quasi-Experimental Evidence from Beijing." *The Journal of Politics* 80 (1): 327–331.

Andresen, Steinar, and Shadrul Agrawala. 2002. "Leaders, Pushers and Laggards in the Making of the Climate Regime." *Global Environmental Change* 12 (1): 41–51.

Arias Cañete, Miguel. 2018. *Opening Remarks by Climate Action and Energy Commissioner Miguel Arias Cañete at the Second Ministerial on Climate Action (MoCA) by the EU, China and Canada*. Brussels: European Commission. http://europa.eu/rapid/press-release_SPEECH-18-4236_en.htm.

Averchenkova, Alina. 2019. *Legislating for a Low Carbon Transition: A Comparison of International Experiences*. Madrid: Elcano Royal Institute. www.realinstitutoelcano.org/wps/portal/rielcano_en/contenido?WCM_GLOBAL_CONTEXT=/elcano/elcano_in/zonas_in/policy-paper-2019-legislating-low-carbon-climate-resilient-transition.

Bäckstrand, Karin, and Ole Elgström. 2013. "The EU's Role in Climate Change Negotiations: From Leader to 'Leadiator'." *Journal of European Public Policy* 20 (10): 1369–1386.

Bloomberg. 2019. "China's Far from Done with Coal as Regulator Eases New Plant Ban." April 19. www.bloomberg.com/news/articles/2019-04-19/china-s-far-from-done-with-coal-as-regulator-eases-new-plant-ban.

Bloomberg Philanthropies. 2018. "Fulfilling America's Pledge. How States, Cities, and Businesses Are Leading the United States to a Low-Carbon Future." www.bbhub.io/dotorg/sites/28/2018/09/Fulfilling-Americas-Pledge-2018.pdf.

Carraro, Carlo, and Marianella Davide. 2016. "Do Climate Policies Hurt the Economy? Lessons from the EU Experience." In *Building a Climate Resilient Economy and Society*, edited by K.N. Ninan and Makoto Inoue, 265–278. Cheltenham: Edward Elgar.

Casarini, Nicola. 2019. *US-China Trade War: Why the EU Should Take Sides and Favour the Rules-Based Order*. Rome: Instituto Affari Internazionali. www.iai.it/en/pubblicazioni/us-china-trade-war-why-eu-should-take-sides-and-favour-rules-based-order.

Ceic Data. 2018. "China Coal Consumption." www.ceicdata.com/en/indicator/china/coal-consumption.

Chai, Qimin, Sha Fu, Huaqing Xu, Weiran Li, and Yan Zhong. 2017. "The Gap Report of Global Climate Change Mitigation, Finance, and Governance After the United States Declared Its Withdrawal from the Paris Agreement." *Chinese Journal of Population Resources and Environment* 15 (3): 196–208.

Chestnoy, Sergey, and Dinara Gershinkova. 2017. "USA Withdrawal from Paris Agreement —What Next?" *International Organisations Research Journal* 12 (4): 215–225.

Climate Action Tracker. 2019. "China." https://climateactiontracker.org/countries/china/.

Dai, Hancheng, Yang Xie, Haibin Zhang, Zhongjue Yu, and Wentao Wang. 2018. "Effects of the US Withdrawal from Paris Agreement on the Carbon Emission Space and Cost of China and India." *Frontiers in Energy* 12 (3): 362–375.

Dai, Hancheng, Haibin Zhang, and Wentao Wang. 2017. "The Impacts of US Withdrawal from the Paris Agreement on the Carbon Emission Space and Mitigation Cost of China, EU, and Japan Under the Constraints of the Global Carbon Emission Space." *Advances in Climate Change Research* 8 (4): 226–234.

Ding, Sai, John Knight, and Xiao Zhang. 2016. "Does China Overinvest? Evidence from a Panel of Chinese Firms." *The European Journal of Finance* 25 (6): 489–507.

EEAS (European External Action Service). 2013. "EU-China 2020 Strategic Agenda for Cooperation." http://eeas.europa.eu/archives/docs/china/docs/eu-china_2020_strategic_agenda_en.pdf.

EEAS (European External Action Service). 2016. *Shared Vision, Common Action: A Stronger Europe. A Global Strategy for the European Union's Foreign and Security Policy*. Luxembourg: Publications Office of the European Union.

Elcano Royal Institute. 2018a. *39ª Oleada BRIE, enero 2018*. Madrid: Elcano Royal Institute. www.realinstitutoelcano.org/wps/portal/rielcano_es/encuesta?WCM_GLOBAL_CONTEXT=/elcano/elcano_es/barometro/oleadabrie39.

Elcano Royal Institute. 2018b. *Barómetro de la imagen de España. 7º Oleada*. Madrid: Elcano Royal Institute. www.realinstitutoelcano.org/wps/wcm/connect/7cb3a69f-1f93-4dd3-b0dd-0b7c0d7d6672/7BIE_Informe_mayo2017.pdf?MOD=AJPERES&CACHEID=7cb3a69f-1f93-4dd3-b0dd-0b7c0d7d6672.

Elcano Royal Institute. 2018c. *Barómetro del Real Instituto Elcano. 40ª Oleada*. Madrid: Elcano Royal Institute. www.realinstitutoelcano.org/wps/wcm/connect/8504de38-4426-4b65-8c72-ca2b3a9d50db/40BRIE_Informe_Diciembre2018.pdf?MOD=AJPERES&CACHEID=8504de38-4426-4b65-8c72-ca2b3a9d50db.

Engels, Anita. 2018. "Understanding How China Is Championing Climate Change Mitigation." *Palgrave Communications* 4. doi:10.1057/s41599-018-0150-4.

Environmental Protection Agency (EPA). 2019. "EPA Collaboration with Europe." www.epa.gov/international-cooperation/epa-collaboration-europe#addressing.

Esteban, Mario. 2017. *The Foreign Policy of Xi Jinping After the 19th Congress: China Strives for a Central Role on the World Stage*. Madrid: Elcano Royal Institute. www.realinstitutoelcano.org/wps/portal/rielcano_es/contenido?WCM_GLOBAL_CONTEXT=/elcano/elcano_in/zonas_in/ari87-2017-esteban-foreign-policy-xi-jinping-19th-congress-china-central-role-world-stage.

Esteban, Mario et al. 2020. "Europe in the Face of US-China Rivalry." European Think-Tank Network on China Report. www.ifri.org/en/publications/publications-ifri/europe-face-us-china-rivalry.

European Commission. 2017. "2020 Climate & Energy Package." https://ec.europa.eu/clima/policies/strategies/2020_en.

European Commission. 2019. *Special Eurobarometer 490: Climate Change.* Brussels: Directorate-General for Communication. https://ec.europa.eu/clima/sites/clima/files/support/docs/report_2019_en.pdf.

European Commission. 2020. *Commission Communication on the Sustainable Europe Investment Plan.* Brussels: European Commission. https://ec.europa.eu/commission/presscorner/detail/en/fs_20_48.

European Council. 2018. *Joint Statement of the 20th EU-China Summit.* Beijing: European Council. www.consilium.europa.eu/media/36165/final-eu-cn-joint-statement-consolidated-text-with-climate-change-clean-energy-annex.pdf.

European Council. 2020. *European Council meeting (10 and 11 December 2020)—Conclusions.* https://www.consilium.europa.eu/media/47296/1011-12-20-euco-conclusions-en.pdf.

Eurostat. 2019. "Development of Greenhouse Gas Emissions Compared to GDP and Population, EU-28, 1990–2017." https://ec.europa.eu/eurostat/statistics-explained/index.php?title=File:Development_of_greenhouse_gas_emissions_compared_to_GDP_and_population,_EU-28,_1990-2017_(index_1995_%3D_100).png.

Falkner, Robert. 2018. "Climate Change, International Political Economy and Global Energy Policy." In *Handbook of the International Political Economy of Energy and Natural Resources*, edited by Andreas Goldthau, Michael F. Keating, and Caroline Kuzemko, 77–88. Cheltenham: Edward Elgar Publishing.

Finamore, Barbara. 2010. "China Records Its Climate Actions by Copenhagen Accord Deadline." *Natural Resources Defense Council.* www.nrdc.org/experts/barbara-finamore/china-records-its-climate-actions-copenhagen-accord-deadline.

Frankfurt School-Unep Collaborating Centre. 2019. "Global Trends in Renewable Energy Investment 2019." www.fs-unep-centre.org.

Gao, George. 2015. *As Smog Hangs Over Beijing, Chinese Cite Air Pollution as Major Concern.* Washington, DC: Pew Research Center, December 10. www.pewresearch.org/fact-tank/2015/12/10/as-smog-hangs-over-beijing-chinese-cite-ai年-pollution-as-major-concern/.

Garcia-Herrero, Alicia. 2019. "Europe in the Midst of China-US Strategic Economic Competition: What Are the European Union's Options?" *Bruegel.* www.bruegel.org/2019/04/europe-in-the-midst-of-china-us-strategic-competition-what-are-the-european-unions-options/.

GCF (Green Climate Fund). 2018. "Status of Pledges and Contributions Made to the Green Climate Fund." www.greenclimate.fund/documents/20182/24868/Status_of_Pledges.pdf/eef538d3-2987-4659-8c7c-5566ed6afd19.

Godement, François, and Abigaël Vasselier. 2017. *China at the Gates: A New Power Audit of EU-China Relations.* London: European Council on Foreign Relations. https://ecfr.eu/publication/china_eu_power_audit7242/.

Goulder, Lawrence H., Richard D. Morgenstern, Clayton Munnings, and Jeremy Schreifel. 2017. "China's National Carbon Dioxide Emission Trading System: An Introduction." *Economics of Energy & Environmental Policy* 6 (2): 1–18.

Grantham Research Institute on Climate Change and the Environment and Sabin Center for Climate Change Law (n.d.). "Climate Change Laws of the World." www.lse.ac.uk/GranthamInstitute/law/13th-five-year-plan/.

Green, Fergus, and Nicholas Stern. 2016. "China's Changing Economy: Implications for Its Carbon Dioxide Emissions." *Climate Policy* 17 (4): 423–442.

Gupta, Joyeeta, and Michael Grubb, eds. 2000. *Climate Change and European Leadership: A Sustainable Role for Europe?* Dorecht: Springer.

Heberer, Thomas, and Gunter Schubert. 2017. "Political Reform and Regime Legitimacy in Contemporary China." In *Critical Readings on Communist Party of China*, edited by Kjeld Erik Brodsgaard, 978–997. Leiden: Brill.

Hilton, Isabel, and Oliver Kerr. 2017. "The Paris Agreement: China's 'New Normal' Role in International Climate Negotiations." *Climate Policy* 17 (1): 48–58.

IEA (International Energy Agency). 2017a. *Coal Information 2017: Overview*. Paris: OECD.

IEA (International Energy Agency). 2017b. *Key World Energy Statistics 2017*. Paris: OECD.

IEA (International Energy Agency). 2019. *Key World Energy Statistics*. Paris: International Energy Agency. https://webstore.iea.org/key-world-energy-statistics-2019.

IEA (International Energy Agency). 2020. *Energy Security. Reliable, Affordable Access to All Fuels and Energy Sources*. Paris: International Energy Agency. www.iea.org/topics/energysecurity/.

Kopra, Sanna. 2019. *China and Great Power Responsibility for Climate Change*. New York: Routledge.

Lázaro Touza, Lara. 2017. *The Paris Agreement After Trump and the Future of Climate Action*. Madrid: Elcano Royal Institute. www.realinstitutoelcano.org/wps/portal/rielcano_es/contenido?WCM_GLOBAL_CONTEXT=/elcano/elcano_es/zonas_es/cambio-climatico/commentary-lazaro-paris-agreement-trump-future-climate-action.

Lázaro Touza, Lara. 2018. "Governing the Geopolitics of Climate Change After the Paris Agreement." In *Handbook of Energy Politics*, edited by Jennifer I. Considine, 435–482. Cheltenham: Edward Elgar.

Lázaro Touza, Lara, and Mario Esteban. 2016. *China and Climate Change: The Good, the Bad and the Ugly*. Madrid: Elcano Royal Institute. www.realinstitutoelcano.org/wps/portal/web/rielcano_en/contenido?WCM_GLOBAL_CONTEXT=/elcano/elcano_es/especiales/especial+cambio+climatico/ari70-2016-lazaro-esteban-china-climate-change-good-bad-ugly.

Liu, Xinsheng, Feng Hao, Kent Portney, and Yinxi Liu. 2019. "Examining Public Concern About Global Warming and Climate Change in China." *The China Quarterly* 1–27. doi:10.1017/S0305741019000845.

Niblett, Robert. 2018. *How Europe Will Try to Dodge the US-China Standoff in 2019*. London: Chatham House. www.chathamhouse.org/expert/comment/how-europe-will-try-dodge-us-china-standoff-2019.

Parker, Charles F., Christer Karlsson, and Mattias Hjerpe. 2017. "Assessing the European Union's Global Climate Change Leadership: from Copenhagen to the Paris Agreement." *Journal of European Integration* 39 (2): 239–252.

Pence, Mike. 2019. "Remarks by Vice President Pence at the Frederic V. Malek Memorial Lecture." *The White House*. www.whitehouse.gov/briefings-statements/remarks-vice-president-pence-frederic-v-malek-memorial-lecture/.

Peters, Glen P., Robbie M. Andrew, Josep G. Canadell, Sabine Fuss, Robert B. Jackson, Jan Ivar Korsbakken, Corinne Le Quéré, and Nebojsa Nakicenovic. 2017. "Key Indicators to Track Current Progress and Future Ambition of the Paris Agreement." *Nature Climate Change* 7 (2): 118–122.

Roberts, Jane. 2011. *Environmental Policy*, 2nd ed. London: Routledge.

Roberts, Timmon. 2018. *One Year Since Trump's Withdrawal from the Paris Climate Agreement*. Washington, DC: Brookings Institution Press. www.brookings.edu/blog/planetpolicy/2018/06/01/one-year-since-trumps-withdrawal-from-the-paris-climate-agreement/.

Skovdin, Tora, and Steinar Andresen. 2006. "Leadership Revisited." *Global Environmental Politics* 6 (3): 13–27.

Sussams, Luke. 2018. "Carbon Budgets Explainer." *Carbon Tracker*. www.carbontracker.org/wp-content/uploads/2018/02/Carbon-Budgets_Eplained_02022018.pdf.

Taraska, Gwynne, Susan Biniaz, Leonardo Martinez-Diaz, Niranjali Amerasinghe, Joe Thwaites, and Howard Marano. 2017. *How the United States Can Remain Engaged in International Climate Finance: A Discussion Paper*. Washington, DC: Center for American Progress. www.americanprogress.org/issues/green/reports/2017/09/06/438436/united-states-can-remain-engaged-international-climate-finance/.

Thwaites, Joe. 2020. "2020 Budget Shows Progress on Climate Finance, But US Continues to Fall Behind Peers." World Resources Institute. www.wri.org/blog/2020/01/2020-budget-shows-progress-climate-finance-us-continues-fall-behind-peers?utm_campaign=wridigest&utm_source=wridigest-2020-2-4&utm_medium=email&utm_content=title.

UNSG (United Nations Secretary-General). 2019. "Press Statement on Climate Change Following the Meeting Between the State Councilor and Foreign Minister of China, Foreign Minister of France and the United Nations Secretary-General. 29th of June 2020." www.un.org/sg/en/content/sg/note-correspondents/2019-06-29/press-statement-climate-change-following-the-meeting-between-the-state-councilor-and-foreign-minister-of-china-foreign-minister-of-france-and-the-united.

Wang, Jinnan. 2016. "Environmental Costs: Revive China's Green GDP Programme." *Nature* 534 (37). doi:10.1038/534037b.

We Are Still In. 2017. "'We Are Still In' Declaration." www.wearestillin.com/we-are-still-declaration.

The White House. 2014a. *Fact Sheet: U.S.-China Joint Announcement on Climate Change and Clean Energy Cooperation*. Washington, DC: Office of the Press Secretary. https://obamawhitehouse.archives.gov/the-press-office/2014/11/11/fact-sheet-us-china-joint-announcement-climate-change-and-clean-energy-c.

The White House. 2014b. *US—China Joint Announcement on Climate Change*. Beijing: Office of the Press Secretary. https://obamawhitehouse.archives.gov/the-press-office/2014/11/11/us-china-joint-announcement-climate-change.

The White House. 2015. *U.S.-China Joint Presidential Statement on Climate Change*. Beijing: Office of the Press Secretary. https://obamawhitehouse.archives.gov/the-press-office/2015/09/25/us-china-joint-presidential-statement-climate-change.

Wu, Gang, Lancui Liu, Zhiyong Han, and Yiming Wei. 2012. "Climate Protection and China's Energy Security: Win—Win or Tradeoff." *Applied Energy* 97: 157–163.

Xi, Jinping. 2017a. "Full Text of Xi Jinping Keynote at the World Economic Forum." *China Global Television Network America*. https://america.cgtn.com/2017/01/17/full-text-of-xi-jinping-keynote-at-the-world-economic-forum.

Xi, Jinping. 2017b. "Secure a Decisive Victory in Building a Moderately Prosperous Society in All Respects and Strive for the Great Success of Socialism with Chinese Characteristics." *Xinhua*, October 18. www.xinhuanet.com/english/download/Xi_Jinping's_report_at_19th_CPC_National_Congress.pdf.

Xu, Muyu, Michael Martina, and Shri Navaratnam. 2019. "UPDATE 1-China Expects First Trade in National Emissions Scheme in 2020." *Reuters*, March 30. www.reuters.com/

article/climate-change-china/update-1-china-expects-first-trade-in-national-emissions-scheme-in-2020-idUSL3N21H02B.

Yao, Lixia, and Youngho Chang. 2014. "Energy Security in China: A Quantitative Analysis and Policy Implications." *Energy Policy* 67: 595–604.

Zhang, Hai-Bin, Hancheng Dai, Huaxia La, and Wentao Wang. 2017. "U.S. Withdrawal from the Paris Agreement: Reasons, Impacts, and China's Response." *Advances in Climate Change Research* 8 (4): 220–225.

Zhu, Lia, and Chang Jun. 2018. "China Reaffirms Climate Commitments." *China Daily*, September 18. www.chinadailyhk.com/articles/231/87/253/1537242579558.html.

Part IV

Concluding remarks

12 Sustaining the European project in an age of Sino-American confrontation

An end to complacency

Sebastian Biba and Reinhard Wolf

The introductory chapter to this volume has already made clear that, in light of the growing and multi-faceted US-China rivalry, Europe is increasingly faced with enormous challenges and tough decisions. Subsequently, the contributors to this volume have comprehensively analysed these challenges across a number of crucial issues and have thoroughly weighed Europe's possible responses. In doing so, they have also made both general and specific suggestions for how Europe should deal with the unfolding of this grave situation. As a first step in this concluding chapter, we would like to take the opportunity to summarise our contributors' key points (from a meta-level perspective). It is quite revealing in this regard that there is more agreement than disagreement between our authors' arguments, especially concerning the major trends, their implications and consequent broader policy recommendations. There are also, of course, nuanced and important differences between the authors' lines of reasoning.

First of all, all contributors, some more explicitly than others, share the sentiment that, in the current international climate, the general trend towards a weakening of global norms and institutions has been considerably fuelled by the intensifying US-China confrontation in recent years. Moreover, the authors also find that the international security environment, particularly in the Asia-Pacific region, has been noticeably deteriorating as a result of the worsening US-China relationship—even the prospect of open military hostilities between the two sides can no longer be easily rejected.

That said, one significant overall finding from the contributions to this book is that there is widespread agreement that Europe remains closer to the United States (US) than to China and that, consequently, the US is a more important partner for Europe than China. One illustrative example in this respect is Le Corre's contribution on foreign direct investment. He emphasises that, "[t]he EU and US share a substantial interest in jointly developing a common approach to Chinese investment, one focused on the rule of law and reciprocity". At the same time, however, the contributors to this volume also largely concur that transatlantic ties have substantially weakened over recent years such that a unity of purpose and values can no longer be ascertained. Consequently, Le Corre represents a minority view among our contributors in that he favours Europe teaming up with the US against China.

For the great majority of our authors, however, the current state of transatlantic relations does not, or no longer, justifies Europe sacrificing profitable ties with China for the sake of transatlantic unity. Instead, they generally suggest that Europe continue cooperating with China as well. Even Tunsjø, who is close to Le Corre in advocating that "with growing US-China confrontation, Europe should side with the US", acknowledges that "[s]uch a grand strategic approach does not imply that Europe cannot trade with China". A more obvious example of promoting continued Sino-European cooperation is Kaminski and Ciesielska-Klikowska's chapter, which states that while "the position of the European Union (EU) towards the US cannot be confrontational, . . . it cannot be closed to other global partners [China]", either. Hence, in a context of escalating conflict between the US and China, maintaining and enhancing cooperative channels between Europe and China, especially on the subnational level, "might be very useful" for the former. Similarly, Esteban and Lázaro explain that Europe should "consider both countries [the US and China] as potential climate partners in order to promote ambitious international climate action". These authors even go a step further when they point out that joint "EU-China climate leadership" would be welcome and possible because, unlike with other issues, "climate cooperation between the EU and China does not presently entail a significant values-interests dilemma".

It is, therefore, one of the major recommendations of this volume's contributors that Europe should avoid taking sides in the intensifying US-China rivalry (with the exceptions, once again, of Le Corre and Tunsjø). Instead, Europe should concentrate on its own preferences and thus choose partners on a case-by-case basis. Most outspoken in this regard is probably Pacheco Pardo, whose chapter discusses the North Korean nuclear issue. As he highlights, Europe should take a "pragmatic approach", that it "must put its [own] interests first" and hence "mix both cooperation with China and the United States . . . as well as, in some cases, divergence".

At the same time, the contributors are certainly aware that not taking sides will be tricky for Europe. In a recent Project Syndicate piece, former German foreign minister Sigmar Gabriel mentioned a conversation he had with an ambassador from a Southeast Asian country. The ambassador told Gabriel, "[w]e small countries know the feeling of sitting between stools, and we have learned to keep the balance. For you Europeans, this is new. You'd better learn to keep the balance quickly" (cited in Gabriel 2019). Against this backdrop, Kirchner's chapter, for instance, cautions that Europe "will have to carefully balance the interests it has with China and the US". Kirchner moreover advises that a potential "brokering role between the US and China [in the Asia-Pacific] would need support from other states such as Australia, Canada, Japan and South Korea". Concurrently, Kirchner, like other authors, admits that in the event of open military hostilities between the US and China, Europe could no longer stay neutral and "would most likely support the US position". Another example that recognises the difficulty for Europe of staying out of the US-China conflict is Schüller's contribution, which frankly concedes that "Europe [simply] is not prepared to take sides in the

US-China geopolitical rivalry. To balance the US and China, the EU needs, how-ever, to become less dependent on both economies".

Given that, in the opinion of our authors, the transatlantic bond has been fading and Europe should (try to) remain neutral in the beginning of this US-China con-test for supremacy, a crucial question that has crystallised from the chapters in this book is what does Europe's new positioning entail for its geostrategic priorities. It is probably here where we see the greatest degree of diverging opinions between this volume's contributors. On the one hand, some straightforwardly argue that Europe should now focus its attention and resources on itself and its immediate neighbourhood. Tunsjø's chapter, for example, maintains, "[c]ore is Europe's abil-ity to sustain security and stability in Europe and its neighbourhood". As Europe would not currently be able to fulfil this objective, it "should retrench from Asia" instead of "pursuing a stronger security role" in the Asia-Pacific. In a similar vein, Zanardi asserts that "the EU lacks the resources to . . . get deeply involved in a region as distant as the Asia-Pacific". Consequently, Europe "should rather focus on strengthening its relations with its immediate neighbourhood".

On the other hand, there are those who may not (explicitly) question Europe's primary focus being on its home turf but nonetheless favour more European engagement in Asia-Pacific (security) affairs. The chapters by Odgaard and Paul are prominent examples of this point of view. Paul insists that the "EU should examine the possibility of a stronger security policy engagement [in the South China Sea] and concern itself more urgently with questions of maritime security in the region". He concedes that, in view of Europe's "limited ability to project military forces, it is unrealistic to assume that the EU will play a significant secu-rity role in Asia". Nevertheless, he asserts that Europe "should play a larger role in reinforcing international legal norms" and also "by increasing [its] own naval presence". For Odgaard, it is clear that Europe's approach of "combin[ing] deter-rence with reassurance . . . provides a positive contribution to an increasingly crisis-prone Asia-Pacific theatre". She even goes so far as to contend that "[t]he successful use of Europe's potential as a middle power [with regard to ameliorat-ing great power dispute in the South China Sea] deserves to be pursued across a wider range of security issues in Central, South, Southeast and Northeast Asia as tensions between the US and China continue to grow".

These diverse viewpoints reflect both different theoretical understandings of international relations (e.g., realism vs. the English school) and differences in Europe's goals, means and alignments, depending on the issue area at hand. They show that it will be far from easy to form a coherent European approach out of diverse challenges and imperatives. Meanwhile, the serious question of Europe's geostrategic priorities is certainly not the only one arising from the explorations and recommendations in this book: a number of other and equally important issues suggest themselves and deserve further analysis. Among them are:

- What exactly does it mean—and take—for Europe to pursue the much favoured "pragmatic approach" in view of the US-China rivalry? What are, or should be, Europe's own vital interests and preferences? And what can and

should Europe do to safeguard these interests and preferences in an increasingly fragmented and post-liberal world?
- Can Europe really avoid choosing sides between the US and China? And is the related idea of its equidistance between Washington and Beijing a realistic option? Or should Europe try to build in some kind of "safety net" by maintaining, and even further investing in, its military alliance with the US?
- What can, and should, Europe do in order to mediate between the US and China? How can Europe help avoid military confrontation between the two? Or, coming full circle, should Europe not get involved in such matters, as they might not be part of following a "pragmatic approach"?

In the next part of this Conclusion, we will (try to) address such questions in some detail. We do so by returning to and answering (in light of our authors' analyses combined with our own ideas) the five guiding questions raised in the Introduction.

Addressing Europe's unpleasant alternatives

As the reader may recall, our five questions raise five alternatives that Europe can no longer ignore but must face:

Firstly, should Europe principally opt for one side in global governance or should it pursue pragmatic case-by-case cooperation, closely collaborating with China on some problems while partnering with the US on others?

Global governance can be understood as "the collective management of common problems at the international level" (Biba 2016, 47). However, it is exactly this *collective* management of common, and urgent, problems that seems to no longer happen between the US and China. The fact that climate cooperation between the two sides has been stalled in recent years (see Esteban and Lázaro Touza in this volume), that economic synergies gave way to harsh disputes over trade and technology and that Washington and Beijing have engaged in mutual finger-pointing instead of providing joint leadership during the COVID-19 pandemic (see Introduction to this volume) speaks volumes in this regard. The world's two foremost powers can no longer work together even on the most pressing international issues, so Europe must decide on its own future course on global governance.

While Europe's traditional and almost reflexive choice had been siding with the US, Europe from now on should *not* generally opt for one side, neither American nor Chinese. This would only further fuel bipolar thinking, which Europe should not encourage (also see Esteban et al. 2020; Lippert and Perthes 2020). Instead, Europe should pursue pragmatic case-by-case cooperation. Such cooperation should be primarily based on Europe's own interests and should, moreover, depend on who is promoting multilateral institutions and solutions, contributing to the provision of public goods (for example, in the areas of security, trade, aid, health and climate) and—ideally—who is supporting a rules-based global order as understood by Europe.

Even though this may represent an unwelcome truth for some obdurate "transatlanticists", Europe's traditional approach can no longer be the preferable option. While this option has been losing its attraction for some time now (see Biba 2016), as of 2020, the advantages of such an approach are in further retreat, whereas its disadvantages have become even more pronounced. Two aspects stand out. The first is that one of Europe greatest advantages in siding with the US had been that it could "hide" behind US military capabilities while concentrating on being a "civilian power" (Maull 1990). This is no longer the case, as the US—most notably under the Trump administration—has made clear its expectation of greater burden sharing and hence its demand for Europe to spend more on defence. While it is reasonable, if not imperative, for Europe to enhance its own military capabilities in these uncertain times (also see Question 3 below), this also reduces the need to habitually follow US positions because Europe would then gradually become more independent in the global arena. A second aspect of abandoning Europe's traditional adherence to the US is that the Trump administration has further weakened the current, and outdated, global governance system because it is no longer seen as beneficial to US interests. Despite the US' key role in constructing this system decades ago, America today shows a national penchant for bi- and minilateralism, especially among members of Congress. This is not a way to solve global problems and it is certainly not Europe's way, which is multilateral almost by default (Dworkin and Gowan 2019).

That Europe should no longer automatically side with the US is, however, not to say that it should about-face and fully align with China. In fact, this alternative approach is an even bigger non-starter, with corridors for substantial cooperation often remaining "clearly circumscribed" (Biba and Holbig 2017). Even though China has arguably shown more interest in global governance and multilateralism than the US under Trump, the former treats multilateralism as merely a means and not an end, unlike the EU (Men 2012). Disagreements remain prevalent even in areas where Europe and China should jointly step into the breach left by the US, such as climate cooperation or the world trading system (see Esteban and Lázaro Touza as well as Schüller in this volume). The fact that China continues to play divide-and-rule with Europe is evidence enough that Europe has failed to socialise China into its preferred behavioural norms. If anything, then, Europe and China have grown further apart in recent years. This is also reflected by contemporary views that EU citizens have of China, who see the country "largely as a competitor", and who "continue to feel a bond with the US" (Bertelsmann Foundation 2020, 4). Under such circumstances, Europe can have no interest in furthering China's global interests while also becoming a potential "junior partner" to a country that has no intentions, or capabilities, of providing security backing if the worst comes to worst. In sum, this is no basis for an all-out European alignment with China in terms of global governance.

Rather than binding itself to one of the rival parties, Europe has much more to gain by following a case-by-case strategy. The benefits are obvious: a case-by-case approach makes Europe a potential "neutral" partner for both the US and China. Given Europe's weight in most areas of global governance, Washington and Beijing would be well advised to convince Europe of their respective positions. In order for them to have Europe on their side and thus increase their leverage *vis-à-vis* the other, both the US and China may be willing to compromise and accommodate European interests much more than if Europe threw itself at one of the two in the first place. Consequently, a case-by-case rationale can help ensure that Europe, as the weakest of the three players, remains a relevant and influential actor in global governance that is able to promote its own interests and principles. Europe would most likely not be downgraded to a mere norm follower but could rather hope to become a significant player in advancing the necessary changes in the current system (Biba 2016). To make this happen, however, Europe must be predictable, reliable and coherent as well as sharpening the contours of what its own interests actually are.

At the same time, if Europe were no longer a sometimes naïve player in international relations, it would not to turn a blind eye to the fact that full equidistance between the US and China is difficult and unlikely. It is more likely that Europe would remain a closer and more frequent partner with the US than China (also see Biba 2020 and the chapters in this volume). Reasons for this include the greater normative and cultural affinity between Europe and the US as well as European military and technological (see Schulze and Voelsen 2020) dependence on the US. However, the crucial difference with previous European cooperation with the US on global governance should be that future cooperation not arise from tradition or be reflexive but should rather be dependent on its compatibility with European interests and values.

To the extent that the US seeks to exploit European vulnerabilities, Europe should increase its efforts to reduce them. Here again, however, a necessary admission is that reducing European dependence on the US militarily and technologically will not be quick or easy (see Question 3). What is more, as long as such dependence exists, it is possible that the US might try to force Europe to choose its side, both on specific global governance issues and US-China rivalry more generally. While this may be a costly endeavour for the US itself, it may realistically also entail Europe facing limitations to putting a case-by-case approach into practice until it has emerged as a fully emancipated actor in international relations.

Secondly, should Europe concentrate on salvaging or promoting global institutions or should it be resigned to the latter's stagnation and decay? Should it thus rather hedge its bets by building regional order(s) to prevent (further) destabilizing developments in its vicinity, which otherwise might hurt it?

The current system of global governance has been under pressure for some time now, mostly due to ongoing power shifts from the Global North to the Global South which have not been reflected well in most international regimes and organisations. With the intensifying US-China rivalry, particularly its global dimension (see Introduction of this volume), global governance is becoming even more challenging, with the fragmentation of the system and competition regarding the modes of governance further increasing (Biba 2016). While the US under Trump severely undermined the system it created, China has long been building the pillars of parallel structures. At the same time, however, global governance has not lost its importance. If anything, it has become even more critical and urgent recently, given, for example, accelerating climate change and the COVID-19 pandemic.

Consequently, Europe should not yet give up on global governance, particularly if the new US administration returns to a somewhat more multilateral posture. But even if the US continues to withdraw from the current system and China seeks to further erode some of its underpinnings, Europe should invest some resources into trying to salvage and simultaneously improve a number of key global institutions (also see Dworkin and Gowan 2019). This is not least because a world with global problems in which, however, all of its largest powers forsake global governance, or seek to exploit it in the rivalries among themselves, is a more dangerous and less stable place—including for Europe. Meanwhile, as Europe can most certainly not hope to save all global governance, it should particularly focus on those institutions that are of a primary concern to its own vital interests and where the EU has some capacity to act, such as the World Trade Organization or the global climate regime.

Frankly, however, functional and *truly* global governance in many areas is likely to become extremely hard to achieve, given the intensifying US-China rivalry, so Europe must not waste its resources on such efforts. Consequently, it must not assume the task of salvaging and reforming specific global institutions by itself. Instead, Europe should actively seek the support of others and build various coalitions of those willing to work against tendencies to force multilateralism and a rules-based international order to their knees. Fortunately for Europe, there still is a number of like-minded states (including Canada, Australia, Japan and South Korea) that are interested in the functioning of global governance, have a proven predilection for multilateralism and share Europe's preference for a rules-based order. Europe should establish regular exchange mechanisms with such like-minded states by, for example, setting up so-called "minilaterals" or "plurilaterals" that could routinely meet in the run-up to major international meetings, thus increasing the group's agenda-setting and bargaining power through enhanced policy coordination. At a minimum, this could help to keep some basic foundations of "global" governance alive until a new situation might emerge.

That said, while global governance should remain a concern for Europe going forward, it is imperative that it increases its attention on its own periphery and invests more resources on promoting peace and stability in its own neighbourhood. This is not only because a new cold war and the effects of the COVID-19 pandemic may generally increase the role for regions and regional governance in international relations. More specifically, it is also because tensions and instability have long been on the rise in several parts of Europe's neighbourhood and are beginning to have adverse effects on Europe's security and welfare. As this negative trend has coincided with the US gradually shifting its military focus away from Europe, the old continent must eventually fully take the reins in its own hands (Wolf et al. 2016).

However, in stabilizing its vicinity, Europe is confronted with no small task that, moreover, admits no delay. What makes this task difficult is that Europe must look in different directions at the same time—with each needing its own specifically tailored strategy. To begin with, the elephant in the room is a resurgent Russia. Despite unease about Russia's intentions (see Kirchner in this volume), Europe must overcome its internal disunity regarding its most powerful neighbour and hammer out a new and, if possible, more cooperative *modus vivendi* with Moscow. In doing so, Europe must learn from past mistakes, such as its policy disaster in Ukraine, which completely underestimated Russian resolve to maintain spheres of influence and was driven by an overly ambitious and naïve values-based approach implemented without care or necessary resources. Europe must perform much better when it comes to the Western Balkans, where it should prevent the creation of strong Russian—and, for that matter, Chinese (see Zanardi in this volume)—footholds by providing immediate benefits and offering well-designed and considered long-term perspectives that make it clear, especially for current non-EU states, that the future of this subregion is tied to Europe.

Beyond its geographical boundaries, Europe must above all look south. Hence, it should accelerate and lead efforts to enhance cooperation and build institutions in the (wider) Mediterranean. This region is home to several countries (whether in the Levant or North Africa) with great instability which has the potential to immediately affect Europe; geographic proximity therefore demands that Europe increase its focus on this region (also see Dworkin and Gowan 2019). What is more, the promotion of cooperation in the Mediterranean should include Turkey and could represent a significant step towards mending fences with Ankara, binding it closer again to Europe after missed opportunities in the past. At the same time, a new European "look south" policy must not stop in the Mediterranean. In fact, Europe should make a long-term investment in the future of all Africa, not just its north. Africa was long exploited, then neglected; the migration issue has brought it back into European minds. Now that Africa may also be turning into one of the new theatres of intensifying US-China global rivalry (Rudolf 2020), Europe must finally get involved more fully there and go to great lengths to ensure that the rivalry of these two distant powers will not be to Europe's detriment. Consequently, Europe's engagement in Africa must be comprehensive, comprising elements of the historical Marshall Plan but also focusing on other aspects such as climate mitigation, education and cultural exchange. Significantly, in doing all this, Europe must avoid a patronizing "teacher-student" approach and should not be too selective about its partners. What now matters most are common interests (e.g., a future for Africans in Africa) rather than not always common values (also see Question 5).

All of these are tremendous challenges that Europe must face and tackle. Unfortunately, global and regional governance are only one part of the equation. Europe has an equally full plate of immediate tasks and another set of tough military and geostrategic decisions to make.

> *Thirdly, should Europe prioritise efforts to strengthen the North Atlantic Treaty Organization (NATO) or should it rather focus its initiatives and resources in a quest for strategic autonomy—even though this policy might (further) undermine US commitment to European security?*

In a volatile international environment where it can place far less confidence in the stabilizing influence of alliances and other international institutions, Europe must eventually accept the fact that it must substantially strengthen its own capacities to react to unforeseen circumstances. When external developments are harder to predict and control, systems must increase their internal resources for reaction to limit their exposure to vulnerabilities. For Europe, this key imperative entails two essential challenges: firstly, as a conglomerate of supranational bodies and semi-sovereign nation states, Europe must enhance its political cohesion and streamline its rules for decision-making. Secondly, it must improve the instruments at its disposal.

The first requirement, of course, has been the subject of numerous debates ever since the EU launched its Common Foreign and Security Policy in the wake of the Cold War. Basically, it calls for updated decision-making procedures with fewer veto players (e.g., through more qualified majority voting or more scope for coalitions of the willing) along with other institutional reforms that would facilitate cross-border agreements on the nature of common challenges and required responses (e.g., through a pro-active pooling of foreign policy expertise within EU institutions and more intensive exchanges between national security elites). While it can often take years to harmonise national perspectives (if at all), the streamlining of decision-making procedures can happen much faster. There are previous situations where the EU succeeded in building new institutions under great pressure (e.g., the European System of Financial Supervision, and the European Stability Mechanism). To some extent, the history of institutional EU reforms is indeed the history of European crises. Accordingly, there is some hope that the EU could become more united and agile as the need for greater cohesion deepens over the coming years.

Unfortunately, relations with NATO further complicate the EU's necessary institutional reforms. While the EU must definitely enhance its foreign policy cohesion, it also needs to avoid procedural reforms that would marginalise consultations within NATO. Therefore, the EU should ensure that greater EU cohesion does not mean less policy flexibility *vis-à-vis* non-members by, for instance, confronting other NATO governments with rigid EU positions on a take-it-or-leave-it basis. This would not only estrange the US and Canada, thereby further jeopardizing the transatlantic bond, but would also complicate policy coordination with European non-EU members, such as the United Kingdom (UK), Norway and Turkey, which might otherwise contribute vital resources to common

European actions. Improved mechanisms for consultations with other NATO members should thus accompany any streamlining of EU decision-making.

The most urgent problem, however, is Europe's inadequate capabilities, especially in the security domain (including cyber defence and infrastructure resilience). Europe's deficiencies are much more precarious in the realm of means, particularly when it comes to military capacities, because substantial improvements in this field take many years, if not decades (Witney 2019). Europe's military dependence on the US can only be reduced with determined effort, which will not bear fruit any time soon. Necessary programs must start now if the EU is seriously concerned about a US shift to growing confrontation in the Asia-Pacific, and if it sees this trend as a reason to build an independent ability to defend all of its members and safeguard its southern periphery. Otherwise, Europeans may soon be confronted with scenarios where Washington proves unwilling or feels incapable to protect vital European interests (Gareis and Wolf 2016).

Such European capacity building should preferably be coordinated within NATO (Howorth 2018; Witney 2019). As long as NATO staff perform this function adequately, EU bodies should take a back seat (albeit an influential one). NATO force-planning is the most experienced in this field, and it also ensures a role for the US and Britain, whose military capabilities even a strengthened Europe will need for some years to come. Performing force planning chiefly within the EU would needlessly marginalise NATO and thus precipitate the very fraying of transatlantic ties, which Europe should try to at least delay. Therefore, the build-up of Europe's forces should be primarily geared to creating a more capable European pillar within NATO, which would alleviate US concerns about insufficient burden-sharing and facilitate a new division of labour, with Europe assuming greater responsibility for its own security (see Tunsjø in this volume). In the long run, multinational forces need to be augmented by fully integrated units ("European Army") as combinations of small and medium national forces become increasingly inefficient.

Moving to a genuine division of labour, however, implies that some duplication of capabilities is unavoidable, at least for an interim period in which the US remains an essential guarantor of European security (Howorth 2018). If Europe really wants to relieve deployed or assigned US forces for engagements in other theatres—such as the Asia-Pacific—EU members must acquire capabilities that, as of now, remain an American monopoly. In that respect, preparing for some form of US disengagement can only undermine the value of existing US deployments in Europe. All sides thus need to accept that moving to greater European self-reliance may also facilitate transatlantic decoupling. The alternative, however, would be opting for a Europe that permanently bets on an unrelinquished US commitment to the burdensome defence of a wealthy but weak continent which no longer aspires to control its own destiny. Moreover, it seems unlikely that its US ally will object to duplication as forcefully as it did in the 1990s. An America that is locked into a serious struggle with China will, after all, want to free up military and financial resources for the Asia-Pacific (see Tunsjø in this volume).

That said, it is far from certain that Washington will welcome every step towards European "strategic autonomy". It could conceivably obstruct some efforts within NATO planning bodies or might even demand greater NATO support in the Asia-Pacific. Even worse, a US administration could try to undermine European unity by pressuring EU members, which are particularly exposed and thus most dependent on US security guarantees. All these contingencies could hamper Europe's efforts to make itself less dependent on the US for carrying out vital missions in Europe and its vicinity. Nevertheless, Europe should not be too concerned about such eventualities. After all, in a confrontation with an autocratic China, Washington could hardly wish to be seen as a bullying ally which is prepared to provoke a rupture with fellow democracies. Moreover, Europe also enjoys some leverage with the US: the latter needs Europe's diplomatic support within international institutions and its cooperation in constraining Chinese access to sensitive technologies (Walt 2019). Hence, Europe (or at least the key promoters of more strategic autonomy) should try to seek an agreement with Washington on such issues and—if Washington proves too intransigent—face the unpleasant fact that common interests have receded to a point where its erstwhile ally can no longer be relied upon.

Fourthly, and related to the previous question, should Europe try to play a more meaningful diplomatic or military role in the Asia-Pacific or should it concentrate its military assets and activities even more on Europe and its neighbourhood?

Europe cannot stay out of major disputes in the Asia-Pacific because it has a strong stake in the stability and openness of that region. As pointed out in Michael Paul's contribution to this volume, Europe's prosperity depends on open sea lanes in this economically most dynamic region of the world. Thus, it cannot ignore developments in the South China Sea and beyond that might impair the free movement of merchant vessels. A military conflagration involving China and the US would be even worse because it would entail unfathomable military, economic and environmental risks for Europe as well. Even if this worst-case scenario is avoided, Europe has a crucial interest in an orderly resolution of these disputes on the basis of international law and multilateral principles (where appropriate); a successful resort to military or economic blackmail would further undermine the rules-based international order so important to Europe's welfare.

Europe should thus remain engaged in the region, even if disputes over the South China Sea, the East China Sea, Taiwan, and North Korea were to become more acrimonious. This applies particularly to the first two disputes, where the EU could offer its good offices as a party with no territorial stakes or political alignments (Stanzel 2016). The EU could raise the costs of selfish power politics by explicitly promising its diplomatic support to parties which adhere to international law and support peaceful dispute resolution (including, of course, the US and its regional partners). Such a principled stance might also entail synergies for Europe's global governance approach, as it would enhance its credibility with regional partners with similar stakes in the future of multilateralism (e.g., Japan, South Korea, ASEAN or even India).

A limited military presence in the region would bolster such a constructive role. As argued in Odgaard's and Paul's contributions, the intermittent deployment of European frigates or destroyers is not only useful for underscoring Europe's profound interests in a peaceful Western Pacific and signalling its solidarity with governments that commit themselves to diplomatic dispute resolution, but it can also make the point that unfettered freedom of navigation is a truly global concern rather than just a matter for regional parties with territorial stakes or for rival superpowers competing for strategic advantage. Moreover, European vessels operating in the South China Sea can also help spread best practice for mitigating the risks of dangerous naval incidents.

However, Europe should resist the temptation or possible foreign demands to substantially increase its military deployments to the Asia-Pacific, be it to further enhance its diplomatic clout or to provide meaningful military support to its American ally. Seeking a significant military role in the Western Pacific would probably overburden Europe's resources and encounter strong public resistance (Stanzel 2016). Hence, it would risk derailing vital efforts to strengthen its military autonomy for operations in Europe and its environs. Europe cannot achieve both, especially when it also needs to cope with the political and economic fallout of COVID-19. It will be challenging enough to overcome the entrenched complacency that has so far prevented Europe from assuming greater responsibility for deterring aggression in its own region.

At any rate, European participation in combat operations in the Western Pacific would hardly make sense from a military perspective. It would be a logistical nightmare, especially if such a task force were to be little more than a collection of single ships or submarines operated by various European navies. Interoperability with regional US allies would also pose a major challenge, as would tactical (and political) coordination with the US military and its regional supporters. For these reasons, it seems unlikely that Washington would demand the aid of its NATO allies in a military confrontation with China. Judging by previous American complaints about the encumbering involvement of allied forces in the air operations against Serbia and Libya, it is rather to be expected that Washington would prefer other forms of European support, in particular European efforts to replace US capabilities in Europe, so that they could be redeployed to the Pacific theatre (Cohen and Scheinmann 2014; Riddervold and Rosén 2018). The most important consideration, however, is that Europe could hardly afford a military engagement in the Western Pacific in a high-stakes conflict that would divert US attention from the European theatre. In such a contingency, Europe would need to focus on dealing with its own military vulnerabilities.

All of this suggests that, in the event of war, Europe would have much better options of demonstrating solidarity with its American ally and regional combatants by upholding established principles rather than by sending combat forces to the Far East. Should Europe deem it expedient to express its support to these actors, it could eventually free US forces in Europe and its vicinity, such as parts of the Atlantic fleet, for combat roles in the Asia-Pacific by improving the regional division of labour. It also could provide diplomatic support in international bodies and could bolster US war efforts on the economic front and in the cyber domain. Should Washington nevertheless insist on a substantial engagement of European forces in the Asian theatre, Europe would face a dire choice between weakening the US commitment to Europe's security and prosperity on the one hand, and weakening its own military at a time when it would need it more than ever in its own region. Again, a pro-active effort to attain strategic autonomy would be the best way to guard against such a contingency.

Finally, will Europe still be able to afford the "luxury" of promoting its values in the global arena, particularly in the Asia-Pacific, or should it accept that material interests must take precedence whenever interests and values are at odds?

In this rougher and more diverse international environment, Europe needs to find a new balance between championing universal values and pursuing its narrow self-interest. We no longer live in the 1990s, when market-powered liberal democracy seemed to be the unrivalled socio-political model and North American and West European states were widely regarded as its best embodiments and most authentic teachers. Back then, Europe in particular appeared to have found a "magic formula" for tackling the basic problems of humankind: it had overcome centuries of warfare by building ever-tighter multilateral institutions; it had tamed the antagonistic forces of modern nationalism by creating a common space for economic and cultural exchange; it had provided decent incomes and social security for (almost) everyone by building and adapting competitive welfare states; and it had guaranteed citizens' liberty by firmly entrenching democratic norms, basic rights and the rule of law among the EU Member States. Unsurprisingly, many came to regard the EU, if not quite as a "shining city on the hill", than at least as a "normative power" (Manners 2002), which they increasingly saw as a kind of human *avant garde*, whose values and policies were widely emulated.

Today, however, things look rather different. Instead of pondering the promises of the "end of history", pundits now worry about the "retreat of western liberalism" (Luce 2017). Brexit and the election of autocratic, illiberal populists in Italy, Hungary, Poland and the US have dramatically demonstrated that even in the West, and above all within its historic Anglo-American core (Buruma 2016), liberal democracy and cosmopolitan values have lost their electoral appeal. Western belief in the superiority of liberal ideas has thus given way to harsh ideological disputes both within and between Western nations. Meanwhile, autocratic systems, most prominently China's state-permeated capitalism, have often delivered for their citizens, at least in the sense of raising living standards and lessening dependence on the West. Recently, diverse national responses to the common curse of COVID-19 suggest that Asian societies may increasingly question Western role models: whereas prominent Western liberal democracies (including Britain, France and the US) appeared to perform rather poorly in the beginning of the health crisis, less liberal Asian states, such as China, Singapore and Vietnam, were widely perceived as coping more effectively (Gilchrist 2020; VOA News 2020; Wintour 2020).

In addition, the growing antagonism between the US and China further undermines prospects for spreading Europe's values. Superpower rivalry threatens to bring about a tougher ("realist") environment where normative and institutional constraints gradually give way to unabashed competition and self-help. When major international organisations are marginalised and global governance can no longer provide many collective goods, Europe's call for multilateralism, self-restraint and lawful conduct loses much of its international appeal. When national egotism prevails over mutual accommodation, principled behaviour within and across national boundaries tends to lose its normative grip. Moreover, in such a harsher and more volatile environment, every major actor, including the EU and European states, needs to ponder whether it still can afford to put values before interests. In a messy self-help world, actors need to safeguard and enhance their own capabilities for coping with unexpected events and unprincipled transgressions. Therefore, standing up for values may increasingly appear as a noble "luxury" that is beyond the means of the vulnerable.

Flatly sacrificing its values on the altar of expediency, however, is not an option for Europe, least of all for the EU and its members. More than most nation states, the EU was founded as a "community of values". Institutionalizing and protecting Enlightenment political values has always been a crucial to the EU's *raison d'être*. Thus, Europe cannot repudiate or ignore such values without undermining itself (Smith 2018). In any event, liberal norms and procedures also guide decision-making within the EU. It cannot function without the rule of law, mutual accommodation and respect for minority interests. However unforgiving the international environment may become, the European project can only endure as a normative project.

The question is nevertheless relevant as to where, how and to what extent Europe should champion its values in the international sphere. For instance, as already mentioned previously (see Question 2), can Europe really afford to be choosy when it comes to collaborating with repressive states in its unstable periphery or with authoritarian governments that support productive efforts for safeguarding global and regional governance (e.g., for combating climate change or effectively managing regional disputes)? Does it make sense to spend scarce resources and political capital on the global promotion of Europe's political model when liberal values have lost so much appeal both within the EU itself and beyond? Can the EU or its Member States retain restrictive arms exports policies when the need for more strategic autonomy calls for a strong European defence sector? These are inconvenient questions which defy easy answers.

Basically, Europe needs to face the unpleasant reality that, in a world where US security guarantees have weakened, the EU and European states need to pay greater attention to their own vulnerabilities. When Washington can be less relied upon to rescue threatened Europeans, commitments to general principles need to give way more to considerations of actual consequences. Thus, when (global) promotion of its values and norms might come at the expense of safeguarding its values or its fundamental interests in its own realm (e.g., by jeopardizing or using up key resources), Europe should clearly prioritise safeguarding its "base" on the old continent. In a harsher environment with fewer like-minded partners, "normative power" should become more defensive (and thus, at times, more self-ish), if this is needed to protect the viability of the European project. High-minded Europeans need to realise that defending the EU is itself a moral policy, even if doing so may sometimes require resort to means and policies that until now were preferably left to the "less scrupled" Americans.

To be sure, such a more defensive approach should not be mistaken for a value-free external policy. There is a difference between being a missionary for one's own values against others' preferences and the strengthening of such val-ues among like-minded countries, including states in the Asia-Pacific. The latter policy should certainly remain on Europe's agenda, not least because it can func-tion as glue for other areas of potential cooperation. Europe's sincere commit-ment to its values will often be a policy asset, in that it furthers trust and mutual understanding, which in turn helps advance more mundane European interests. As Kaminski and Ciesielska-Klikowska remind us in their chapter, there may be less intrusive ways for Europe to spread its normative ideas and practices, simply by the power of example that Europeans may provide through repeated subnational contacts.

Nevertheless, in the foreseeable future there is no alternative to a less ambitious and more cautious approach to championing European values. In fact, we have already seen this more "defensive" posture in recent action in, for example, Euro-pean reactions to China's draconic "handling" of the Uighurs in Xijiang and the protest movements in Hong Kong. At the same time, in the case of Ukraine, we witnessed where an over-ambitious promotion of values can lead us, in prompting an unexpected confrontation with Russia that produced nothing but losers. Finally, growing value controversies *within* Europe (especially between Brussels and the illiberal governments in Budapest and Warsaw) severely constrain Europe's nor-mative outreach. Such quarrels open channels of influence for authoritarian states (notably China and Russia), weaken Europe's normative cohesion and also under-mine its normative appeal. They make it less likely that EU members can agree on external value promotion and make it more imperative for Europe to focus on defending its values on its home turf. Hence, these internal differences likewise suggest a more inward-looking value policy.

Lessons for Europe and Europeans

Altogether, these recommendations amount to a veritable paradigm shift, which, above all, needs to be persuasively communicated to European citizens. Whereas elites have become gradually aware of these new challenges, constituents still have to learn—and accept—that Europe is about to enter a new era in which the old continent must increasingly fend for itself. They must face the fact that exter-nal developments might well jeopardise the mid-term viability of the European project and most of the benefits it has realised for all of us. Indeed, this is for Europeans a question of sustainability, as grave in the political sphere as climate change is in the realm of the environment—perhaps even more so, because a collapsing or powerless Europe might end multilateral cooperation in many vital fields, including the environment. Voters must realise that the future of the European way of life is at stake unless they and their leaders overcome a deeply ingrained strategic complacency, nourished by decades of habitual reliance on US support.

That said, coping with the challenges caused by a (likely) Sino-American cold war requires, above all, strengthening of the EU itself—both politically and militarily. Josep Borrell, EU High Representative for Foreign Affairs and Security Policy, recently drove the point home when he correctly stated that, in order "[t]o avoid being the losers in today's US-China competition, we must relearn the language of power and conceive of Europe as a top-tier geostrategic actor" (Borrell 2020). While managing the social and economic consequences of COVID-19 will be Europe's priority for some time, elites must educate their publics that there can be no return to business as usual. Once the worst is over, they need to make the case for more economic and—crucially—political integration. Political integration is, for example, about expanding EU-internal systems of majority voting and establishing supranational elements in security-related fields. This obviously requires increased defence spending. Perhaps, the experience of mutual interdependence and of economic solidarity between Member States in times of COVID-19 can yet again boost common identification with the European project, thus enhancing citizens' support for a more cohesive and autonomous EU. Europeans must learn once more that their nation states will be unable to thrive in a more hazardous environment unless they are again prepared to pool more sovereignty.

At the same time, European leaders must also recognise that, on its way to becoming a "geopolitical Commission", as was put by European Commission President Ursula von der Leyen in her first press conference in December 2019, Europe and the EU have a number of potential tools already at their disposal—the degree of integration already achieved just has to be used more strategically. For example, Europe should more readily employ the regulatory and norm-setting power of its huge single market *vis-à-vis* external actors. Similarly, Europe should deploy greater financial firepower through the current euro zone that could, of course, be strengthened further and gradually enlarged.

What is more, Europeans must become keenly aware that they need to take far more responsibility for the security and welfare of their own neighbourhood. In a world of intense superpower rivalry, neither global governance nor its US ally can be relied upon to provide the necessary stability to Europe's periphery. In the worst case, Washington may even be unable, or unwilling, to offer meaningful support for the defence of its NATO partners. While Europeans should seek to maintain transatlantic security ties, they also need to seriously prepare to meet challenging military contingencies effectively on their own.

In addition, Europeans are well advised to realise the need to cultivate new foreign partners. The era of close and easy alignment with the US may well be over, even with the advent of the Biden administration. The days of a cohesive West, unified by common purposes and American leadership, could be over once and for all. Leaders on both sides of the Atlantic must prepare for a scenario where they might be opposed on numerous international issues. While Europe should try to strengthen US advocates of multilateral global governance so as to enhance prospects for renewed transatlantic partnerships, it also needs to look for new (middle power) partners to salvage the liberal international system where possible. As indicated by some of our contributors, European capitals should also keep an eye on opportunities for cooperation with Beijing, provided any such alignment strengthens the rules-based order or facilitates the provision of collective goods.

Last but not least, in order to successfully shift the paradigm following from our recommendations, Europe requires two more fundamental assets that it has lacked, particularly more recently: one is more decisive leadership and the other is the ability and willingness to think long term. As for leadership, it will be crucial that the Franco-German tandem reforms and picks up pace again, so as to lead the way to a stronger Europe. At the same time, though, this tandem should always strive to include others—not least because Europe is much more than just France and Germany. Moreover, Europe's governments and the EU can no longer afford to think in short four-to five-year administrative cycles, from one national or European election to the next. Instead, Europe needs to build the capacity for strategic long-term planning that outlasts democratic election cycles and can rival those of authoritarian regimes like China.

In sum, Europe, increasingly faced with intensifying US-China rivalry, must find its own distinct way to respond. Essentially, this way is one of not aligning too closely with, or relying too much upon, either of the superpower antagonists. However, it should not be confused with a policy of strict equidistance, either. Rather, it is a way that strongly centres on a pragmatic and relatively flexible approach that, above all, puts more emphasis on Europe's own interests and preferences, its own security and welfare. At the end of the day, this entails nothing less for Europe than reinventing some of the cornerstones of its external affairs. In the 21st century, European nations will only thrive if they start to realise that a post-Western world shaped by Asia-Pacific rivalries will necessitate a European foreign and security policy that is genuinely post-national. The sooner leaders and their publics accept this paradox, the greater will be the chances for Europeans to determine their own future, both within national societies and in matters relating to Europe as a whole.

References

Bertelsmann Foundation. 2020. "Survey: Europe's View of China and the US-Chinese Conflict." www.bertelsmann-stiftung.de/fileadmin/files/BSt/Publikationen/Graue Publikationen/eupinions_China_DA_EN.pdf.

Biba, Sebastian. 2016. "Global Governance in the Era of Growing US-China Rivalry: What Options Exist for Europe?" *European Foreign Affairs Review* 21 (3/1): 47–64.

Biba, Sebastian. 2020. "Ganging Up on Trump? Sino-German Relations and the Problem with Soft Balancing Against the USA." *Journal of Chinese Political Science* 25 (4): 531–550.

Biba, Sebastian, and Heike Holbig. 2017. "China in the G20: A Narrow Corridor for Sino-European Cooperation." *Giga Focus Asia* 2, May. www.giga-hamburg.de/en/publication/china-in-the-G20.

Borrell, Josep. 2020. "Embracing Europe's Power." *Project Syndicate*, February 25. www.project-syndicate.org/commentary/embracing-europe-s-power-by-josep-borrell-2020-02?barrier=accesspaylog.

Buruma, Ian. 2016. "The End of the Anglo-American Order." *New York Times Magazine*, November 29. https://www.nytimes.com/2016/11/29/magazine/the-end-of-the-anglo-american-order.html.

Cohen, Raphael S., and Gabriel M. Scheinmann. 2014. "Can Europe Fill the Void in US Military Leadership?" *Orbis* 58 (1): 39–54.

Dworkin, Anthony, and Richard Gowan. 2019. *Rescuing Multilateralism*. London: European Council on Foreign Relations. www.ecfr.eu/page/-/7_Rescuing_multilateralism.pdf.

Esteban, Mario, Miguel Otero-Iglesias, Una Aleksandra Bērziņa-Čerenkova, Alice Ekman, Lucrezia Poggetti, Björn Jerdén, John Seaman, Tim Summers, and Justyna Szczudlik, eds. 2020. "Europe in the Face of US-China Rivalry." European Think-Tank Network on China Report. www.ifri.org/sites/default/files/atoms/files/etnc_report_us-china-europe_january_2020_complete.pdf.

Gabriel, Sigmar. 2019. "Europe in the Shadows." *Project Syndicate*, March 8. www.project-syndicate.org/onpoint/europe-in-the-shadows-by-sigmar-gabriel-2019-03?utm=&barrier=accesspaylog.

Gareis, Sven Bernhard, and Reinhard Wolf. 2016. "Home Alone? The US Pivot to Asia and Its Implications for the EU's Common Security and Defence Policy." *European Foreign Affairs Review* 21 (3/1): 133–150.

Gilchrist, Karen. 2020. "China Gets Top Score as Citizens Rank Their Governments' Response to the Coronavirus Outbreak." *CNBC*, May 6. www.cnbc.com/2020/05/07/coronavirus-china-vietnam-uae-top-list-as-citizens-rank-government-response.html.

Howorth, Jolyon. 2018. "Strategic Autonomy and EU-NATO Cooperation: Threat orOpportunity for Transatlantic Defence Relations?" *Journal of European Integration* 40 (5): 523–537.

Lippert, Barbara, and Volker Perthes. 2020. "Strategic Rivalry Between United States and China: Causes, Trajectories, and Implications for Europe." SWP Research Paper, April. www.swp-berlin.org/fileadmin/contents/products/research_papers/2020RP04_China_USA.pdf.

Luce, Edward. 2017. *The Retreat of Western Liberalism*. London: Little, Brown.

Manners, Ian. 2002. "Normative Power Europe: A Contradiction in Terms?" *Journal of Common Market Studies* 40 (22): 235–258.

Maull, Hanns. 1990. "Germany and Japan: The New Civilian Powers." *Foreign Affairs* 69 (5): 91–106.

Men, Jing. 2012. "The EU and China: Mismatched Partners?" *Journal of Contemporary China* 21 (74): 333–349.

Riddervold, Marianne, and Guri Rosén. 2018. "Unified in Response to Rising Powers? China, Russia and EU-US Relations." *Journal of European Integration* 40 (5): 555–570.

Rudolf, Peter. 2020. "The Sino-American World Conflict." SWP Research Paper, February. www.swp-berlin.org/fileadmin/contents/products/research_papers/2020RP03_rdf_Web.pdf.

Schulze, Matthias, and Daniel Voelsen. 2020. "Strategic Spheres of Influence." In *Strategic Rivalry Between United States and China: Causes, Trajectories, and Implications for Europe*, edited by Barbara Lippert and Volker Perthes, 30–34. SWP Research Paper, April. www.swp-berlin.org/fileadmin/contents/products/research_papers/2020RP04_China_USA.pdf.

Smith, Michael E. 2018. "Transatlantic Security Relations Since the European Security Strategy: What Role for the EU in Its Pursuit of Strategic Autonomy?" *Journal of European Integration* 40 (5): 605–620.

Stanzel, Volker. 2016. "Need Disputes Turn into Armed Conflicts? East Asia's Maritime Conflicts in a New Environment: Consequences for the European Union." *European Foreign Affairs Review* 21 (3/1): 65–80.

VOA News. 2020. "China, Vietnam Top Virus Response Survey, but for Different Reasons." May 21. www.voanews.com/covid-19-pandemic/china-vietnam-top-virus-response-survey-different-reasons.

Walt, Stephen M. 2019. "Europe's Future Is as China's Enemy: The Continent Can Save NATO—But Only if It Takes Washington's Side in Its Growing Struggle with Beijing." *Foreign Policy*, January 22. https://foreignpolicy.com/2019/01/22/europes-future-is-as-chinas-enemy/.

Wintour, Patrick. 2020. "Only Three Out of 53 Countries Say US Has Handled Coronavirus Better Than China." *The Guardian*, June 15. www.theguardian.com/world/2020/jun/15/only-three-out-of-53-countries-say-us-has-handled-coronavirus-better-than-china.

Witney, Nick. 2019. "Building Europeans' Capacity to Defend Themselves." *European Council on Foreign Relations*, June. www.ecfr.eu/page/-/5_Building_Europeans%E2%80%99_capacity_to_defend_themselves.pdf.

Wolf, Reinhard, Markus Liegl, and Sebastian Biba. 2016. "Introduction: Perils of US-China Confrontation—Implications for Europe." *European Foreign Affairs Review* 21 (3/1): 1–10.

Index

Note: Page numbers in *italic* indicate a figure, page numbers in **bold** indicate a table, and page numbers followed by an 'n' indicate a note on the corresponding page.

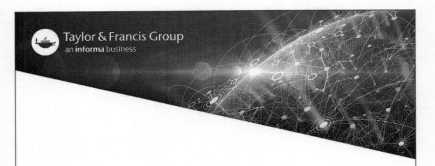